KKAA
KENGO KUMA AND ASSOCIATES
ARCHITECTURE AS SPIRIT OF NATURE

EDITED BY MAURIZIO MUCCIOLA

Beijing TEAHOUSE ©Koji Fujii/Nacasa & Partners Inc.

KENGO KUMA BIOGRAPHY

2008- Established Kuma & Associates Europe (Paris, France)
1990 - Established Kengo Kuma & Associates
1987 - Established Spatial Design Studio
1979- Completed the Master Course, Department of Architecture, Graduate School of Engineering, The University of Tokyo
1954 - Born in Yokohama, Kanagawa Prefecture, Japan

TEACHING AND PROFESSORSHIPS

2009 – present
Professor at the Graduate School of Architecture, The University of Tokyo
2007 – 2008
Visiting Professor at the School of Architecture, University of Illinois at Urbana-Champaign (Chicago, USA)
2001 – 2009, Professor at the Faculty of Science and Technology, Keio University
1998 – 1999, Professor at the Faculty of Environmental Information, Keio University
1994, Lecturer at the Graduate School of Architecture, Planning and Preservation, Columbia University (New York, USA)
1985 – 1986, Visiting Scholar Graduate School, Columbia University and Asian Cultural Counci (USA)

PROFESSIONAL AFFILIATIONS

First class Architect in Japan
Architecte DESA (Diplôme de l'Ecole Spéciale d'Architecture); Architecte inscrit au Tableau de l'Ordre des Architectes; International Fellow for Royal Institute of British Architects (RIBA)
Honorary Fellow for The American Institute of Architects (AIA); Received a Ph.D from Keio University,

MAIN LITERARY WORKS

2013, Chisana Kenchiku (Iwanami shoten)
Kenchikuka, Hashiru (Shincho-sha)
2012, Taidanshu Tsunagu Kenchiku (Iwanami shoten)
Nihonjin wa dou sumaubekika? (co-authored with Takeshi Yorou / Nikkei BP)
Basho genron (Ichigaya publishing)
2011, Shin Mura-ron Tokyo (co-authored with Yumi Kiyono / Syuei sha shinsho)
2010, Kyokai (Tanko sha)
Santei Shugi (co-authored with Atsushi Miura / NTT)
2008, The Origins of Materials (Graphic sha)
Shizen na Kenchiku (Iwanami sinsho)
Shin Toshi-ron Tokyo (co-authored with Yumi Kiyono / Syuei sha shinsho)
Studies in Organic (TOTO)

2007, Kengo Kuma: Lecture and Dialogue (INAX)
2004, Kengo Kuma Tokuhon II – 2004 (GA)
Makeru Kenchiku (Iwanami shoten)
2000, Anti-Object (Chikuma shobou)
1999, Kengo Kuma Tokuhon – 1999 (GA)
1995, Kenchiku no Kiki wo Koete (TOTO)
1994, Kenchikuteki Yokubo no Shuen (Shinyou sha), Shin-Kenchiku Nyumon (Chikuma shinsho)
1989, Good-Bye Postmodern Ð11 American Architects(Kajima publishing)
1986, Jutaku-ron (Chikuma Bunko)

SOLO EXHIBITIONS

2009, Studies in Organic (Tokyo, Japan)
2008, Material Immaterial (Chicago, USA)
Build Built (Beijing, China)
2005, Kengo Kuma, Mock-ups (Tokyo, Japan)
Kengo Kuma, The Architecture Between Tradition and Innovation (Siracusa/Milan/Napoli, Italy and Stockholm, Sweden)
KRUG×KUMAÐ℠ÐInfinityÐ (Tokyo, Japan)
2004, Niwa: Where the Particle response (Tokyo, Japan)
Kengo Kuma: Defeated Architecture (Tokyo, Japan)
1995, Velocity of Transmission (Tokyo, Japan)
1992, Tokyo columns (Tokyo, Japan)

AWARDS (FOR KENGO KUMA)

2012, The 6th ASIAGRAPH Award
Japan Information-Cultuology Society Award
2011, The Minister of Education, Culture, Sports, Science and Technology's Art Encouragement Prize for "Yusuhara Wooden Bridge Museum"
2010, Mainichi Art Award for "Nezu Museum"
2009, Decoration Officier de L'Ordre des Arts et des Lettres (France)
2008, Energy Performance + Architecture Award (France); Bois Magazine International Wood Architecture Award (France)
2002, Spirit of Nature Wood Architecture Award (Finland)
2001, Togo Murano Award for "Nakagawa-machi Bato Hiroshige Museum"
1997, Architectural Institute of Japan Award for "Noh Stage in the Forest"
First Place, AIA DuPONT Benedictus Award for "Water/Glass" (USA)

AWARDS (FOR ASSOCIATES)

2014, JIA Award for environmental architecture
Architectual Institute of Japan Prize for Design, Specific Contributions Division for "Nagaoka City Hall Aore"

2009, Conde Nast Traveler Magazine's WorldBest New Hotels 2009 for "The Opposite House" (USA)
2008, Emirates Leaf Award for Public Building for Suntory Museum of Art (UK/UAE)
Design For Asia Award for "Fujiya Ryokan" (Hong Kong)
2007, Detail Prize 2007 special prize for 'Chokkura Plaza and Shelter" (Germany)
International Architecture Award for the Best New Global Design for "Chokkura Plaza and Shelter" (USA)
2005, The Marble Architecture Award 2005 East Asia External Facings 1st prize for "Nagasaki Prefectural Art Museum" (Italy)
2001, International Stone Architecture Award for "Stone Museum" (Italy)
Building Contractors Society Prize for "Nakagawa-machi Bato Hiroshige Museum"
2000, Grand Prize, Inter Intra Space Design Selection for "Kitakami Canal Museum"
Director General of Forestry Agency Prize for "Nakagawa-machi Bato Hiroshige Museum"
Tochigi Prefecture Marronnier Architecture Award for "Stone Museum"
Tohoku Architecture Award for "River/Filter"
1999, Honorable Mention, Boston Society of Architecture, Unbuilt Architecture Design Award (USA)
1997, Grand Prize, Regional Design Award, Kochi Prefecture, for "Yusuhara Visitor's Center"
1995, Grand Prize for JCD Design Award 1995 Cultural / Public Institutions for "Kiro-san Observatory"

COMPETITION PRIZES

2012, First Prize, The competition for "Susa International train station" (Susa valley, Turin, Italy)
First Prize, The competition for "EPFLEspace et pavillions sur place Cosandey" (Lausanne,Switzerland)
First Prize, The proposal for "Tomioka City Hall" (Gunma, Japan)
First Prize, The proposal for "Iiyama Plaza" (Nagano, Japan)
2011, First Prize, The proposal for "the Towada city plaza for social communication" (Aomori, Japan)
First Prize, HIKARI, ILOT-P, Lyon Confluence Competition (Lyon, France)
2010, First Prize, V&A at Dundee Competition (Scotland, UK)
First Prize, Aix en Provence Conservatory of Music Competition (Aix en Province, France)
First Prize, Macdonald Public Facility Complex of General Education and Sports Competition (Paris, France)
2008, First Prize, Granada Performing Arts Center Architectural Competition (Granada, Spain)
First Prize, International Invited Architectural Competition for iconic park and mixed development in Iskandar Malaysia (Johor-Bahru, Malaysia)
First Prize, Asakusa Tourist Information Center Architectural Competition (Tokyo, Japan)
2007, First Prize, Fond Regional d'Art Contemporain Competition (Marseille, France)
First Prize, Besancon City of Arts and Culture Architectural Competition (Besancon, France)
First Prize, Architectural Competition for the Complex of Government Buildings related to the area of the "Eiffel Hall" Western Railway Station of Budapest (Budapest, Hungary)
First Prize, Nagaoka City Hall Architectural Competition (Niigata, Japan)
2004, First Prize, Tobata C Block Urban Design Competition (Fukuoka, Japan)
First Prize, Utsunomiya Station East Plaza Urban Design Competition (Tochigi, Japan)
First Prize, Ondo-cho Learning Center Design Competition (Hiroshima, Japan)
2002, First Prize, (provisional title) Living National Treasure Museum in Ota, City Preliminary Design Outsourcing Proposal (Gunma, Japan)
First Prize, Tokyo University of Agriculture, Exhibition Center Competition (Tokyo, Japan)
2001, First Prize, Nagasaki Prefecture New Museum Design Competition (Nihon Sekkei.inc + Kuma Kengo) (Nagasaki, Japan)
1998, First Prize, Nakagawa-machi Bato Hiroshige Museum Competition (Tochigi, Japan)

Many thanks to Mariko Inaba, for having assisted in this difficult, but fascinating work.

CONTENTS

ARCHITECTURE

PAG. 5 | **CONVERSATION**
Achitettura come Natura, di Pino Scaglione
CONVERSAZIONE
Architecture as Nature, by Pino Scaglione

PAG. 12 | **WOOD**

PAG. 52 | **AIR AND FLOW**

PAG. 94 | **PARTICLES**

PAG. 154 | **FOLDING**

PAG. 188 | **ROOF**

PAG. 236 | **STACKING ELEMENTS**

CONVERSATION

Architecture as Nature
Talking with Kengo Kuma
Rovereto, maggio 2013

Kuma San and I are sitting facing each other, next to him Yuki Ikeguchi, charming young woman architect and his partner at the studio in Tokyo. She is listening to our conversation, nodding sometimes. This is a sign that Kengo Kuma's ideas are extensively shared by his partners and by the studio, as if they were a cultural heritage, already DNA of the studio itself.
And, actually, one cannot disagree with what the architect articulates as founding principles: to love and learn from Nature, to offer "community service" through architecture, to make places and spaces even denser and more evocative thanks to the blending between them and the artifact.
During the business lunch, surrounded by a group of colleagues who follow the project for the former Manifattura Tabacchi – amongst them is Maurizio Mucciola, Italian architect and pillar of the firm – we start the conversation which I am going to report in the next lines.
Kuma is very relaxed, calm and seraphic, he seems to be feeling at ease among this group of people who, in Trentino, gave life to the adventure and international opportunity that is the project of rehabilitating the former Manifattura Tabacchi into the Green Factory; a project that, as a matter of fact, is the first he takes part in in Italy and one he really holds dear.
Kuma asserts that, right from the start – being fascinated by the alpine landscape in its beautiful sequence of fullness and emptiness of mountains and valleys – he has had the idea to literally lift the ground floor of the new building, which will be added to the already existing ones of the old establishment. On the other hand, the project for the new Manifattura is also a concentrated of technology that, combined with quality spaces, natural structures and materials, aspires to design an intelligent, contemporary building which embraces the local alpine tradition avoiding the vernacular.
It comes natural for me to ask him how, even when outside Japan, he manages to stay true to his principle and keep designing landscape-buildings. I'm trying to understand how he deals with such a fundamental aspect of every architect's job: being able to make the building look like it belongs to a specific place and landscape and, at the same time, pointing out its absolute and necessary contemporaneity.
Kuma responds by saying that – before setting any project – he spends some time "smelling", perceiving the "particles" of places and cities in order to find, within them, some recognizable elements to turn into the pieces which create the architecture of the place, like a structure that eventually is embedded in the context, becoming its essential part.
Still, is there anything that recalls the more recent tradition?
The brutalism needed by Japan to reach a further modernist dimension doesn't interest Kuma, and never has – he is also proudly and stubbornly attached to the

CONVERSAZIONE

Architettura come Natura
Conversando con Kengo Kuma
Rovereto, maggio 2013

Siamo seduti di fronte io e Kuma San, a fianco a lui Yuki Ikeguchi, giovane e affascinante donna architetto, sua partner di studio a Tokio, che ascolta la nostra conversazione e ogni tanto annuisce. Segno che le idee di Kengo Kuma sono ampiamente condivise dai suoi partner e dallo studio, come se fossero un patrimonio culturale ormai DNA di KKAA.
E, in effetti, come non essere d'accordo su ciò che l'architetto dispiega come principi fondativi:
amare e imparare dalla natura, fare servizio "civile" con l'architettura, rendere i luoghi, i contesti, ancora più densi e suggestivi, proprio per la fusione tra questi e il manufatto.
Durante il pranzo di lavoro, circondato dal gruppo di collaboratori che seguono il progetto della ex Manifattura Tabacchi, tra i quali Maurizio Mucciola, architetto italiano, e ormai pilastro dello studio, iniziamo la conversazione della quale cerco di dare seguito nelle prossime righe.
Kuma è molto serafico, tranquillo e rilassato, mi sembra sia a suo agio in questo gruppo di persone che in Trentino hanno dato vita ad una avventura/occasione internazionale come il progetto della ex Manifattura Tabacchi, futura Green Factory, e questo progetto -primo al quale attende in Italia- gli sta molto a cuore.
Sostiene Kuma di aver avuto da subito l'intuizione di dover letteralmente sollevare il suolo del nuovo edificio -che si aggiunge a quelli esistenti del vecchio stabilimento- perché affascinato dal paesaggio alpino, dalle montagne e valli che si alternano in un gioco di pieni e vuoti naturali. Allo stesso tempo il progetto della nuova Manifattura è un concentrato di tecnologia fusa con spazi di qualità, strutture e materiali naturali, in un edificio intelligente e contemporaneo, che guarda con attenzione alla tradizione alpina e locale, senza incorrere nel vernacolo.
Mi viene spontaneo chiedergli come riesce fuori dal Giappone a tenere fede al suo principio di fare edifici paesaggio e cerco di capire come si misura con questa parte così fondamentale per ogni buon architetto: saper fare in modo che l'edificio –pur denunciando la sua assoluta, necessaria contemporaneità- sembri appartenere a quel luogo, a quel paesaggio.
Kuma risponde dicendomi che –prima di impostare qualsiasi progetto- passa del tempo ad "annusare", a percepire le "particelle" dei luoghi, delle città, all'interno delle quali trovare elementi di riconoscibilità e tradurli nelle parti che compongono l'architettura: per quel luogo come una struttura che risulti alla fine "incassata" nel contesto, e che ne divenga parte essenziale.
C'è però qualcosa che richiama la tradizione più recente?
Il brutalismo che è servito al Giappone per agganciare una sua dimensione modernista più spinta, non interessa e non è mai interessato a Kuma, -che è anche orgogliosamente e caparbiamente legato all'insegnamento nella Scuola di Architettura di Tokyo- per il suo lavoro la modernità vera è sapere coniugare la semplicità della tradizione giappone-

teachings of Tokyo School of Architecture – according to his job, true modernity lies in the combination of the simplicity of Japanese tradition into pure contemporary elements. In 2009, in Tokyo, Kengo Kuma exhibited his works as architect and, during an introduction of the exhibition, he supported an interesting thesis/antithesis: between Wright and Le Corbusier, the latter is authentically nearer to an intelligent approach between Man and Nature, even though the first is considered to be the pioneer of organic architecture.
In fact, explains Kuma, the organic approach is more of a fetish than a real interest of the American architects in the relationship between living organisms and the act of inhabiting, a sort of metaphor of architecture itself. Le Corbusier's machine/autonomous system can be a real reference model to create intelligent buildings that are in connection with Nature without artificial deceptions, and still show the strength of the beginning of a technological era which would change (as it already is) lifestyles, architecture and city planning.
When we ask Kuma to explain his rather challenging statement, he quietly responds arguing that none in the field of biology, botany or any other similar discipline, can support the full independence of human beings or living creatures; on the contrary, they exist only through active and constant interactions with the environment they live in. The same goes for architecture; thus Wright's buildings are beautifully shaped artifacts attempting a formalist communication with the place without establishing a real osmotic relationship between living and natural space. Instead, Kuma says: "For my architectures it's like that: they try to establish an intense relationship with the environment they will live and grow in by using local materials, enhancing their texture or softness, the smell, the warmth, the surfaces and the membranes."
He continues describing, almost evoking, his first job: "the Observatory of Kiro-san was the first of my works in which the relationship between the local elements has played a key role in deciding spaces, dimensions and connections: the water, the landscape surrounding it, the views, the materials, everything was born after a careful observation of the place and its relationships. It's like architecture was buried in the bowels of Nature, which welcomes and embraces it."
"I'm not interested in a formal relationship with the place – continues Kuma – that simulates the profile of mountains adapting architecture to this or other alleged silhouettes; I'm interested in the ability of architecture to become itself part of a shape or a context."
However, this still reminds of an organic approach and, without bringing up Wright again, what does it mean, to an architect and to Kuma, to build "architectures as Nature"?
"You know when the chameleon – an animal sensitive to the environment – changes its skin color according to the background, especially when it feel it's in danger? To me, for my architectures, this is fundamental: to be able to change, to actually transform their skin, their color, in connection with the surrounding environment; to understand this and to turn it into living spaces, into shapes that are intertwined and blended seamlessly is one of the tasks of my job."
It is clear that for Kuma this is an extreme simplification, an evident similarity; but the reference to the chameleon – knowing that

se in elementi di pura contemporaneità. Nel 2009 a Tokyo, Kengo Kuma ha esposto i suoi lavori di architetto e nel corso di un incontro di presentazione della mostra ha sostenuto una interessante tesi/antitesi: tra Wright e Le Corbusier, il secondo è più autenticamente vicino ad un approccio intelligente tra uomo e natura, malgrado il primo sia considerato il pioniere dell'architettura organica.
Infatti, spiega Kuma, che l'approccio organico è più un feticcio che un reale interesse dell'architetto americano verso il rapporto tra organismi viventi e l'abitare, una sorta di metafora dell'architettura stessa, mentre "la macchina/essere autonomo" di Le Corbusier può essere il vero modello di riferimento per costruire edifici intelligenti e in relazione con la natura, senza inganni artificiali, ma denunciando la forza dell'avvento tecnologico che avrebbe cambiato (come sta cambiando) stili e modi di vivere e così l'architettura e l'urbanistica.
Di questa affermazione –piuttosto impegnativa- chiediamo conto a Kuma che ci risponde pacatamente sostenendo che ne la biologia, la botanica, o altre discipline simili possono sostenere l'autonomia totale di individui-essere umani o forme viventi, al contrario questi esistono solo attraverso l'interazione, piuttosto attiva e costante, con l'ambiente di vita. Lo stesso vale per l'architettura, così che gli edifici di Wright sono splendide forme, artefatti, che tentano un dialogo formalista con il luogo, ma non instaurano una vera relazione osmotica tra spazio abitato e spazio naturale.
"E' così per le mie architetture, che cercano di instaurare sempre una intensa relazione con l'ambiente in cui vivranno e cresceranno, usando materiali del posto, esaltando la loro consistenza o morbidezza, l'odore, il calore, le superfici, le membrane".
E segue descrivendolo, quasi ad evocarlo, il suo primo lavoro: "L'Osservatorio di Kiro-san, è stato il primo dei miei lavori in cui il rapporto con gli elementi del luogo ha avuto un peso determinante nel decidere spazi, dimensioni, superfici e relazioni: l'acqua, il paesaggio che la circonda, le visuali, i materiali, tutto è nato da una attenta osservazione del posto e delle sue relazioni. L'architettura è come se fosse sepulta dentro le viscere della natura, che quasi l'accoglie e la fa sua."
"A me non interessa l'aspetto formale della relazione con il luogo –prosegue Kuma-, simulando un profilo di montagne o adeguando l'architettura a questa o ad altre presunte sagome, ma la capacità dell'architettura di farsi essa stessa parte di una forma e di un contesto".
Ma questo ricorda comunque un approccio organico, e senza voler scomodare di nuovo Wright, cosa vuol dire per un architetto, e per Kuma, costruire "architettura come natura"?
"Hai presente quando il camaleonte –animale sensibile all'ambiente- si mimetizza con lo sfondo in cui si trova, soprattutto quando avverte un pericolo? Per me, per le mie architetture, questa è una modalità importante: essere in grado di cambiare, mutare realmente la propria pelle, il colore, in relazione con l'ambiente circostante; comprenderla e tradurla in spazi di vita, di scambio, in forme che si compenetrano e fondono senza soluzione di continuità è uno dei compiti del mio lavoro".
Ed è chiaro che per Kuma si tratta di una semplificazione estrema, una evidente similitudine; ma il riferimento al camaleonte –sapendo che l'architettura non ha la

architecture doesn't have the same dynamic and active ability as the animal – concerns elements (such as latches, exterior surfaces, materials and finishings) that the architect uses very often with a natural approach, elements which can change the appearance of a building because of the light, the shadows, the changes of the environment, the use of the building itself through time and also because of its exposure and modifications.
Just as when in nature a landscape literally "swallows up" a work, so a building too can become part of the environment.
Almost every one of Kuma's buildings follows this approach, this ever-changing contextual sensitivity that makes them landscape themselves. A landscape which is contemporary and not ordinarily mimetic, one that is sensitive to every modification and effect that it absorbs and produces. Monograph.it, which collects three decades of activity of the international-Japanese studio, shows that each one of the buildings expresses the characteristics of this great sensitivity and attention to design. Even the "inflatable" objects, the temporary architectures, pavilions, displays and stores, are strongly influenced by the constant lesson Kuma has learnt from Nature.
Recently, right in the small Camper store in Milan, in the heart of the "artificial city", one can admire one of the latest skill performances of the Japanese architect: it seems to walk into the hollow of a big light-wooded tree, wooden shelves stretch out and move within the space as if they were uneven branches of the tree; jute sacks – of different forms – lie on a rough floor in dark wood. The simplicity of the arrangement of each element allows to build a space which is as simple as it is appealing and balanced, filled with elegance and sobriety. These are elements that usually only Nature manages to harmonize together, even in compressed spaces; well, it happens also in architecture, like in the case of the shop in question. Experimental structures made of natural or recycled fabrics, which swell only when used, are a way to appropriate places – even temporarily – and to use them in a simple manner, to build, also playfully, a different relationship with Nature. An example of this series of experiments is the Experimental house MEME, where Kuma, playing with a traditional and archetypal form, tries to incorporate transparency and natural softness into the "hardness" which is necessary to architecture.
As described above, in Kuma's architectures every material has an important meaning. At the end of our conversation, talking again about the relationship with the Masters of Modern Architecture, Kuma seeks to distance himself from what we have assimilated as an "undeniable" and timeless lesson and confirms that the difference from Frank Lloyd Wright's organic approach – meant as "organic" especially in the forms – is to be translated as "through all materials, from the most important one to the most hidden one!"
But Nature is also constant invention and reinvention and, among the latest natural ecological architecture experiments which Kuma is trying to carry on, there is a ETFT block system (ethylene tetrafluoroethylene, published among these projects): an alloy between natural and artificial which is usually employed in broad execution facilities, it is made up of membranous elements capable of creating a building by

piling up the little blocks just as bricks, "air bricks", shown for the first time at the personal exhibition Kuma opened in Shanghai in 2010 (during the Expo in June). The success of this great designer, beyond his talent and sensitivity, his adhesion to basic building principles – that translates into original and fascinating spaces – is also the result of an attitude of a full human and intellectual availability and of an anti-star; an attitude, actually, of permanent curiosity, of research and experimentation, of balance between nature and future, added to the thousands of years of Japanese history and culture which, of the "patient" art of listening and building within nature, have made a lifestyle.

by Pino scaglione

Kengo Kuma
Camper Store
in Milan

Kengo Kuma
working at his desk
busy wiht books, object
collected in his world
travels and project to
review

capaci di realizzare un edificio impilando i blocchetti come mattoni, "mattoni d'aria", mostrati per la prima volta alla personale che Kuma ha aperto a Shangai (a giugno, durante Expo) nel 2010.

Il successo di questo grande progettista, oltre al suo talento e sensibilità, della sua adesione a principi elementari del costruire, tradotti in spazi affascinanti e originali, è anche frutto di un atteggiamento di totale disponibilità umana e intellettuale, di anti-star, anzi di curiosità permanente, di ricerca e sperimentazione, di equilibrio tra natura e futuro, sommati ai millenni di storia e cultura giapponese che dell'arte "paziente" di ascoltare e costruire tra la natura, hanno fatto stile di vita.

di Pino Scaglione

KKAA, Cube building

KKAA architects working in the By-Cube building

01 WOOD
MANIFATTURA PROJECT - GREEN INNOVATION FACTORY
PROGETTO MANIFATTURA - GREEN INNOVATION FACTORY

Rovereto, Trento, Italy (2010)

The stone facade of the auditorium is the most prominent public face of a project which is otherwise "hidden" under a green roof

Progetto Manifattura – Green Innovation Factory is transforming a 9-hectare (22-acre) historic tobacco facility into a business, innovation and research hub for green building, renewable energy, and environmental technology. This is a public Project of the "Provincia Autonoma di Trento". Manifattura is located at a key point in the valley, where the Leno River practically flows into the Adige River, and is clearly visible from all the mountains that surround the area.

The perception of the Manifattura from the mountains, a point of view from top to bottom, is the most typical, and it represent therefore the way the buildings is normally perceived, which is a most important to take into consideration.

Generally, when people think about the idea of a "Landmark", an object that marks the territory by being visible from afar, it is common to think of a vertical element. This is a necessary strategy when we are in a "flatland".

Where flat and horizontal directions prevail, something willing to be visible must be higher than the rest, and verticality creates this strength. In this project instead, exactly the opposite happens: the perception is that of a point of view from top to bottom. Here a vertical mark would have no power and would get little visibility. The planar direction becomes the most powerful sign in this complex condition, and therefore the possibility of creating a new type of sign: a Horizontal Landmark, site specific and which merges into the landscape and at the same time becomes visible in all its strength from the surroundings. The second concept that characterizes Manifattura Project comes from analysing the landscape in a closer scale: reading of the lines and shapes of the territory.

The Manifattura complex sits in the valley around Rovereto and it is surrounded by the beautiful vineyards that characterize this area and that appear to be to the eye of a visitor like well-defined areas of thin and delicate parallel lines.

The directionality of the green roof of the new buildings originates from the same idea of integrating the project to its territory with the lines of the vineyards.

This results in a large green roofscape covering the production spaces below and integrating the new buildings with the surrounding nature.

This approach allows us to give back to the city of Rovereto green space that had long been occupied by the factory and made inaccessible to the public.

We wanted to re-open the space of the Manifattura to the city while ensuring the necessary security for the production buildings, and doing so not through physical barriers but gradual changes in levels and green slopes which gives us the opportunity to create the new large accessible green space.

The Manifattura Project target is LEED Platinum certification.

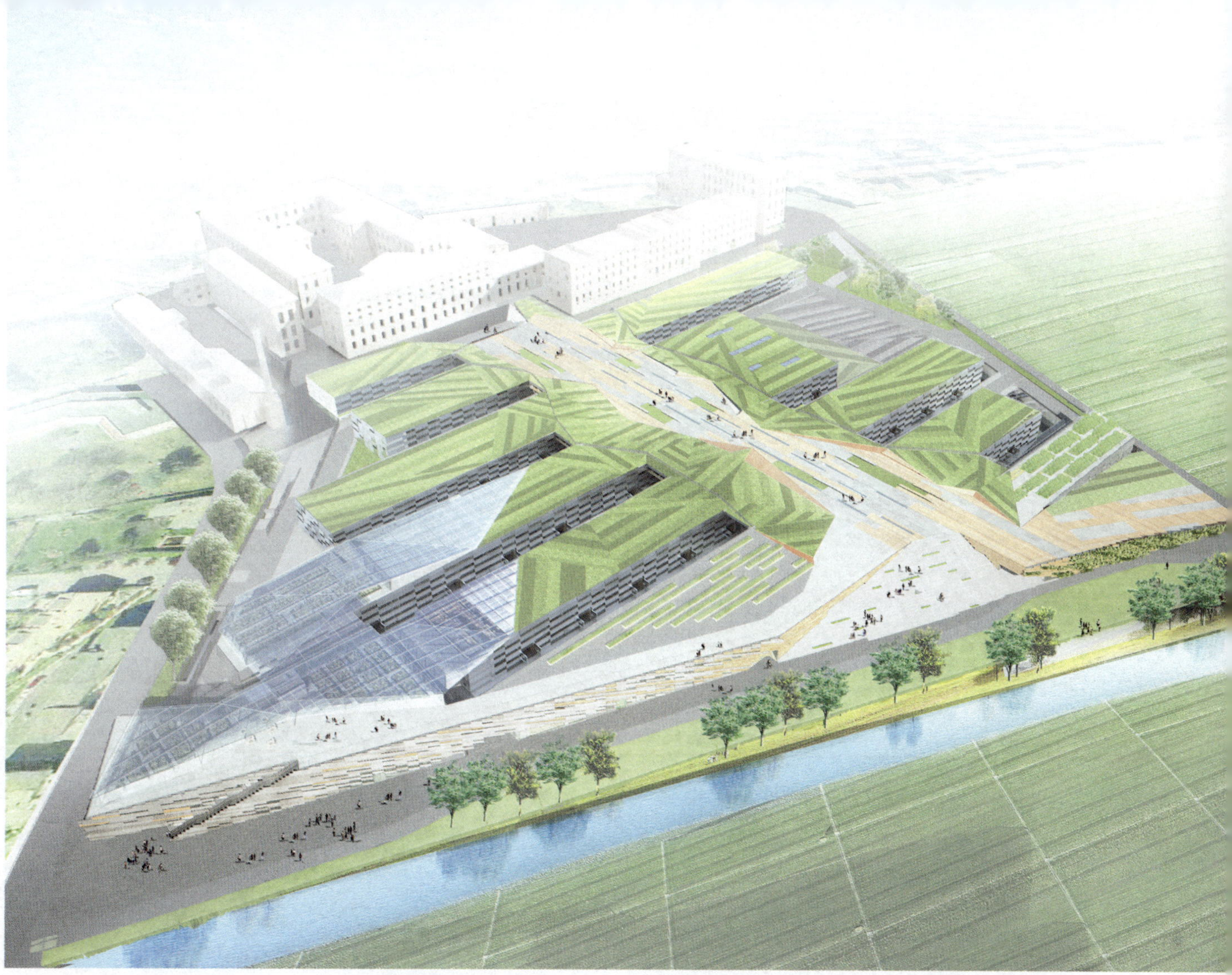

The green accessible roof, is the public heart of the project, wiht its geometry inspired by the surroundign vineyards.

The facade material gradually changes from stone, to wood, and to vegetation along the canal promenade

02 WOOD
YUSUHARA MARKET
MERCATO DI YUSUHARA

Yusuhara, Yusuhara-cho, Takaoka, Kochi Prefecture, Japan (2000)

Yusuhara Machino-eki is a complex of a market selling local products and a small hotel with 15 rooms. Combining the two different functions via atrium, a new core facility was born for the town of 3,900 in the mountains.

Yusuhara is widely known as the town facing a main road used by Sakamoto Ryoma, a high-minded warrior of the region who contributed to the initiation of the Meiji Restoration (big political reform). Along the road, there existed a number of greenrooms called "Chad Do" for travelers, which functioned not only as restrooms but also as a kind of cultural salon, serving teas free of charge. As an attempt to respect this history, we used thatch as the material, which is deeply related to "Cha Do," which worked as a medium to connect the past with the present.

Glass fittings are used for the lower part of the building, including the market's entrance facing the front road, which can be open at any hour of the day, and on top of it come piles of the straw unit in the module of 2,000×980mm, an unprecedented form for a curtain wall. Normally in a thatched roofing, thatch is fixed vertically against the foundation, in which its cut ends face towards outside. In this building, however, the bunch of thatch is bound horizontally to the foundation, with which the cut end won't be exposed to rainfalls, and will last long. As another device, pivots are set on the steel mullion at the both ends of each thatch unit, so that it can rotate and take in fresh air from outside, which will the maintenance of the thatch easier.

For the interior, we used logs of cedar tree with some remained astringent skin. The remain of the astringent was controlled by the pitch of the bark peeler, so that some nuance was added to their texture. Using rough-textured materials, such as thatch and log, we tried to create a new characteristics of Yusuhara.

The small building combines a market of locally grown fresh vegetables and ta boutique hotel.

The hotel rooms facing the market hall.

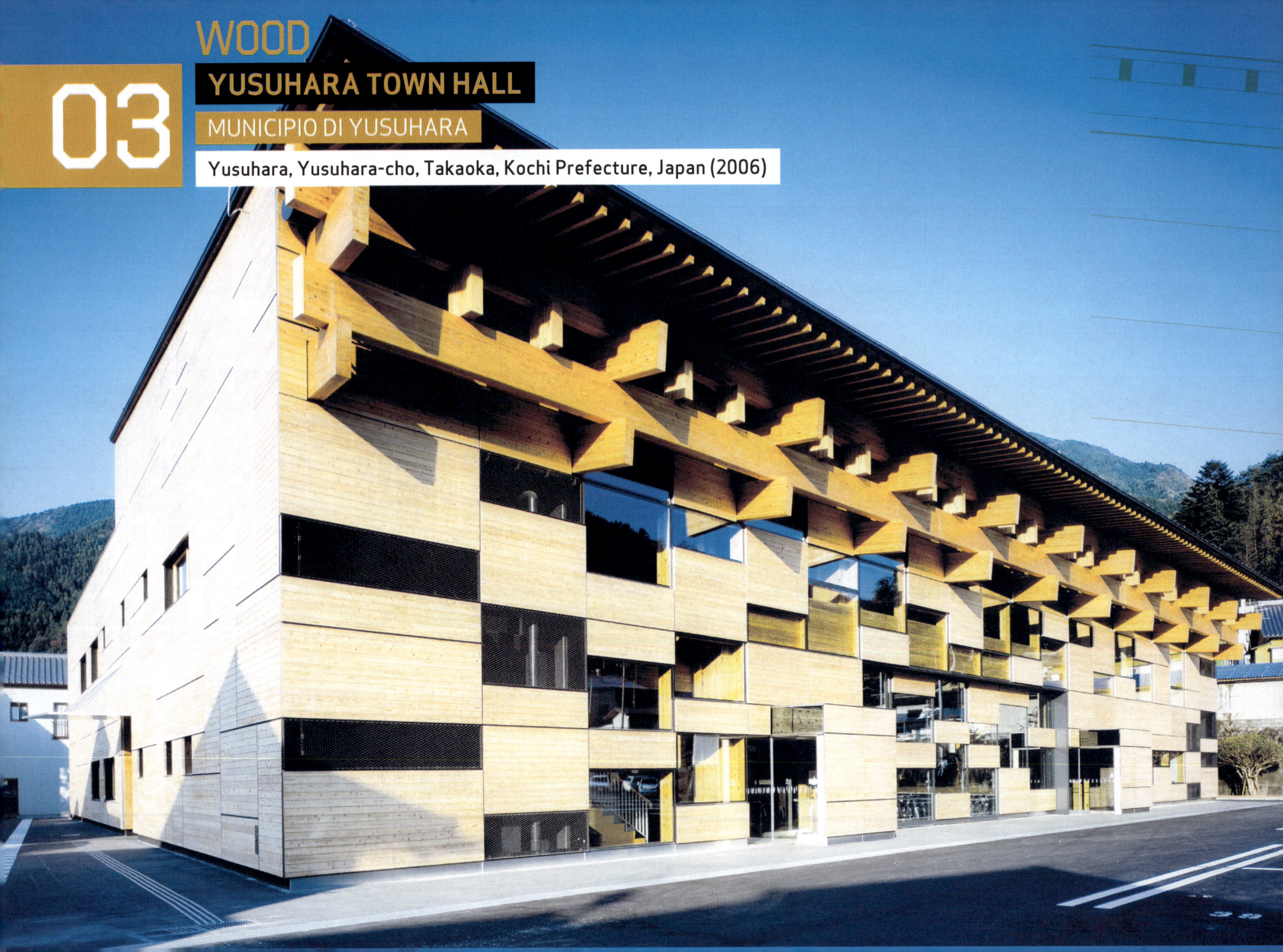

03 WOOD
YUSUHARA TOWN HALL
MUNICIPIO DI YUSUHARA
Yusuhara, Yusuhara-cho, Takaoka, Kochi Prefecture, Japan (2006)

The Town of Yusuhara is known as the river head of the Shimanto River, the longest river in Japan, and also for its snow, despite it being an island in the south. It has a population of 4,700, where one big problem is depopulation. At the center of the town, an "Open Town Hall" and an "Open Wooden Construction" were planned. An open town hall must be open to the town space. When following this definition, it could become a "Glass Town Hall", yet we came to the conclusion of using a door that is "Opened by Everyone" on nice and pleasant days in beautiful seasons. The action of everybody opening the door was important, not the aperture ratio, therefore doors used for hangars and storage rooms were placed on the front side, opening the town hall to the exterior plaza. However, just having an "Opening Door" was insufficient. To "Open" the door, there exist other motives besides the good weather or the clean air. When discussing with the local people, the idea of creating an "Avenue Style" town hall involving people's destinations such as the bank, the JA, and the Association of Commerce and Industry came up. Since all places are equally important, this is especially helpful at winter times when there is a lot of snow. If the motive to "Open" gets higher and the town hall starts to become "Open", the relationship between the local people and the administration would become close. Therefore it could change the atmosphere of the town, and might even change the politics of the town itself. The motive to open the box was gradually prepared, yet what kind of structure and skin should be organized to further open the box remained. Everyone wanted to create a wooden box rather than a heavy concrete one, because Japanese cedar is at the center of the industry of Yusuhara, at the center of the culture. However, a big problem arose.

Japanese cedar lacks strength compared to the cypress and pine, and when a large span is necessary for spaces such as the atrium at the center or the assembly hall, the Japanese cedar must be made into laminated wood to support such large spans. Yet in the local factories it was impossible to create such large section dimensions.

Then I realized that the limitation of only being able to create small parts was in fact the turning point for an "Open" architecture. The benefit of conventional wooden structures is the pleasurable scale that is comfortable to the fragile human body. If we can feel that the structure can be assembled by human hands, the architecture would not reject humans, but should be open to us. On the contrary, the overwhelming heaviness of the large laminated wood matches that of concrete. If the architecture should be felt open to the public, it should be disassembled to a dimension of humble particles.

After I came up with this idea, the façade design, the details, and the structure of the architecture starting pouring out and were decided. An amiable structure, amiable dimensions, warming dimension.

The characteristic of Japanese traditional architectures is its design based on human scales. To combine the requested functionality with the human scale was the ultimate goal for this project.

The town hall was the first KKAA project for the small city of Yushuara.

The small town developed special a relation of trust with KKAA which lead during the years to several projects

WOOD

04 BESANÇON ART AND CULTURE CENTER
CENTRO D'ARTE E CULTURA DI BESANÇON
Besançon, France (2013)

This project is the result of the union between history and architecture, water and light, city and nature.
We wish that the Besancon Art and Culture Center strike a chord with the environment by the fusion of the different scale of reading, from the details to the entire project, by blurring the limit between interior and exterior, to create a building able to enter in resonance with his environment: the hills, the river and the city of Besancon.
The roof creates the link between the building and his environment and makes the project blatant. Semi-transparent, the roof symbolizes the fusion between built and not-built and act as camouflage when people discover it from the Citadelle which is height overlooking. It is an invitation to the citizen to gather below his protection. It symbolized the encounter between the city and the nature, the citizen and the riverbank, the public and the culture.
The site brings with itself both its own history and the history of the city. The riverbank always has been either a protection or a barrier. The project is a continuity of this history, his longitudinal geometry is following the orientation given by Vauban, the warehouse, old storage of wood, is kept and participate in the richness of the building. The Besancon Art and Culture Center perpetuate the notion of protection, but can be read as well as a monumental gate between the city and the river, outstanding object and symbol of the unification of the city and his river.
It is a landmark, recognizable by a sober design and the quality of his materiality. We wish to reinforce the genius loci of the site trough a strong and clearly identifiable building, but still respecting the relationship with the existing bastion, the river and the city.

Unified below the large roof, the two functions are identifiable by subtle differences in the patterns of the façade composed by wood panels and steel panels. The pattern dimensions are for the FRAC: 5000 X 2500 Horizontal while for the CRR 1625 X half floor height vertically.
The Frac is partially located in the old brick warehouse building. After taking out two of the existing slabs, the void created is containing the main exhibition room. The large lobby of the FRAC is as much as possible transparent, open to both "art passage" and city side. The natural top light is diffused thanks to the random positioned glass panels of the roof, in order to achieve to communicate the feeling of being below a canopy of tree, where the light gently come through leaves down to the ground. The CRR is more an introverted space, except for his lobby which is 14 m height and largely transparent. Both lobby of FRAC and CRR are connected by the roof, creating a semi-outdoor space, the "art passage", which is flooded of natural light through the semi-transparent roof. This passage, a large void, is structuring the overall buildings: it acts simultaneously as a gate and a shelter; it emphasizes the particularity of this project witch gathering two different functions. The roof is the emblematic and unifying element of the project. Composed in a random way with different element such as glass, solar panel, vegetation and metal panels with different color finish, the natural light vibrates on its surface, depending of the absorption and reflection of the different elements composing it. It creates a pixelized layer where the apparent aleatory position of the "pixels" define a unique image, abstract and confounded with the environment hue. The transparency is partially defined by the necessity of the program below: opaque on top of the rooms such as class room, administration, or exhibition

room. It gets more transparent when it is on top of the lobby or when it is covering the outdoor spaces. Suspended by a wood framework, this fifth façade made of variation of transparency and opacity represent a unique and innovative design, a thin pixelized layer floating on top of the Doubs river and becoming at night a landmark reinforcing the entrance of the city. The only element emerging from the roof is the old ware house converted in exhibition gallery, reminding the industrial period of the site.

The landscape design takes part in the pedestrian path along the river: it extend and connect the existing promenade. The main constrain of the site is the flood risk. We have reinforced the embankment and built on top of that dike. This is the reason why the building is installed on top of a pedestal. This pedestal can be physically experimented walking below the "art passage" semi-outdoor space, overhanging the street and connected to the river by a large stair. The CRR is organized around a garden, called « harmony garden », a wet garden combining moss and low trees. In continuity with the "art passage", along the FRAC, a water pond planted with filtering rush is creating the soft transition between the city and the building. Partially covered by the semi-transparent roof, the shadow and light variations interweaves with the reflections on the reflection pond.

The interior design is mainly structured by the façade and roof patterns, filtering the natural light. Wood, glass, or metal meshes are combined with subtleties in order to generate a peaceful and relaxing atmosphere. The wood frameworks supporting the roofing appear in the lobbies, terraces and in the last floors witch intensify the presence of the roof. The views to the exterior are precisely framed either to the water pond, the river, the double or triple height spaces manage to offer different space experiences.

This place witch always has been perceived as a physical barrier for the citizens (either fortification or industrial area) we propose to generate an open and welcoming cultural centre, a gate and a roof between the river and the city, in harmony with the environment.

The open public space between the music conservatory and the exhibition buildings creates a spacial connection between the city and the river to the other side.

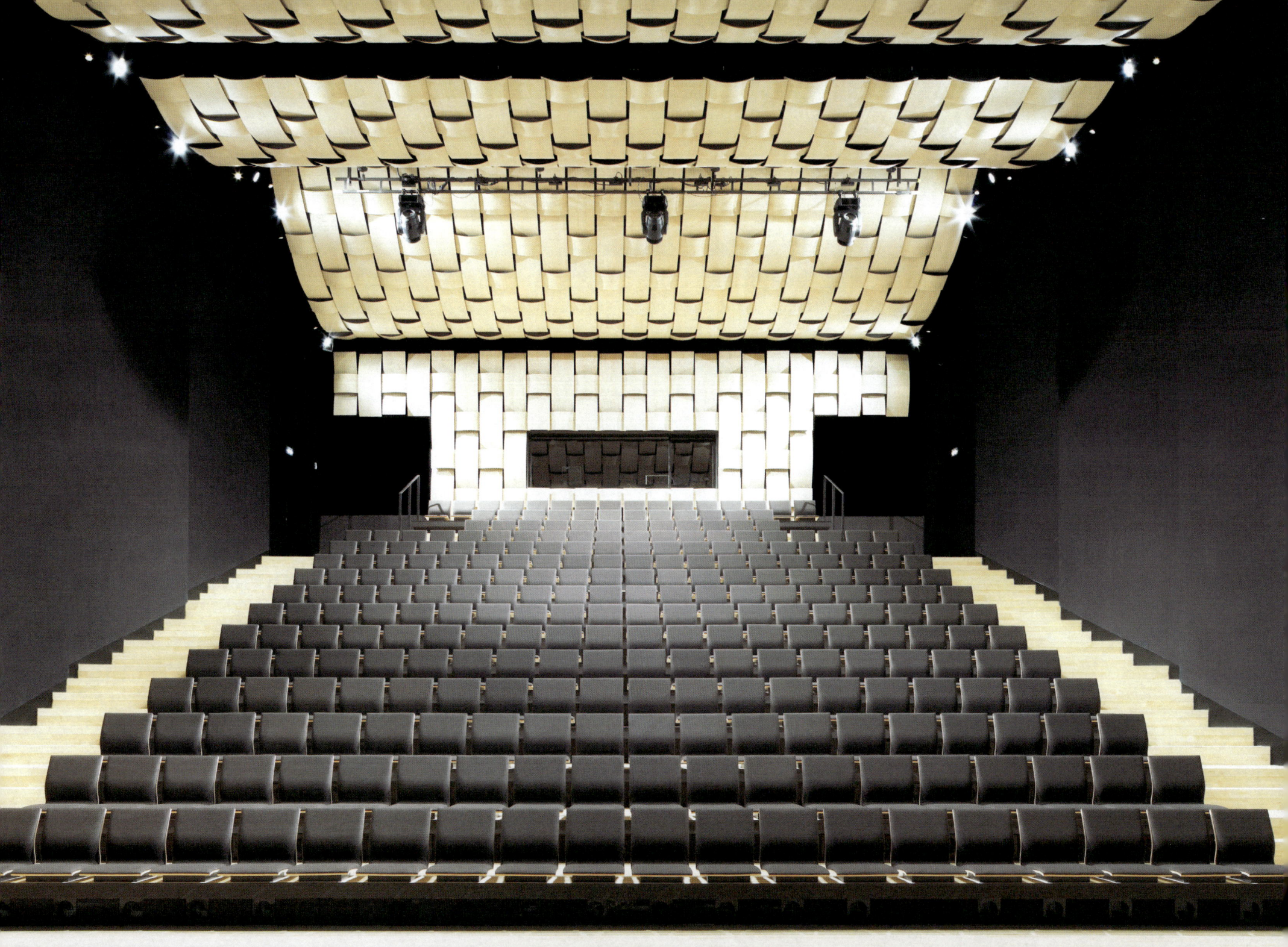

05 WOOD JOINERY
CHIDORI FURNITURE
MOBILE CHIDORI
Fujisato Mokkoujo, Oshu, Iwate Prefecture, Japan (2011)

Chidori is a flexible furniture that can adapt to different uses and life style. Each modular unit can be connected to from all 6 sides, making numerous configurations possible. One Chidori unit consists of 12 timber sticks with different connection details. These special junctions require highly skilled carpenters in the Tohoku region to produce.

This modular furniture is part of the E.JP project set by Kengo Kuma and KKAA after the earthquake and Tsunami of 2011.
This and other object and projects have been designed to help craftsmen from the disaster area who will manufacture them in their local ateliers.

Chidori is a popular child toy and is he inspiration for the structural joint for this furtniture and other KKAA projects

06 WOOD JOINERY
CHIDORI PAVILION
PADIGLIONE CHIDORI

Castello Sforzesco, Milano, Italy (2007)

CIDORI, the literal translation being 1000 birds, does not express how material is dense, but rather the state of birds flying through the sky like particles. This CIDORI KOSHI, or CIDORI Lattice, is a traditional technique lacing thin rectangular wood into a lattice by making a special notch in the wood. By using this technique, a strong structure can be created without using any nails, and at the same time, it is possible to dismantle the structure at once. For this project, we have applied the CIDORI KOSHI in a three-dimensional space, attempting to create an open and transparent "house". This structure has not used any adhesives or nails, and is easy to dismantle. The "house" created by CIDORI KOSHI, is similar to a sentence composed of words. A sentence does not need any nails or adhesives. If carefully composed, a firm, solid sentence can be made. Furthermore, the words can be easily disassembled, creating a new sentence. In this way, words should be a free and eternally-open element. The wood in CIDORI has acquired such infinite liberty.

WOOD JOINERY
07 GC PROSTHO MUSEUM RESEARCH CENTER
MUSEO E CENTRO DI RICERCA GC PROSTHO

Torii Matsu Machi, Kasugai-shi, Aichi Prefecture, Japan (2010)

This is architecture that originates from the system of Cidori, an old Japanese toy. Cidori is an assembly of wood sticks with joints having unique shape, which can be extended merely by twisting the sticks, without any nails or metal fittings. The tradition of this toy has been passed on in Hida Takayama, a small town in a mountain, where many skilled craftsmen still exist. Cidori has a wood 12 mm square as its element, which for this building was transformed into different sizes. Parts are 60mm×60mm×200cm or 60mm×60mm×400cm, and form a grid of 50cm square. This cubic grid also becomes the grid on its own for the showcase in the museum.

Jun Sato, structural engineer for the project, conducted a compressive and flexure test to check the strength of this system, and verified that even the device of a toy could be adapted to 'big' buildings. This architecture shows the possibility of creating a universe by combining small units like toys with your own hands. We worked on the project in the hope that the era of machine-made architectures would be over, and human beings would build them again by themselves.

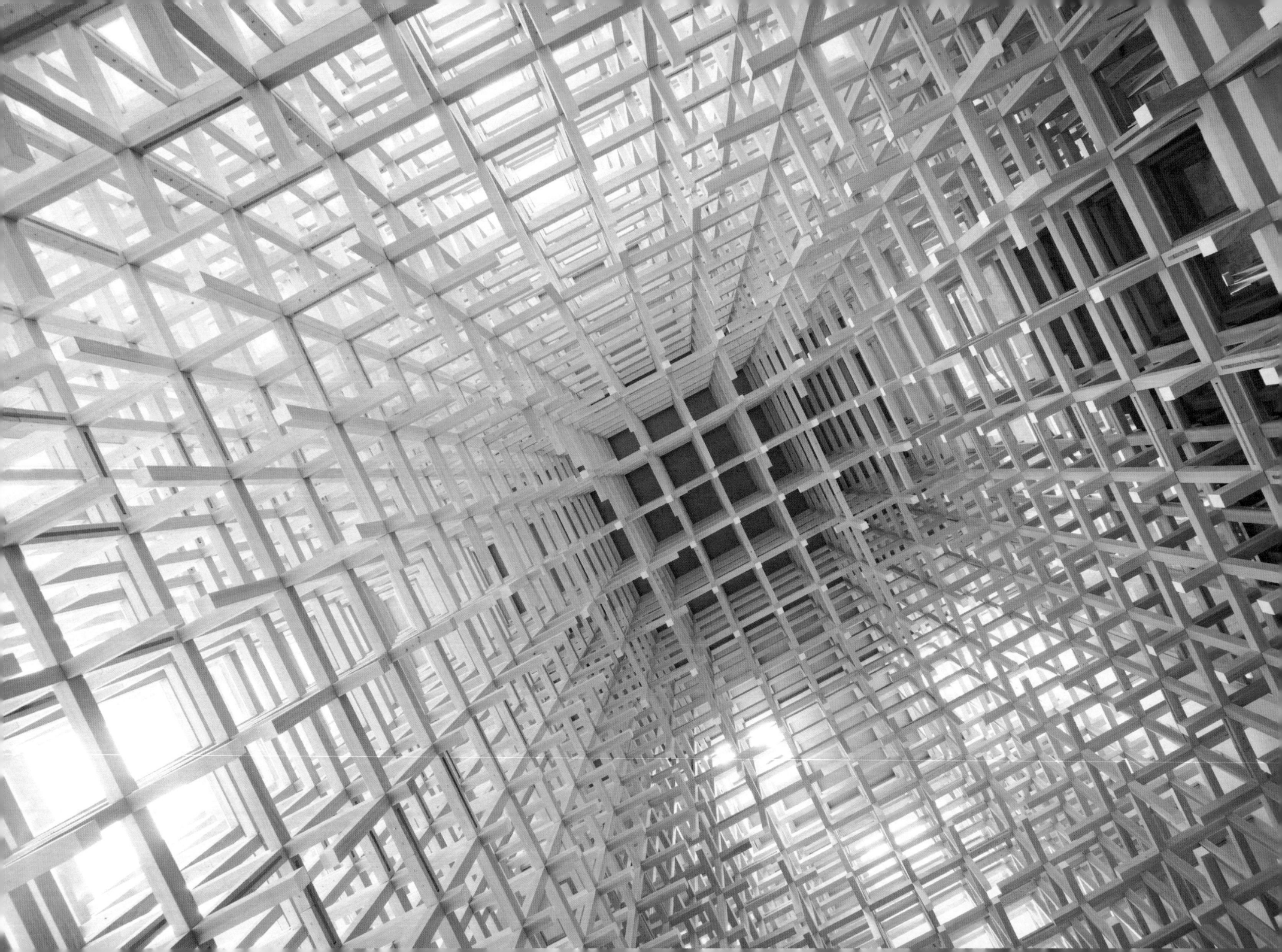

The GC museum represents a bigger scale development of the chidori module, the small structural joint is brought here to the architectural scale of this two stories building

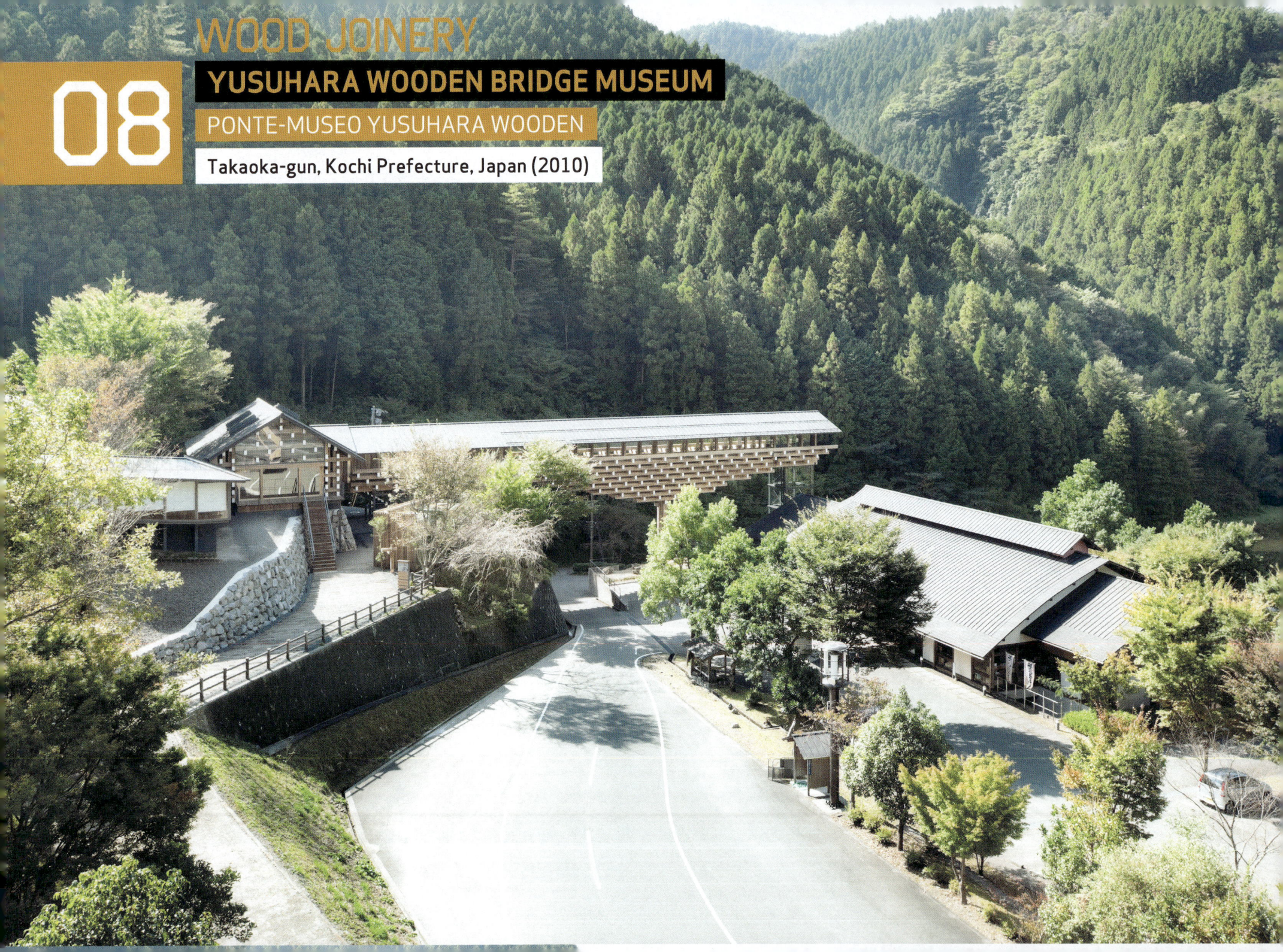

WOOD JOINERY
08 YUSUHARA WOODEN BRIDGE MUSEUM
PONTE-MUSEO YUSUHARA WOODEN
Takaoka-gun, Kochi Prefecture, Japan (2010)

This is a plan to link two public buildings with a bridge-typed facility, which had been long separated by the road in between.
The museum technically bridges communications in this area. It functions not only as a passage between the two facilities but also as an accommodation and workshop, ideal location for artist-in-residence programs. In this project, we challenged a structural system which composes of small parts, referring to cantilever structure often employed in traditional architecture in Japan and China. It is a great example of sustainable design, as you can achieve a big cantilever even without large-sized materials.

A third project in the small town of Yushuara, this architecture combines a bridge and a museum.

09 WOOD JOINERY
STARBUCKS
STARBUCKS
Zaifu, Dazaifu, Fukuoka, Japan (2011)

Location of this Starbucks is somehow characteristic, as it stands on the main approach to the Dazaifu Tenmangu, one of the most major shrines in Japan. Established in 919 A.D., the shrine has been worshiped as "the God for Examination," and receives about 2 million visitors a year who wish their success. Along the main path to the shrine, there are traditional Japanese buildings in one or two stories. The project aimed to make a structure that harmonizes with such townscape, using a unique system of weaving thin woods diagonally.

The building is made of 2,000 stick-like parts in the sizes of 1.3m – 4m length and 6cm section. Total length of the sticks reached as far as 4.4km. We had experimented the weaving of sticks for the project of Chidori and GC Prostho Museum Research Center, and this time we tried the diagonal weaving in order to bring in a sense of direction and fluidity. Three sticks are joined at one point in Chidori and GC, while in Starbucks four steps come to one point because of the diagonal – a more complicated joint. We solved the problem by slightly changing positions of the fulcrums, dividing the four sticks into two groups to avoid concentration on a single point. Piling up of small parts from the ground was highly developed in the traditional architecture of Japan and China. This time the method was greatly improved in combination with state-of-the art technology so that people are brought further into the architecture. It is a fluid, cave-like space.

10 WOOD JOINERY
KYUSHU GEIBUNKAN
KYUSHU GEIBUNKAN
Fukuoka, Japan (2013)

The Annex consists of pieces of small triangle panel in cedar (long side 2.5m, weight 20kg), combinations of which can expand or shrink with no limit. It is a cloud-like work room for pottery. These triangle fragments with slits can corbel out, following the geometry of lattice pattern, and eventually form a roof with the lightness of clouds. The roof is supported by pillars and wall pillars standing at random and ad hoc, and it creates relaxed, humane space underneath that is most appropriate for the people of the town.

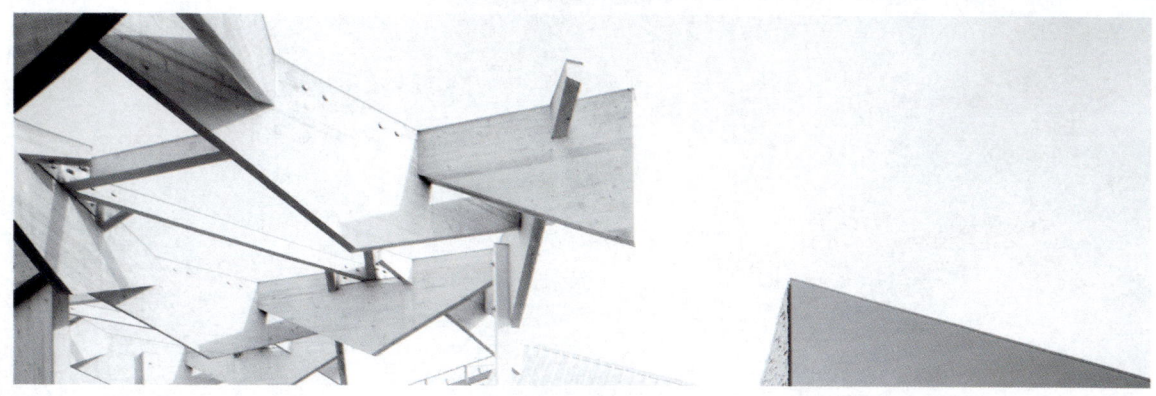

The hexagonal grid created by the structural pattern composition of cedar panels, forms the roof of this pavilion annexed tot he main museum. The wood creates an intimate feeling for the workshop rooms in contrast with the bigger scale of the museum (designed by KKAA at the same time)

WOOD JOINERY
11 SUNNY HILLS
SUNNY HILLS
Omotesando, Tokyo, Japan (2013)

This shop, specialized in selling pineapple cake (popular sweet in Taiwan), is in the shape of a bamboo basket. It is built on a joint system called "Jiigoku-Gumi," traditional method used in Japanese wooden architecture (often observed in Shoji: vertical and cross pieces in the same width are entwined in each other to form a muntin grid). Normally the two pieces intersect in two dimensions, but here they are combined in 30 degrees in 3 dimensions (or in cubic), which came into a structure like a cloud. With this idea, the section size of each wood piece was reduced to as thin as 60mm×60mm. As the building is located in middle of the residential area in Aoyama, we wanted to give some soft and subtle atmosphere to it, which is completely different from a concrete box. We expect that the street and the architectureÐcould be in good chemistry.

The diagonal structural joint developed for the small Starbucks is applied here at a bigger scale in the fashion area of omotesando Tokyo

12 AIR AND FLOW
AIR BRICK
AIR BRICK
Shanghai, China

With the material called ETFE (ethylene tetrafluoroethylene), we created a cell forming a unit, and devised a creature-like structure from these cells. It is a study to realize bigger architecture as a collection of tiny cells of pneumatic structure. In this project, a cell unit was created from ETFE's three-dimensioned transparent membrane, which can be connected without limits. This is the device we used to build the architecture. Each cell is charged with air, and they are linked with tubes. By pouring in and out the air from a single cell, the entire air pressure (in the architecture) can be adjusted and the whole shape can be controlled.

Since the time of Frank Lloyd Wright in 20th century, many architects have advocated "organic architecture." However, what they call "organic" was after all a wavy external form. It was far from the essential softness and flexibility of living things. Cells are joined in different ways and various substances circulate among them. Only such flexibility can cope with the harsh change in our environment, which we call organic softness. Things flow freely there. Life is also a flow. To replace the westernized, highly mechanized wholeness of the last century, we aimed at gaining an Asian-type entirety based on the organic fluidity and flexibility. This project, "Air Brick" was prepared for the exhibition at Shanghai Gallery of Art, Three on the Bund.

Each one of the light elements of this site specific installation for a gallery in Shanghai, is connected to the others with a thin pipe which pumps air into the next element.
the all installation becomes a continuous dynamic flow through the "air bricks"

13 AIR AND FLOW
TEEHAUS
TEEHAUS
Frankfurt, Germany (2007)

Going one step further than "Defeated Architecture", I thought of creating a "Breathing Architecture". A "Defeated" architecture has a one-way passiveness towards the environment. "To Breathe" is to have an interactive communication between the environments.

At times the architecture becomes small as it holds its breath, and at other times it breathes in deeply to become grander. A new dynamic style for the architecture was devised.

Technically, a membrane using a new material called Tenara was used to create a double membrane with air inserted in between. The two membranes are connected by a polyester string. The joints of the membrane and the strings are placed approximately in a 600mm pitch, as they can be seen as dots on the membrane.

Unlike conventional membrane materials, Tenara does not use glass fibers as a base material; therefore it is soft and light. As the membrane expands and contracts as though it breathes, Tenara was chosen as the membrane for this project. Furthermore, as Tenara is highly transparent, it achieves intermediacy between reality and the imaginary world, a distinct texture.

Tatami mats are laid inside to install space for the Tea Ceremony. Tea Rooms originally came from a temporary space called a "Kakoi". This breathing architecture is an attempt to approach the original Tea Room, aiming to oppose to the non-breathing 20th century concrete architectures.

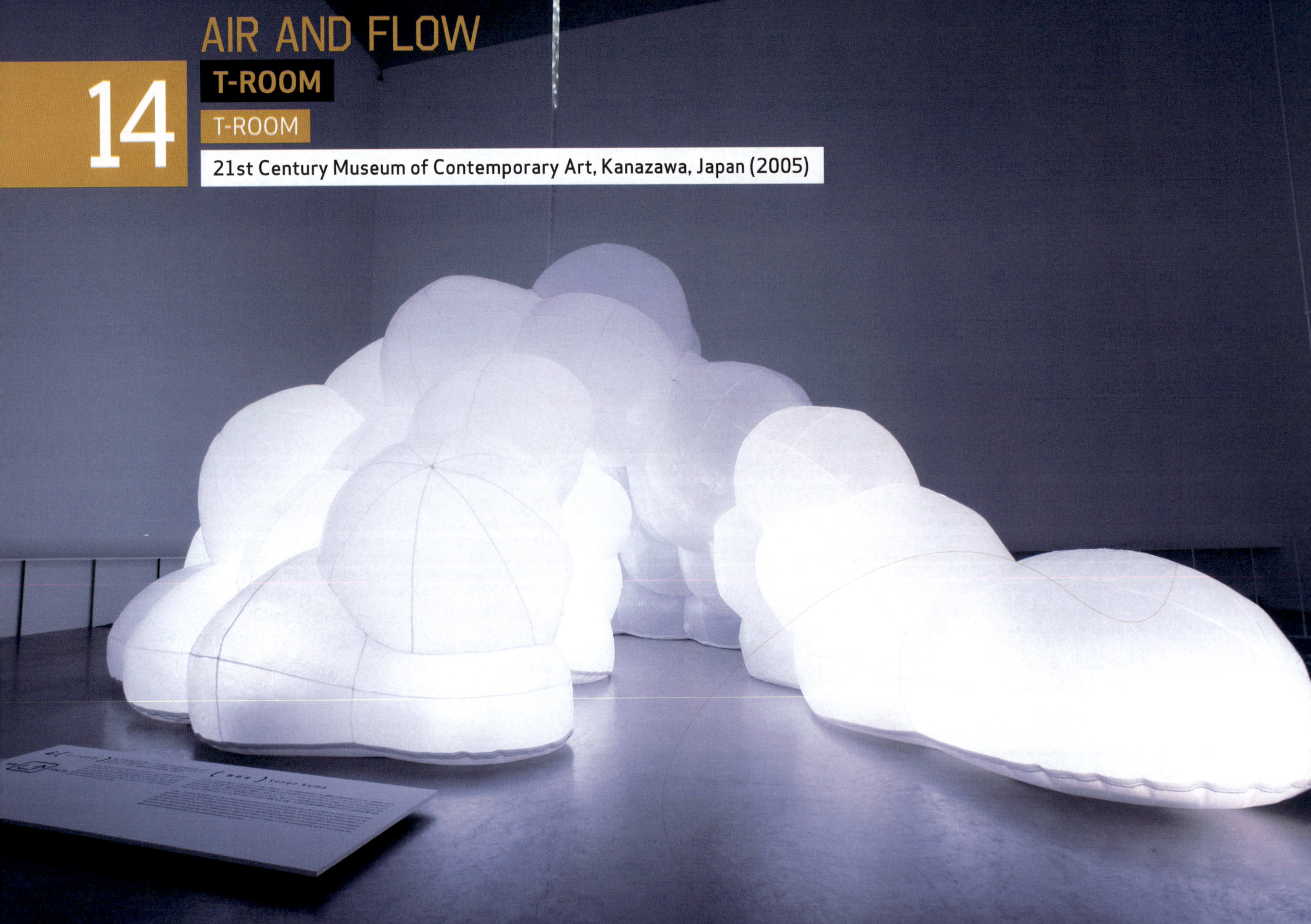

AIR AND FLOW
14 T-ROOM
T-ROOM
21st Century Museum of Contemporary Art, Kanazawa, Japan (2005)

In creating his tearoom Taian, Sen no Rikyu employed coarse walls of earth with plentiful bits of fiber for plastering mixed in. The walls were antithetical in mood to the rigid formality of the shoin (study) style of architecture, dominant at that time. The corners of the walls, instead of forming right angles as might be expected, were rounded and exuded a supple, organic air, like a living thing. I felt that I wanted this tearoom to be soft and supple, in a similar way, for in my mind the tearoom is a place antithetical in character to our rigid and highly regulated society. Instead of bits of fibers I have employed polyester mesh, and instead of earth, silicon, a material used in artificial skin. (Silicon is in fact created from a kind of earth). In form, it is not simply rounded but also moves in a soft, spongy way, like a living organism, through the entry and release of air. The purpose of this tearoom is to destroy the rigidity of architecture (society) and return to it the essential flexibility of living things.

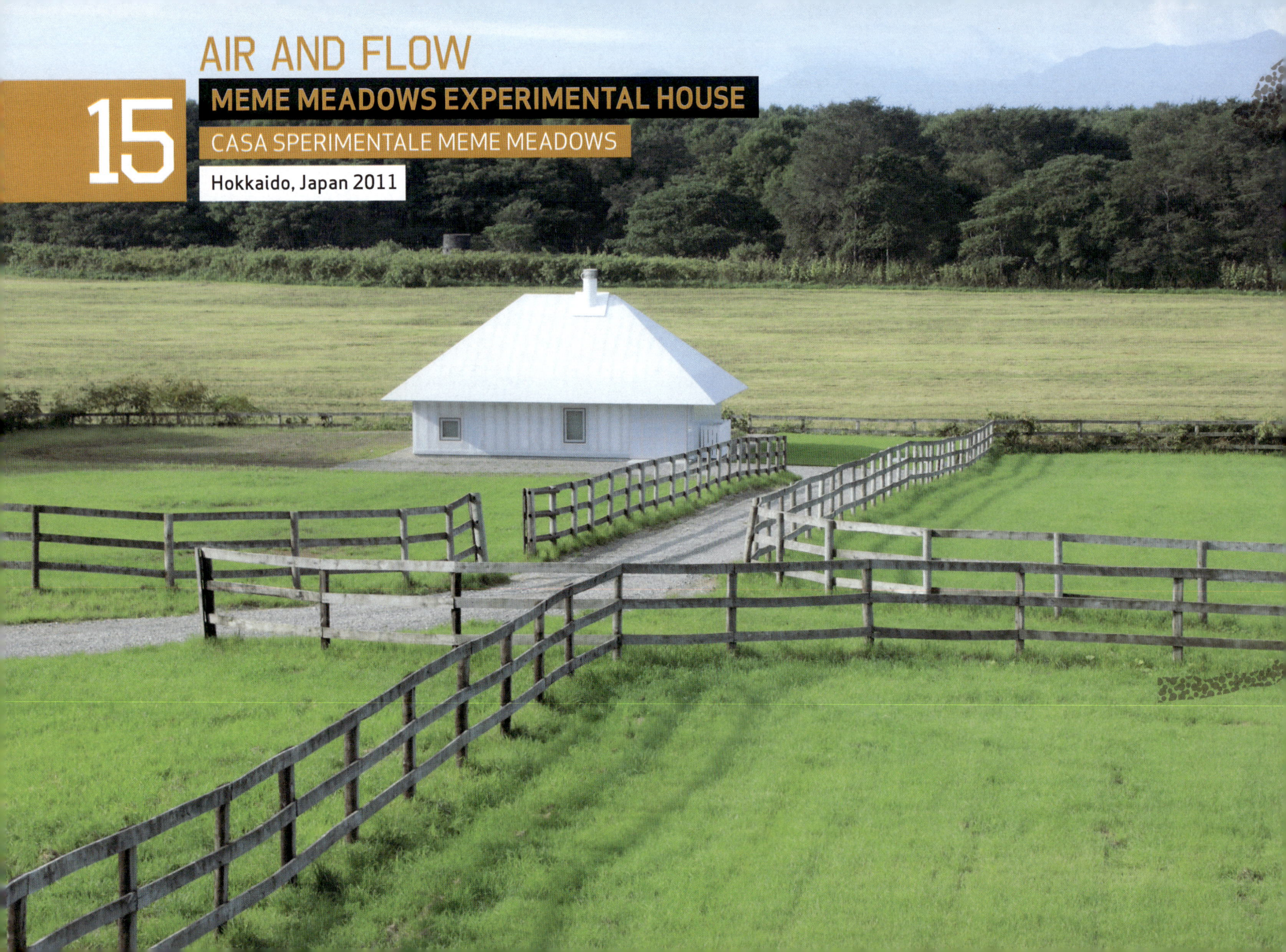

15 AIR AND FLOW
MEME MEADOWS EXPERIMENTAL HOUSE
CASA SPERIMENTALE MEME MEADOWS
Hokkaido, Japan 2011

We were in charge of the first experimental house, and in the process of designing, we got a number of clues from "Chise," the traditional housing style of the Ainu. What is most characteristic about Chise is that it is a "house of grass" and "house of the earth." While in Honshu (the main island) a private house is principally a "house in wood" or "house of earthen wall," Chise is distinctively a "house of grass," as the roof and the wall are entirely covered with sedge or bamboo grass so that it can secure heat-insulating properties. Also, in Honshu the floor is raised for ventilation to keep away humidity, whereas in Chise they spread cattail mat directly on the ground, make a fireplace in the center, and never let the fire go out throughout the year. The fundamental idea of Chise, "house of the earth," is to keep warming up the ground this way and retrieve the radiation heat generated from it Here is how section of the house is structured: We wrapped a wooden frame made of Japanese larch with a membrane material of polyester fluorocarbon coating. Inner part is covered with removable glass-fiber-cloth membrane. Between the two membranes, a polyester insulator recycled from PET bottles is inserted that penetrates the light. This composition is based on the idea that by convecting the air in-between, the internal environment could be kept comfortable because of the circulation.

We do not treat insulation within the thickness of heat-insulation material only, which was a typical attitude of the static environmental engineering in 20th century. What we aim at is a dynamic environmental engineering to replace it for this age. That we utilize the radiant heat from the floor is part of it, and it has been verified that you could spend several days in winter here without using floor heating. The other reason we covered the house with membrane material was our longing for a life surrounded by natural light, as if you were wrapped in daylight on the grassland. Without relying on any lighting system, you simply get up when it gets light, and sleep after dark – we expect this membrane house enables you to lead a life that synchronizes the rhythm of the nature.

In one part of the house, a wooden insulated window sash is installed external to the membrane. It is a new device to monitor the living environment of the house by changing various types of sashes. Likewise, all glass fiber cloth in the interior can be removed so that we can continue many kinds of environmental experiment.

WOOD

01 MANIFATTURA PROJECT - GREEN INNOVATION FACTORY

PROGETTO MANIFATTURA - GREEN INNOVATION FACTORY

Rovereto, Trento, Italy (2010)

CREDITS	
Area	**50,000 sqm**
Client	**Trentino Sviluppo**
Architect + Partner	**Kengo Kuma & Associates (Master Plan with CarloRatti Associati and Arup)** Kengo Kuma, Yuki Ikeguchi, Maurizio Mucciola, Maria-Chiara Piccinelli, Roberto Aparicio Ronda, Miguel Huelga De La Fuente, Jaime Fernandez Calvache
System	**Timber, Concrete**
Construction	**2015-2018**
Project Manager and Client Architect	**Stefano Sani**
Progetto strutture in legno	**ing. Ermanno Acler**
Supporto al progetto delle opere edili	**arch. Marco Giovanazzi**
Supporto al progetto delle strutt. in c.a. e acciaio	**ing. Marco Zanuso**
Consulente per la progettazione sostenibile	**Arup Milano**
Consulente per la mobilità sostenibile	**MIC - Mobility in Chain**

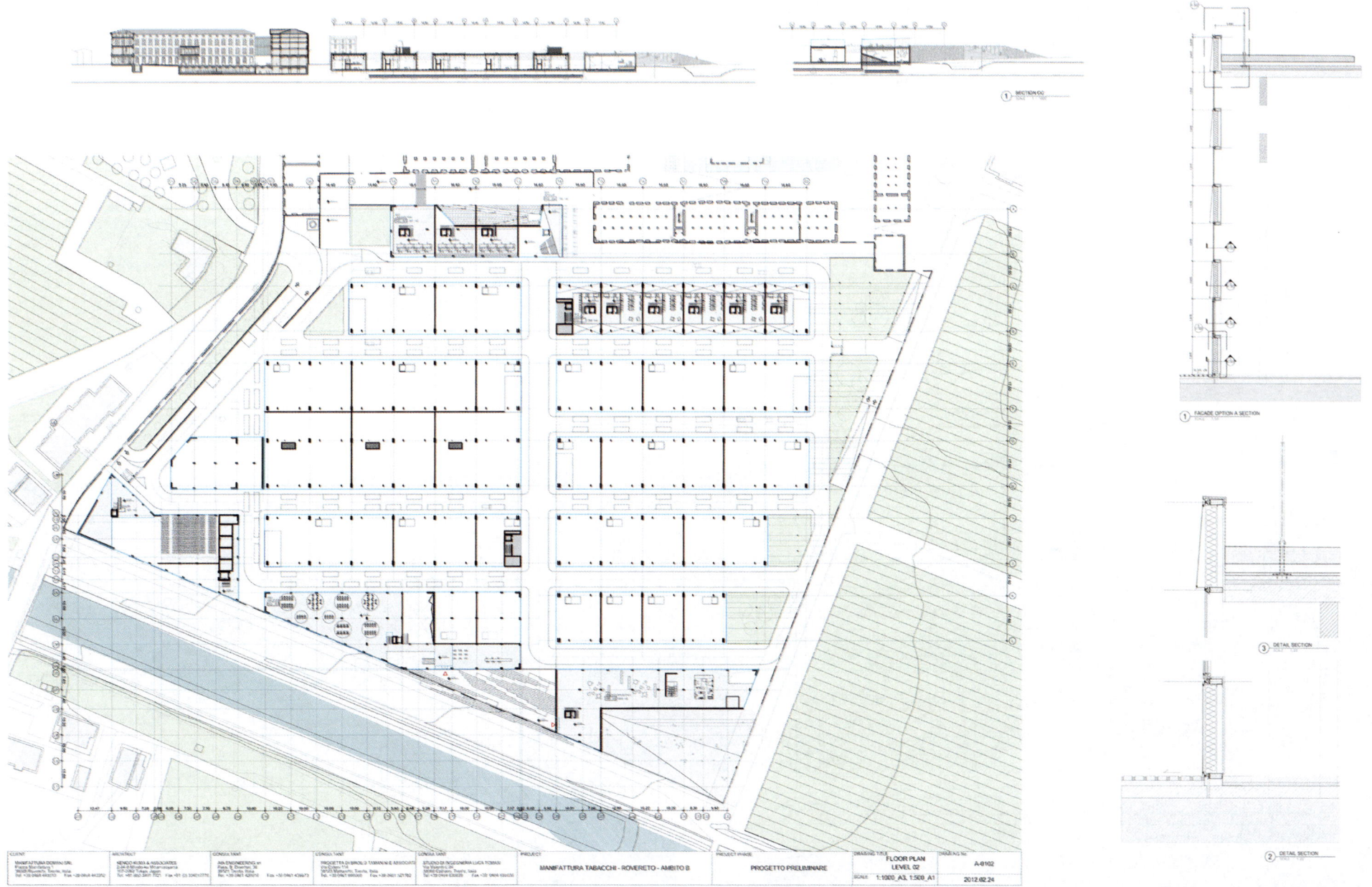

WOOD
02 | YUSUHARA MARKET
MERCATO DI YUSUHARA

Yusuhara, Yusuhara-cho, Takaoka, Kochi Prefecture, Japan (2000)

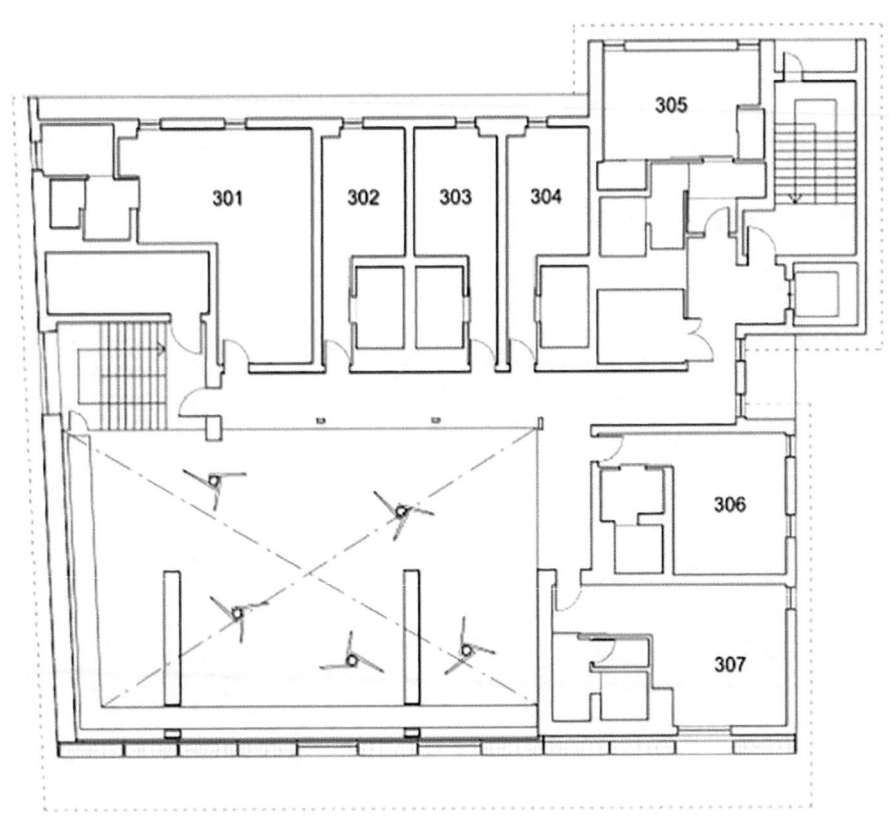
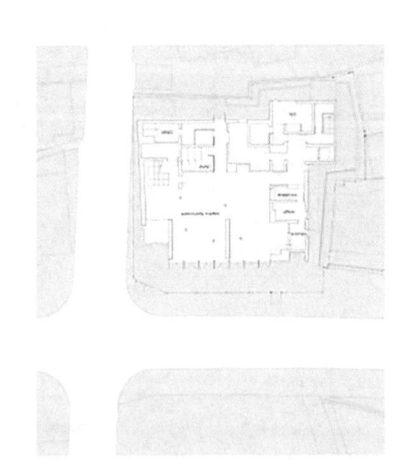

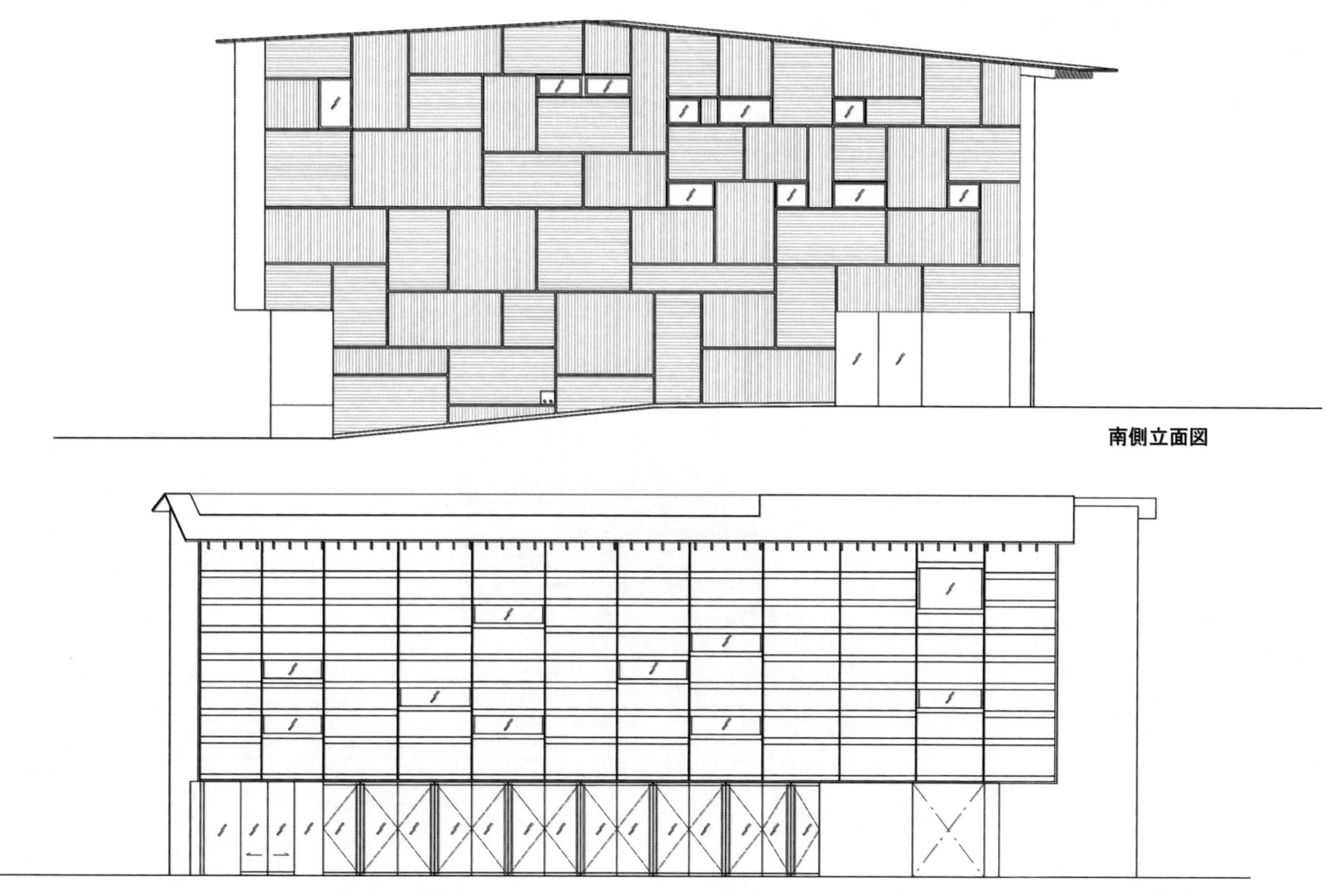

南側立面図

東側立面図
S=1:200(A4)

WOOD

03 YUSUHARA TOWN HALL

MUNICIPIO DI YUSUHARA

Yusuhara, Yusuhara-cho, Takaoka, Kochi Prefecture, Japan (2006)

CREDITS	
Area	**1,132.00m²**
Budget	**360,259,200JPY**
Client	**Tomio Yano, Town Mayor of Yusuhara**
Architect + Partner	**Kengo Kuma & Associates**
ColB. Team	**Ks Design**
Engineer	**Daio Shin-yo (building) Ventilation and Hygiene/Yondenko**
System	**Main structure/reinforced concrete Pile or Foundation / Direct foundation**

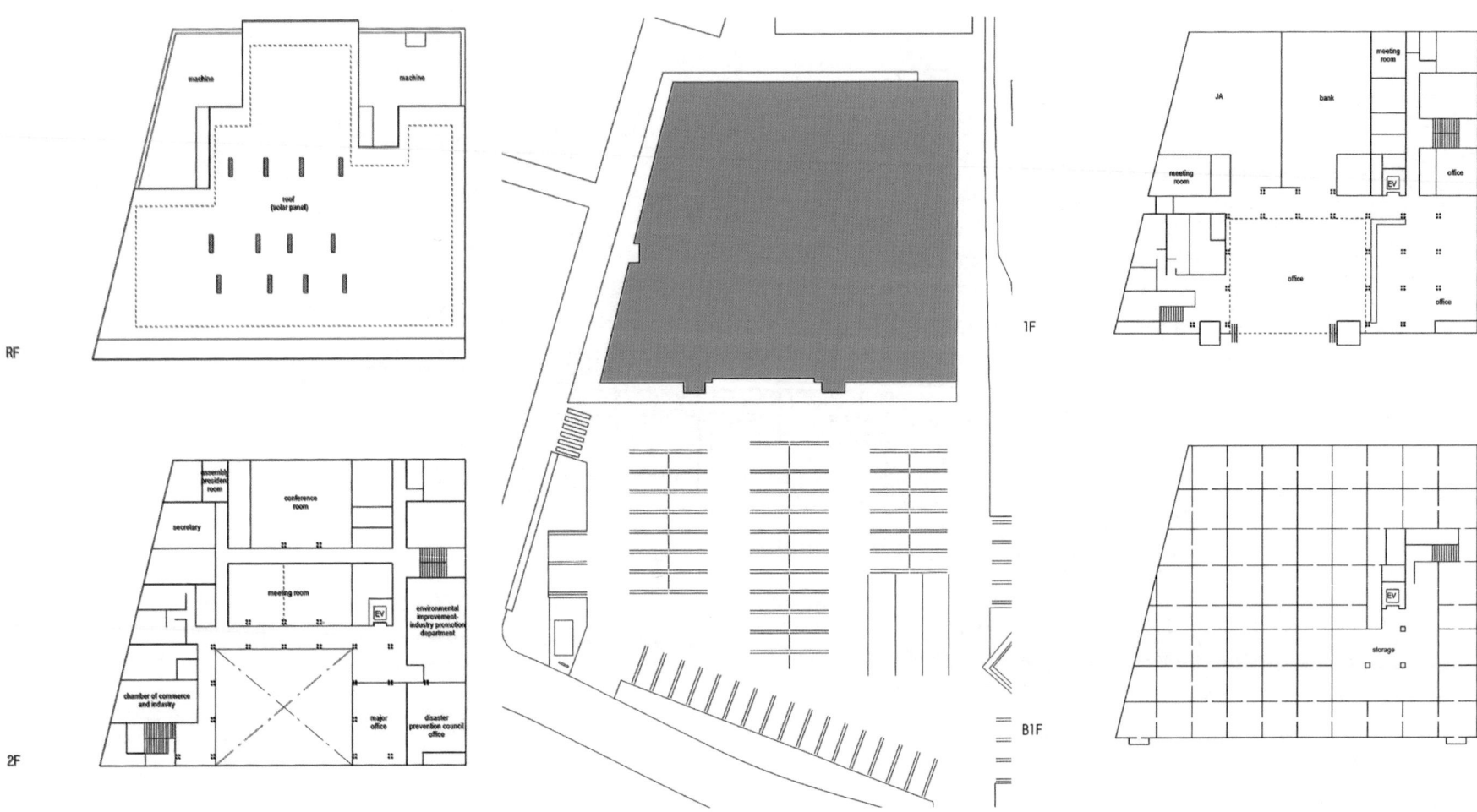

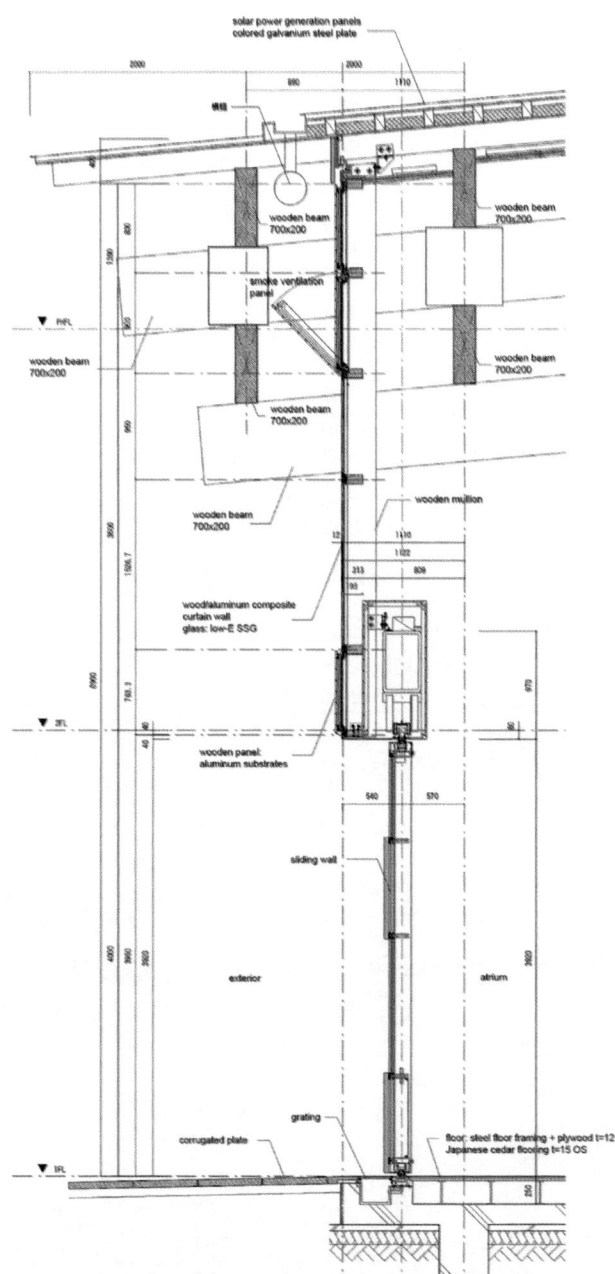

curtain wall detail 1/50

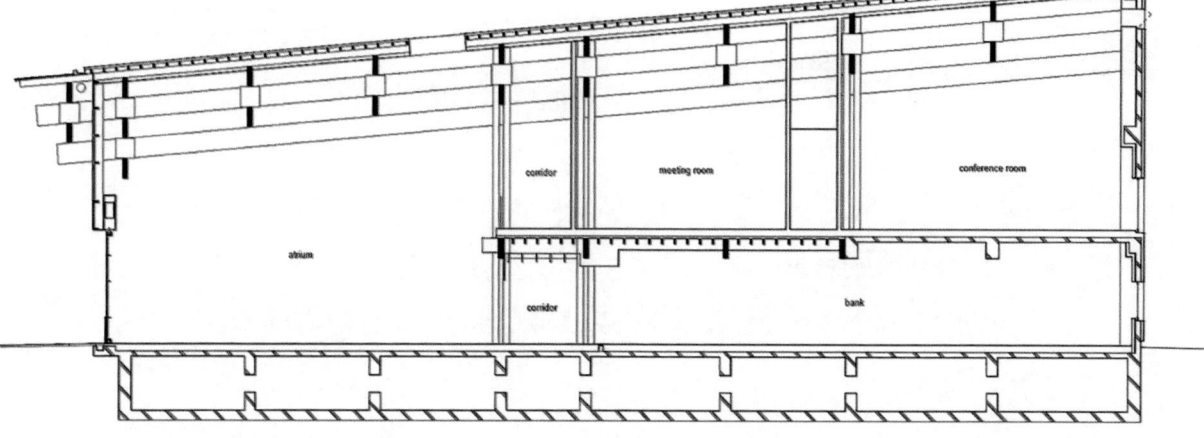

section 1/800

WOOD
BESANÇON ART AND CULTURE CENTER
CENTRO D'ARTE E CULTURA DI BESANÇON

04

Besançon, France (2013)

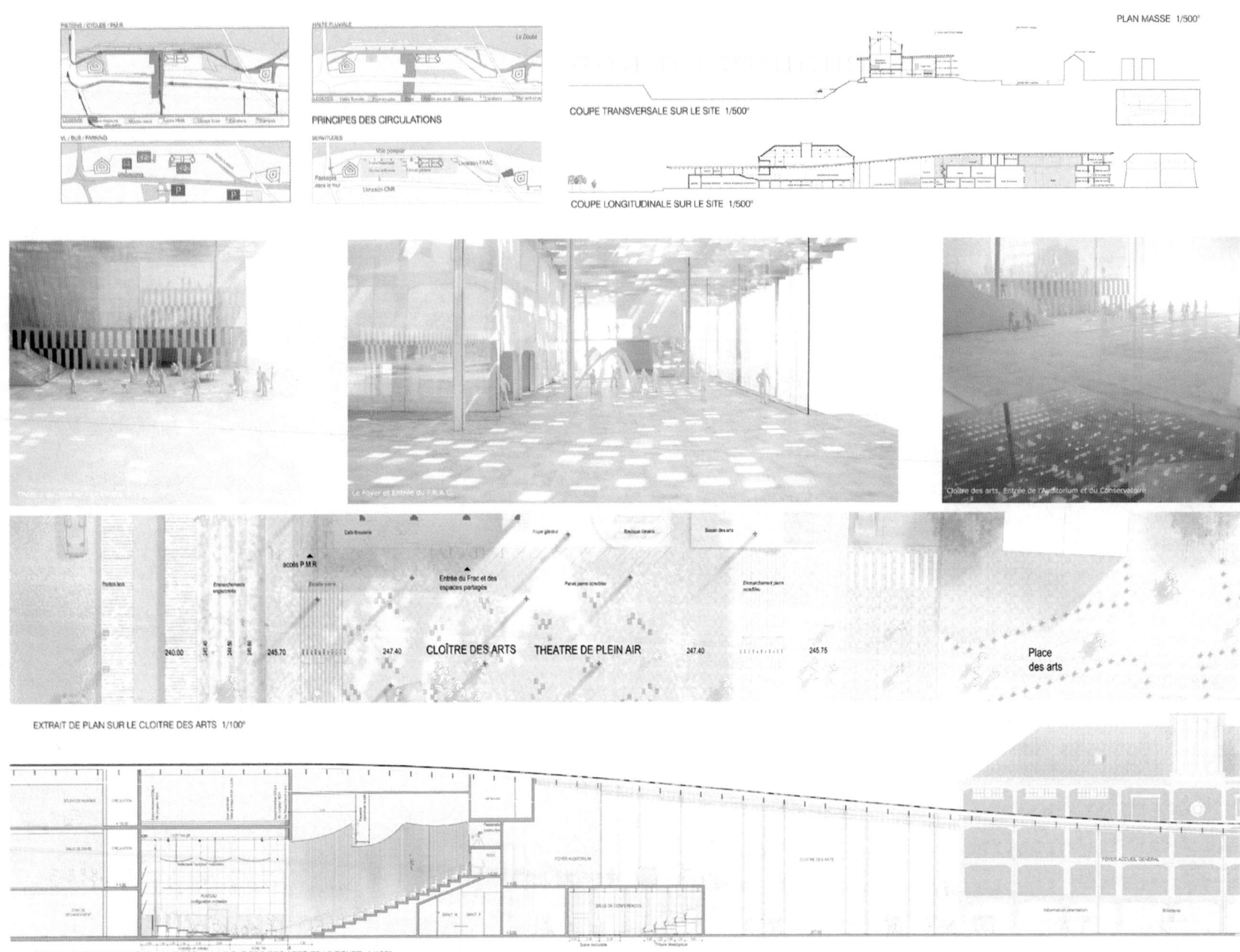

PLAN TOITURE 1/200°

ELEVATION SUD 1/200°

ELEVATION NORD 1/200°

ELEVATION OUEST CNR 1/200°   ELEVATION OUEST FRAC 1/200°   ELEVATION EST FRAC 1/200°   ELEVATION EST CNR 1/200°

WOOD JOINERY
CHIDORI FURNITURE
MOBILE CHIDORI

Fujisato Mokkoujo, Oshu, Iwate Prefecture, Japan (2011)

Assembly Sequence

01

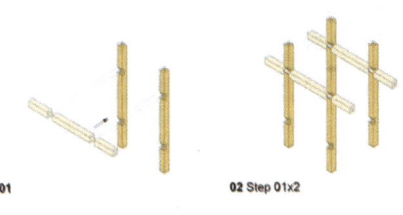
02 Step 01x2

03

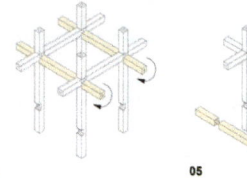
04

05

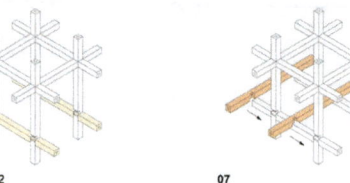
06 Step 05x2

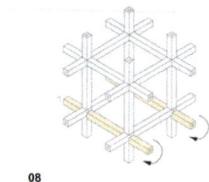
07

08

Components

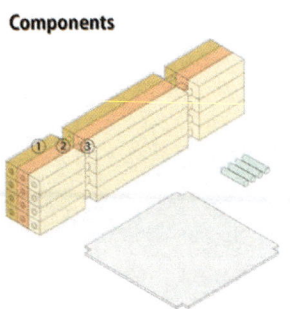

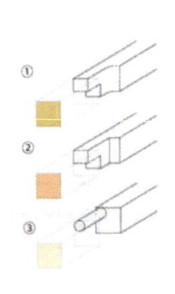

① ② ③

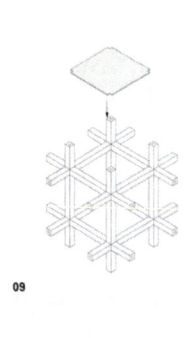
09

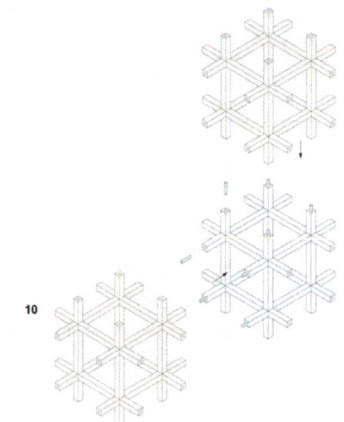
10

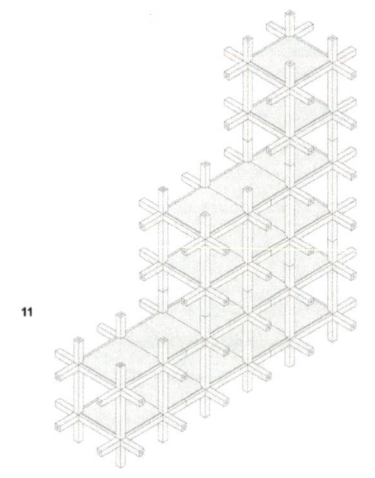
11

WOOD JOINERY
CHIDORI PAVILION
PADIGLIONE CHIDORI

Castello Sforzesco, Milano, Italy (2007)

CREDITS	
Contest	**100 years of Mondadori Milano Capitale del Design**
Client	**BALS Tokyo and Motorola**
Architect + Partner	**Kengo Kuma & Associates**
Project Team	**Jun Satoh Structural Engineers + Matsushita Electric Works**
ColB. Team	**studio KAYA, IKEYA**

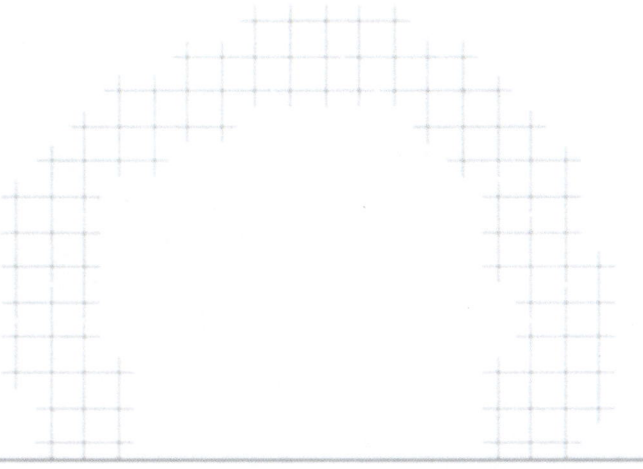
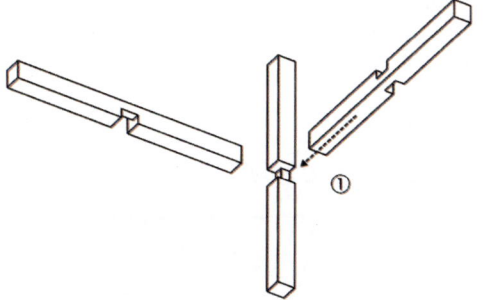
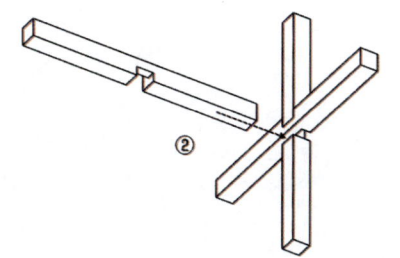
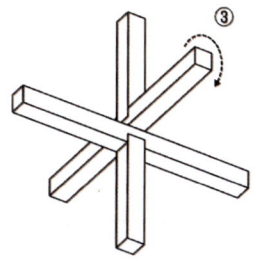
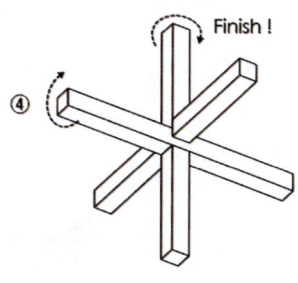
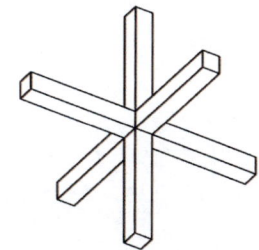

07 WOOD JOINERY
GC PROSTHO MUSEUM RESEARCH CENTER
MUSEO E CENTRO DI RICERCA GC PROSTHO

Torii Matsu Machi, Kasugai-shi, Aichi Prefecture, Japan (2010)

CREDITS	
Contest	**100 years of Mondadori Milano Capitale del Design**
Area	**626.5m²**
Client	**GC Corporation**
Architect + Partner	**Kengo Kuma & Associates**
Project Team	**Design Department of Matsui Construction + Jun Sato Structural Design**
ColB. Team	**Daiko Electrics, Nippon Design Center Inc, Hara Design Institute**
Engineer	**Matsui Construction**
Render + Photos	**Daici Ano**

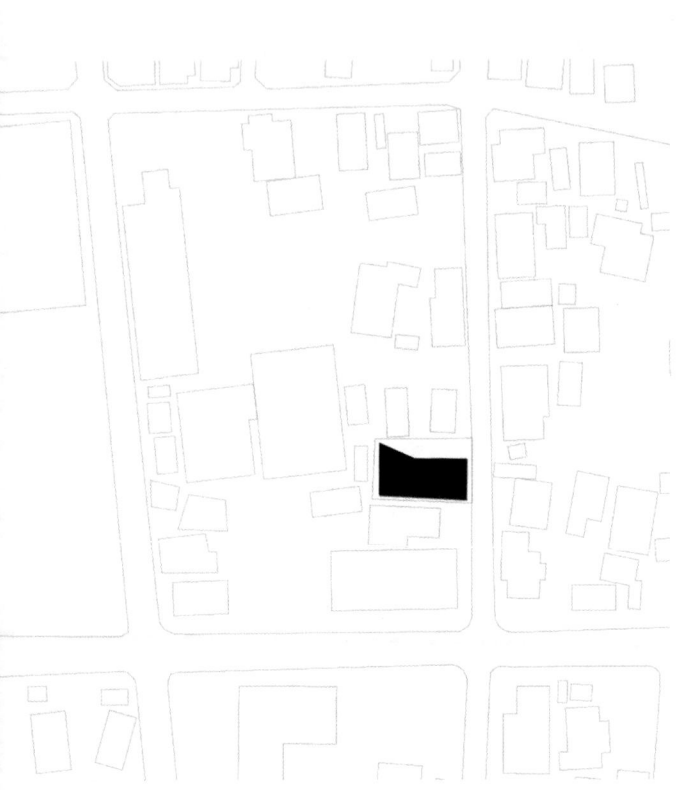
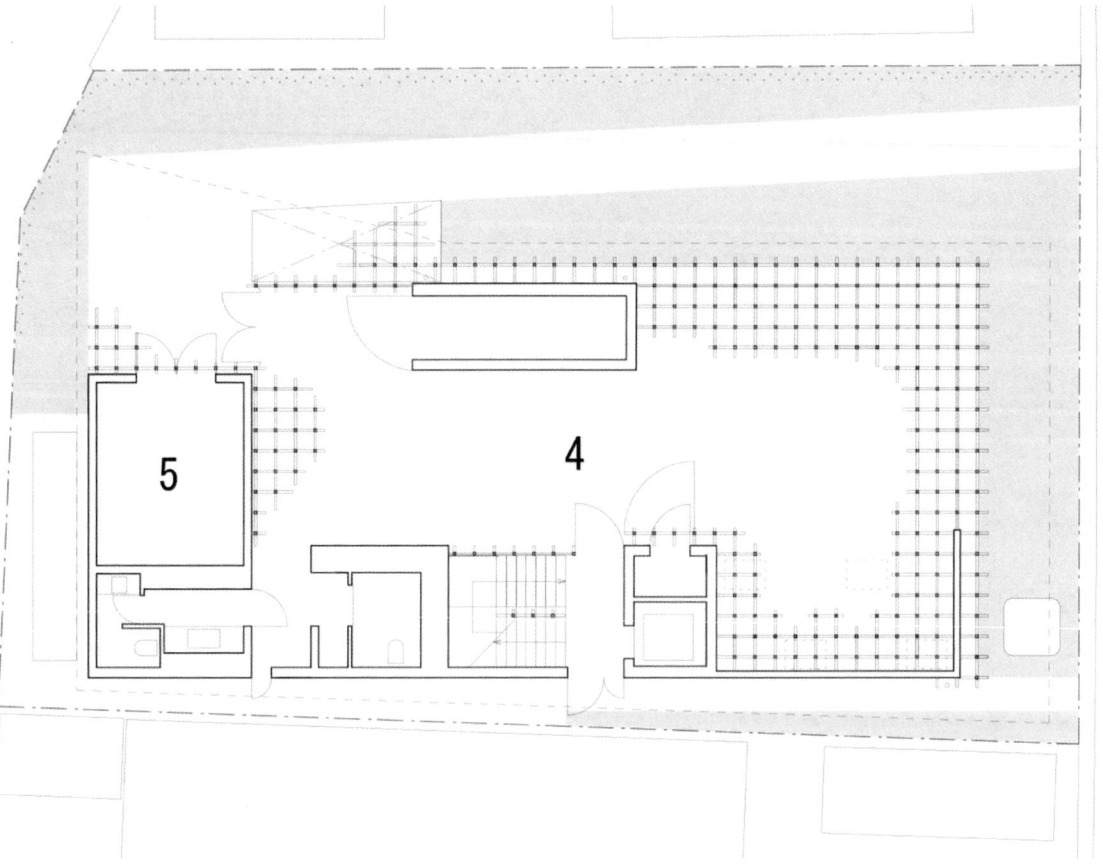

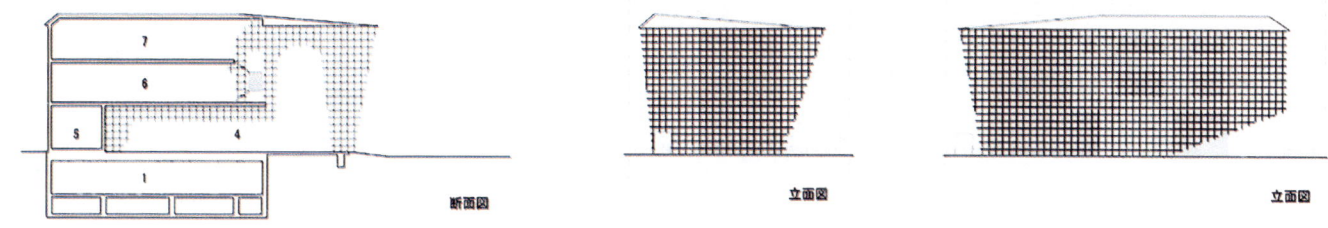

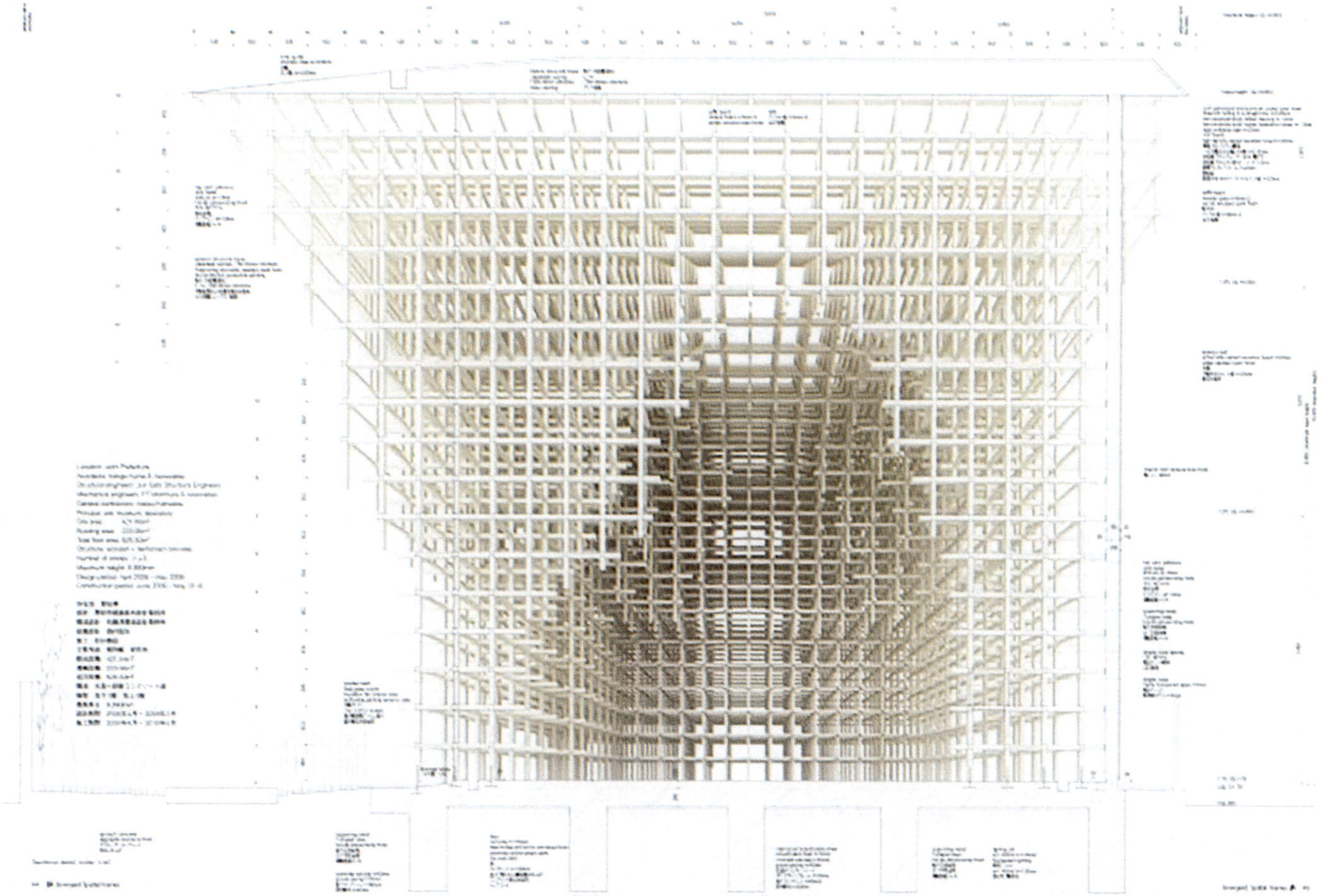

WOOD JOINERY
YUSUHARA WOODEN BRIDGE MUSEUM
PONTE-MUSEO YUSUHARA WOODEN

Takaoka-gun, Kochi Prefecture, Japan (2010)

CREDITS

Contest	Mat and Direct Foundation
Area	574,15m²
Client	Tomio Yano, Town Mayor of Yusuhara
Architect + Partner	Kengo Kuma & Associates
Project Team	K's design
ColB. Team	Katsuo Nakata & Associates + Showa Denki Kogyo + Kansai Setsubi
Engineer	Shimanto Sogo Construction
System	Pile or Foundation / Mat and direct foundation
Render + Photos	Takumi Ota Photography

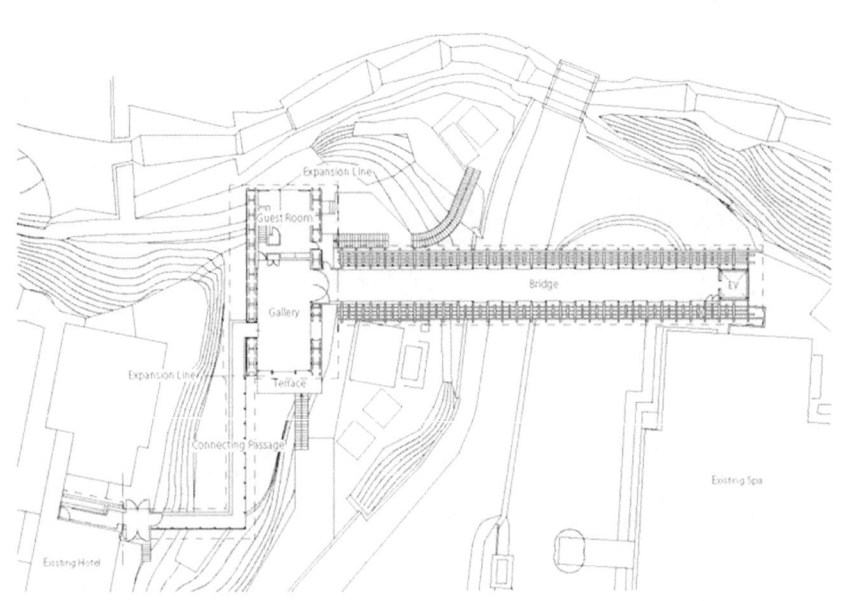

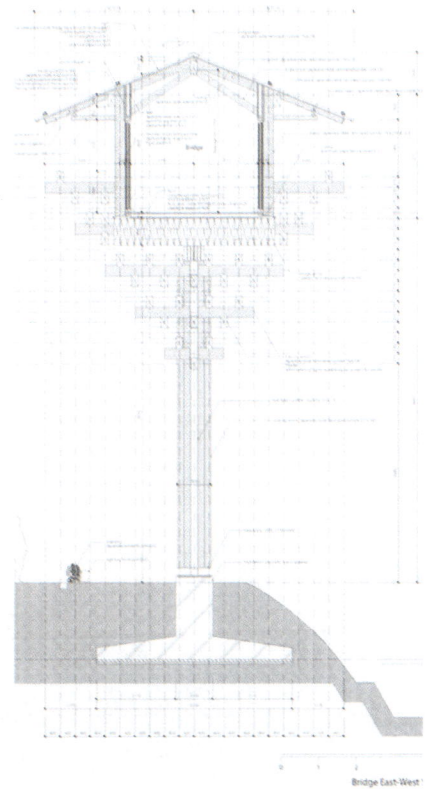

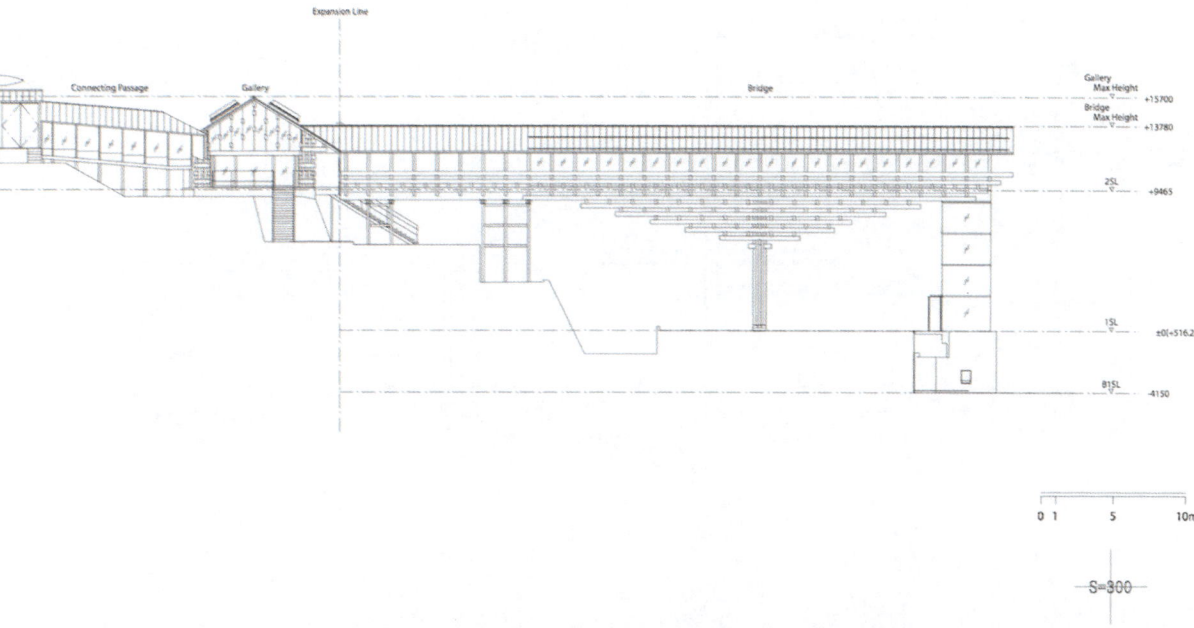

KENGO KUMA & ASSOCIATES | MONOGRAPH.IT | 79

WOOD JOINERY

09 STARBUCKS

STARBUCKS

Zaifu, Dazaifu, Fukuoka, Japan (2011)

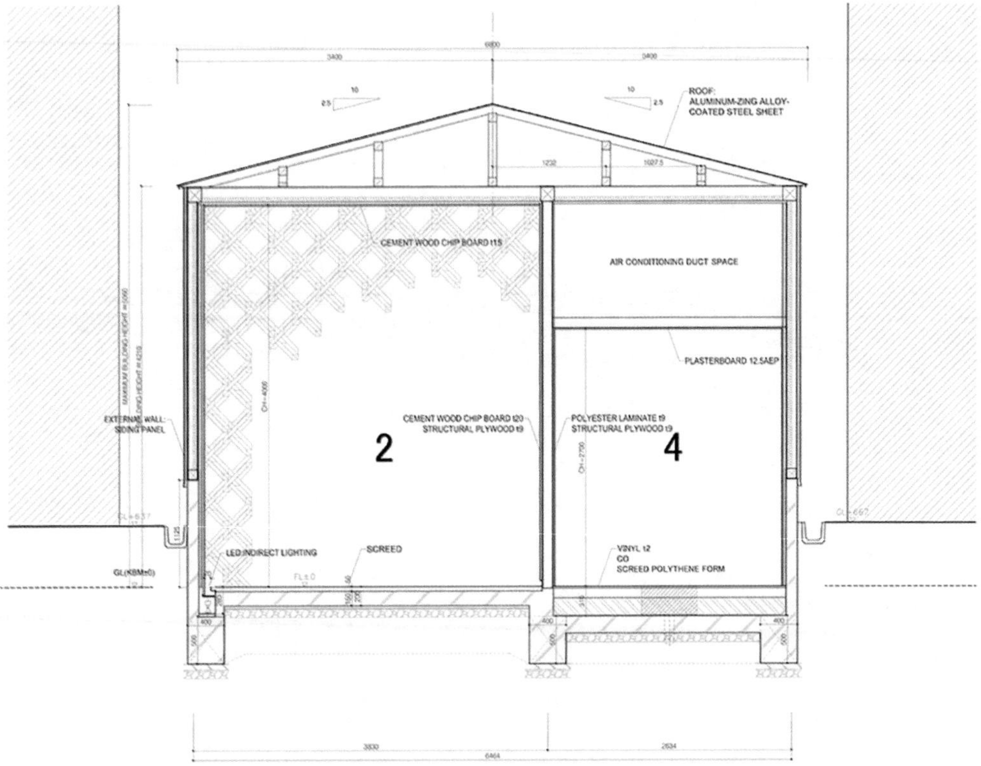

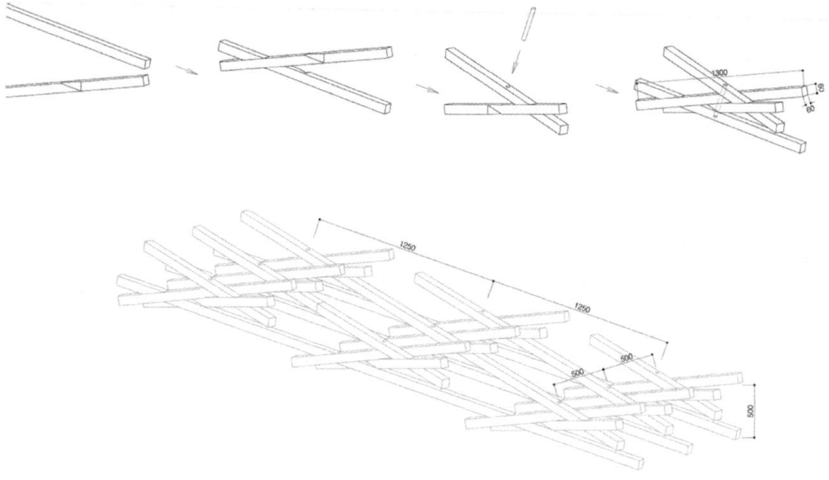

1 ENTRANCE
2 CAFE SEATING
3 BACK BAR
4 WORK ROOM
5 MANAGERS ROOM
6 WC
7 WC
8 MACHINE ROOM
9 GARDEN
10 AIR CONDITIONING UNIT

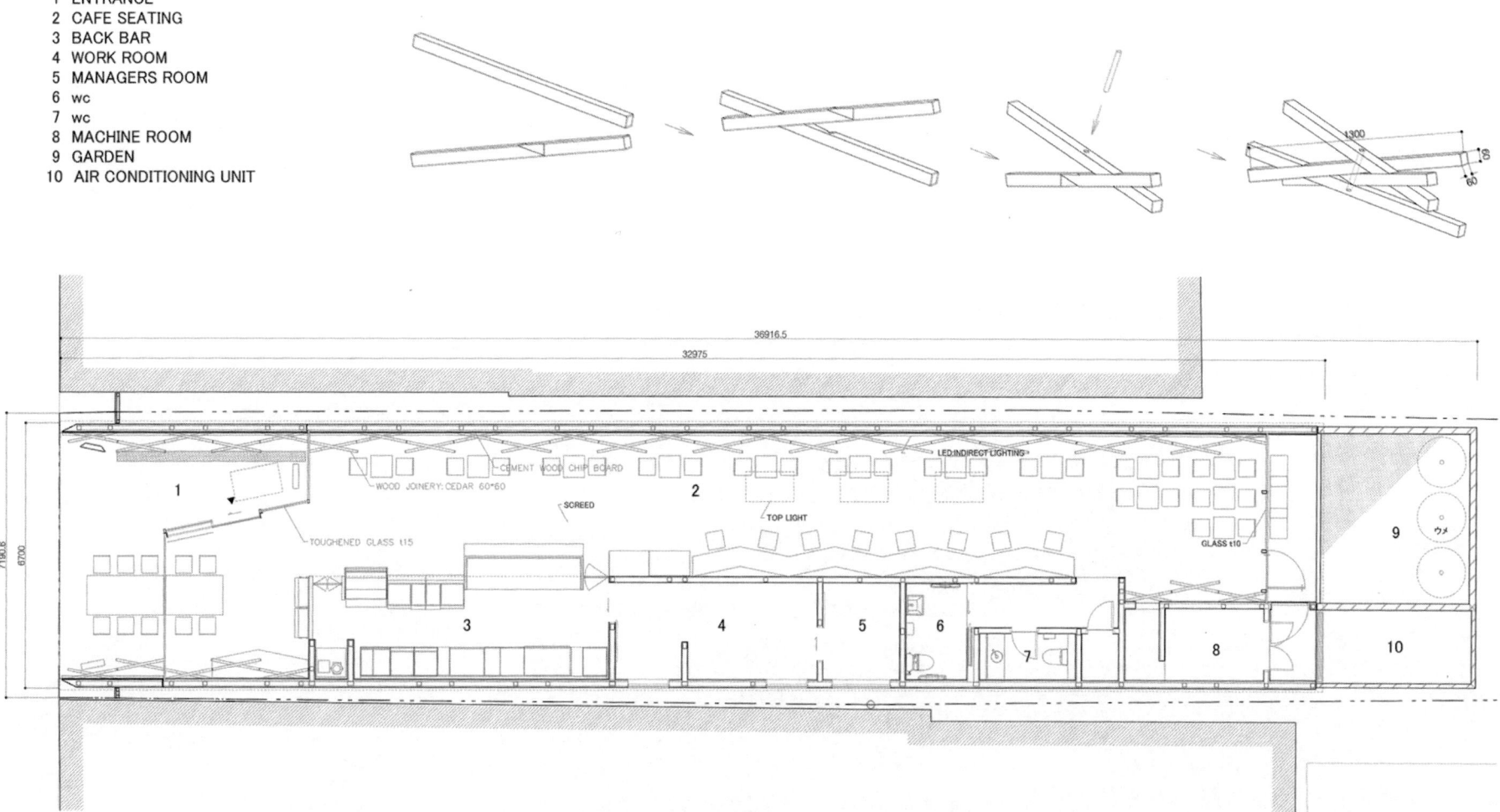

WOOD JOINERY
10 KYUSHU GEIBUNKAN
KYUSHU GEIBUNKAN
Fukuoka, Japan (2013)

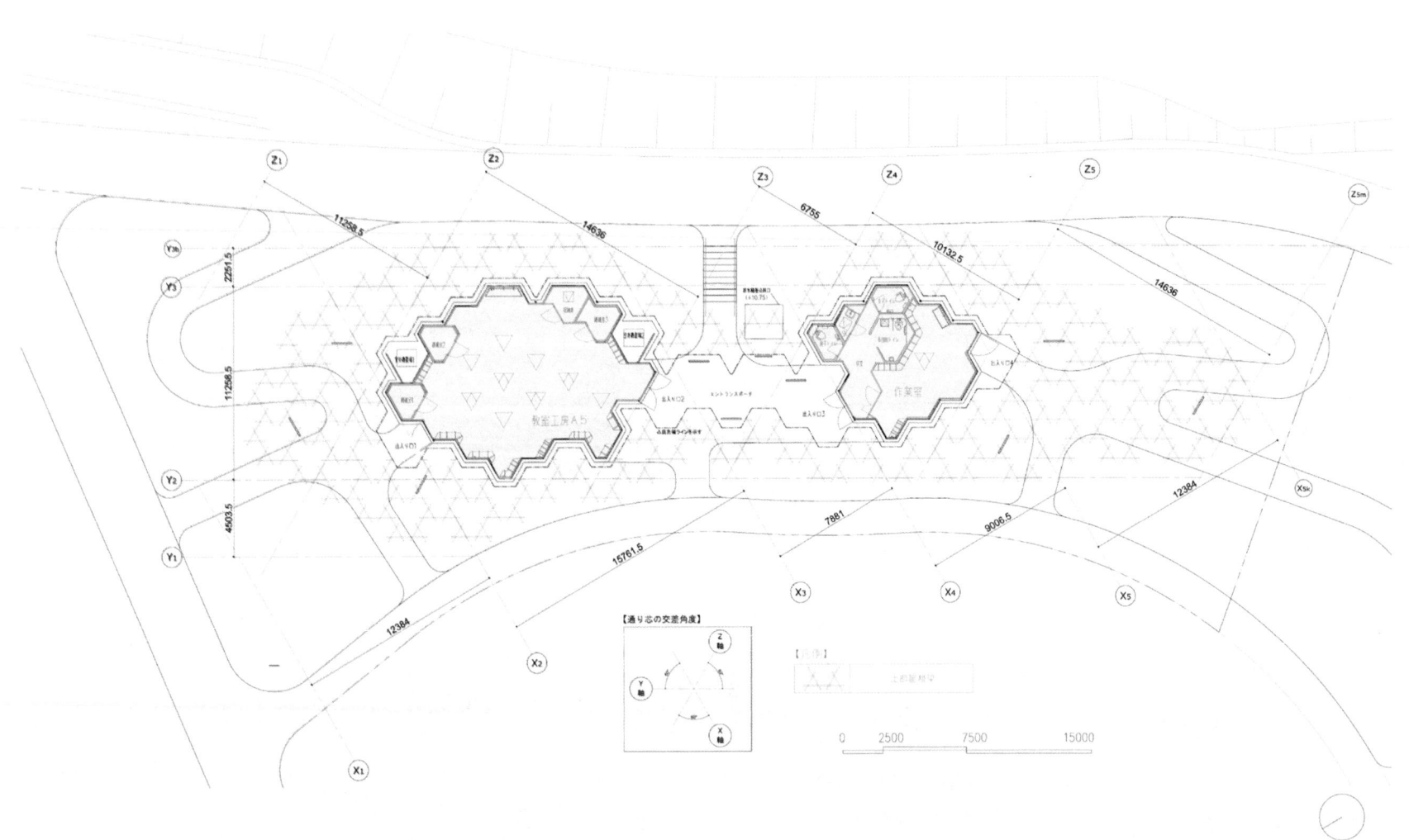

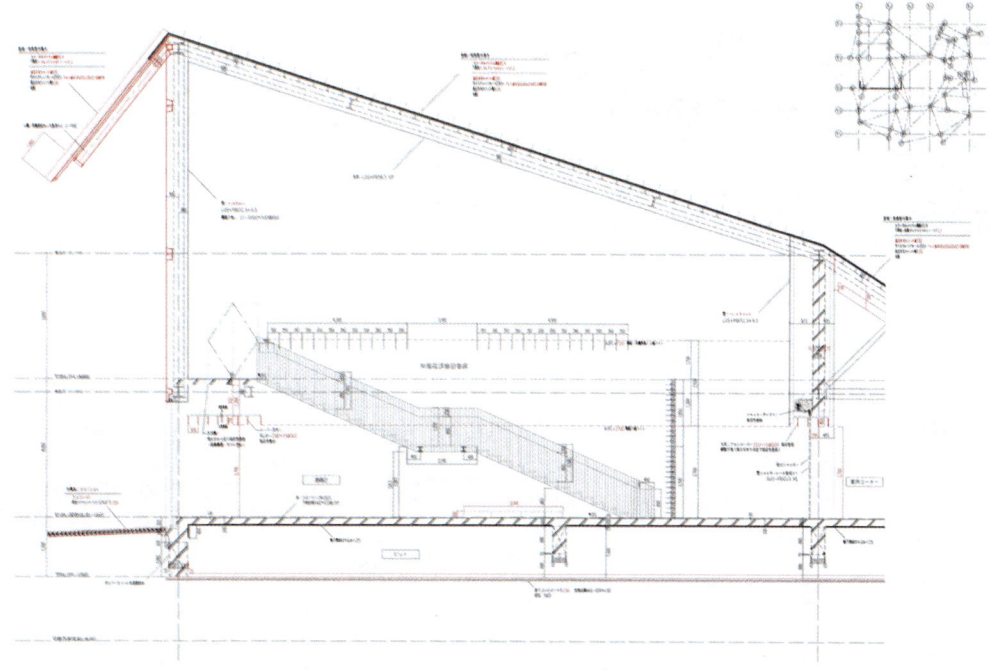
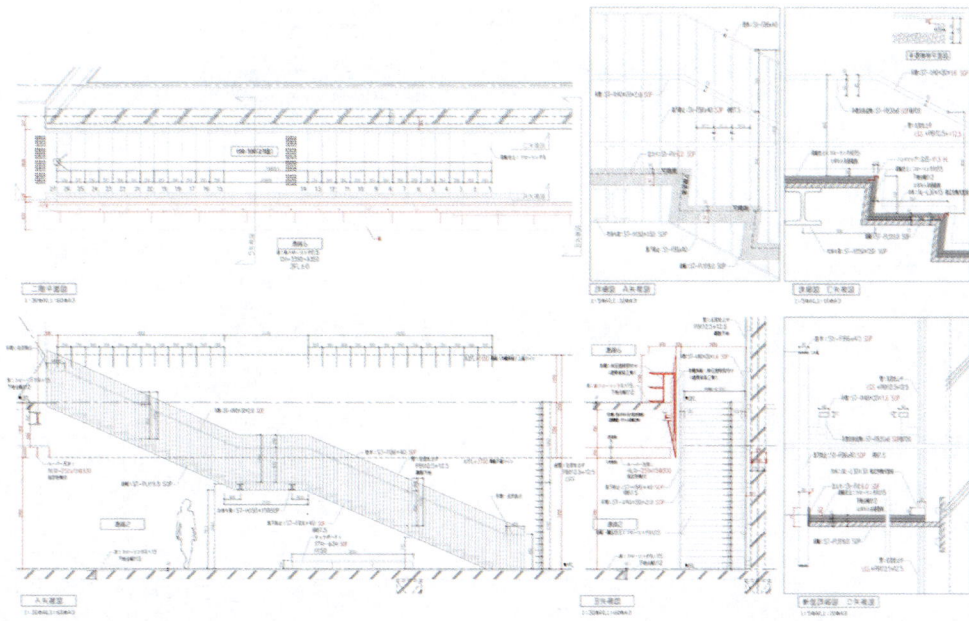

WOOD JOINERY

11 SUNNY HILLS
SUNNY HILLS
Omotesando, Tokyo, Japan (2013)

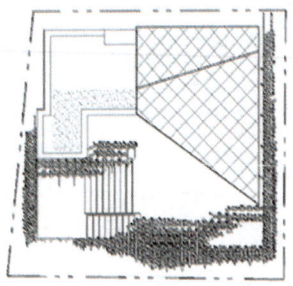
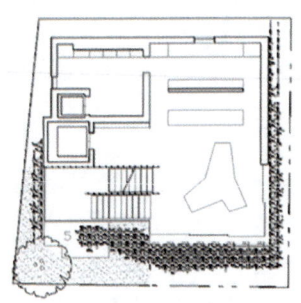
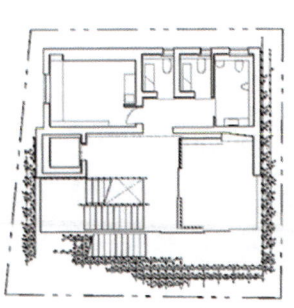
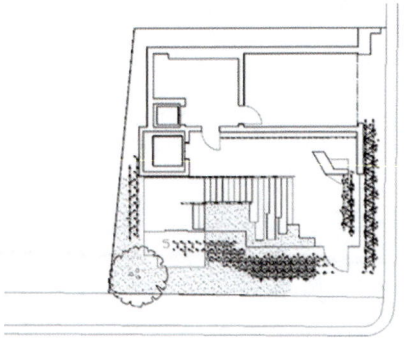
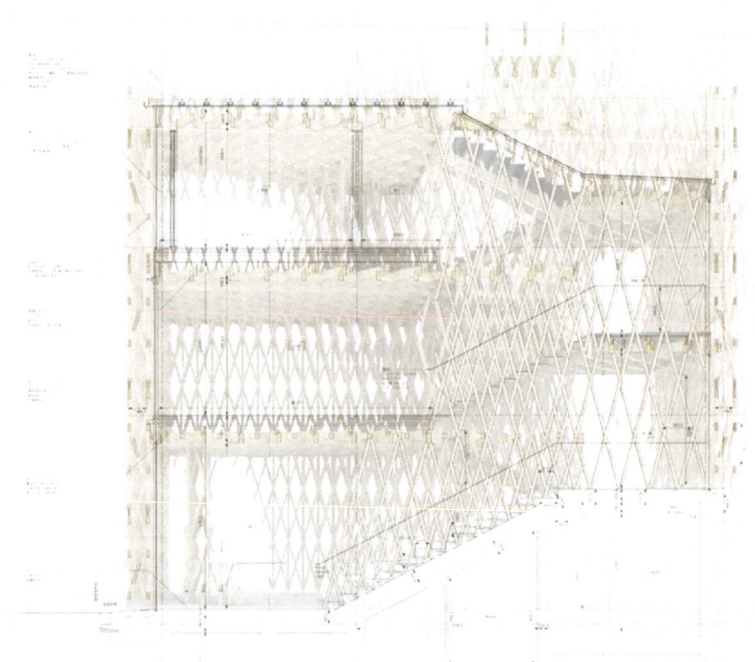

S=1/200

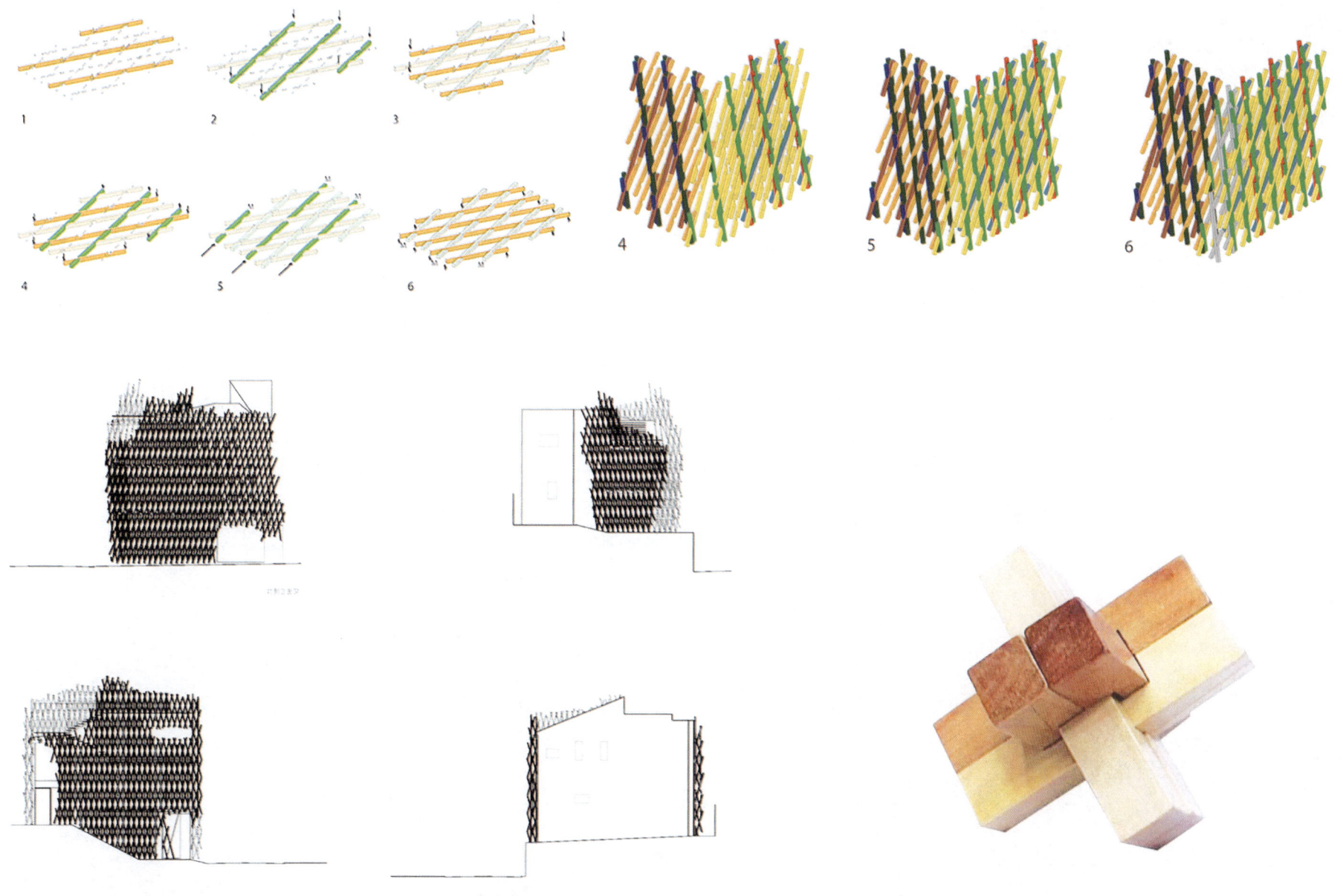

AIR AND FLOW
12 AIR BRICK
AIR BRICK
Shanghai, China

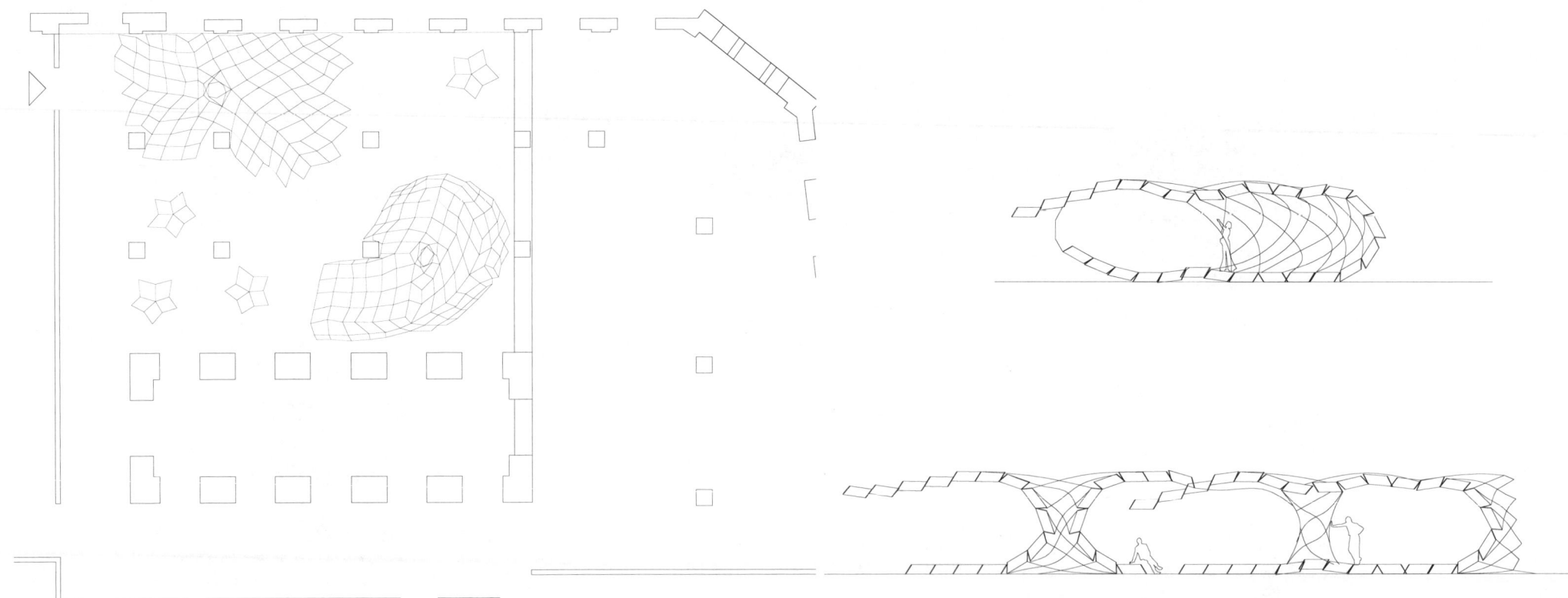

AIR AND FLOW
13 TEEHAUS
TEEHAUS
Frankfurt, Germany (2007)

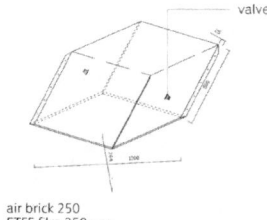

air brick 250
ETFE film 250μm

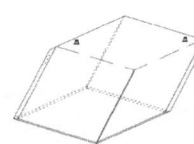

air brick 100
ETFE film 100μm

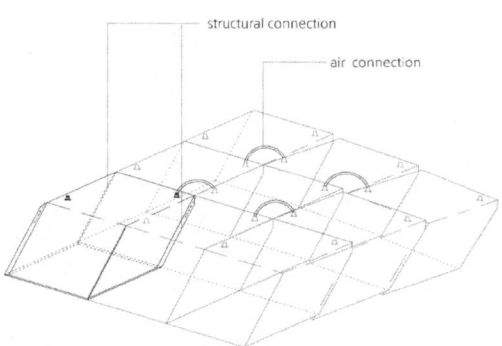

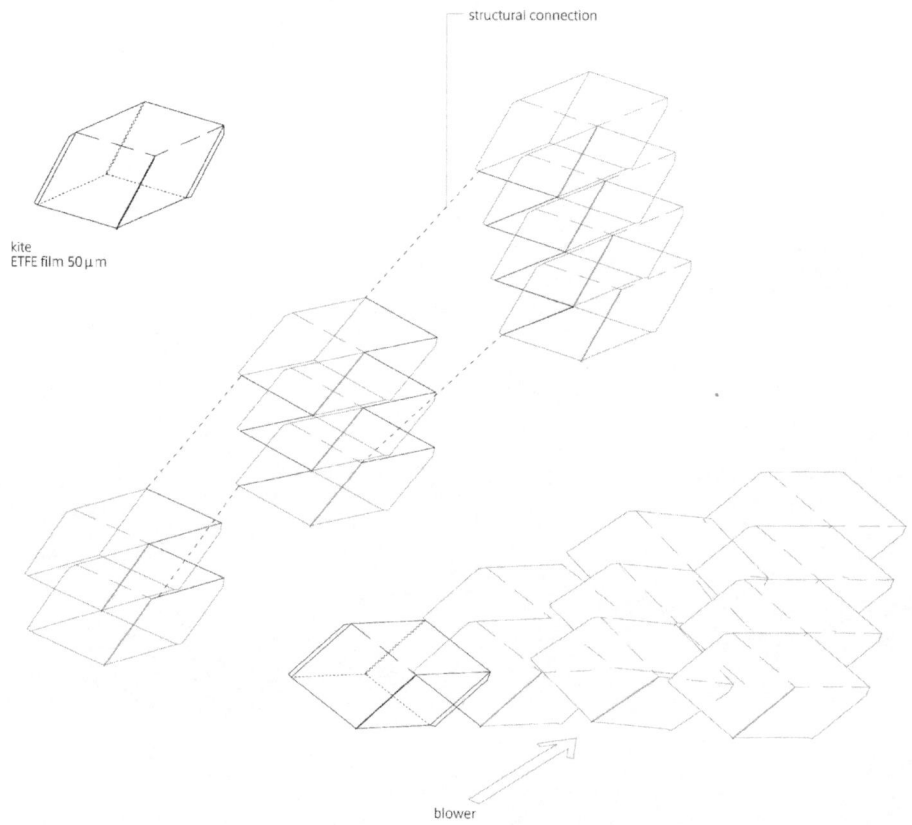

AIR AND FLOW
T-ROOM
T-ROOM

14

21st Century Museum of Contemporary Art, Kanazawa, Japan (2005)

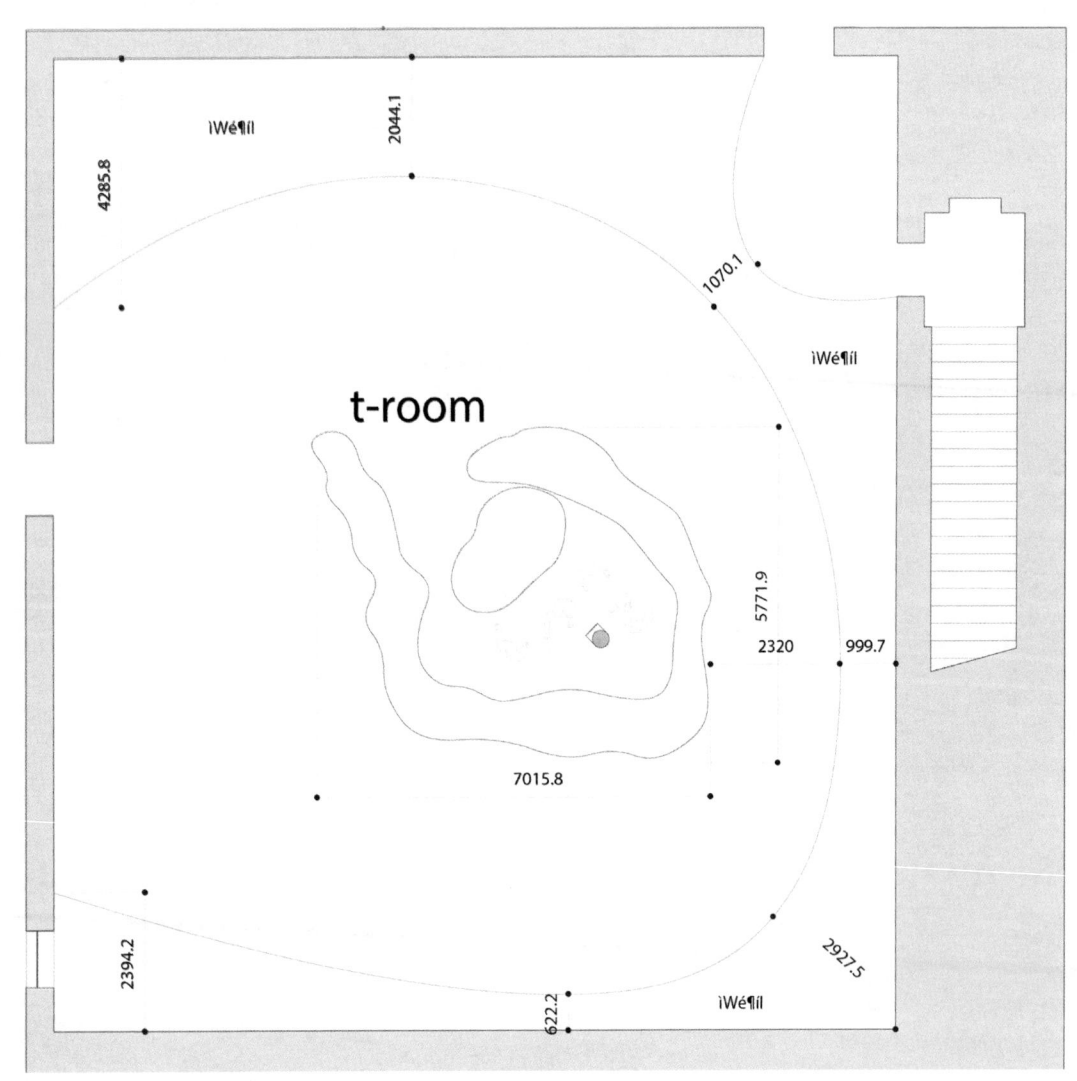

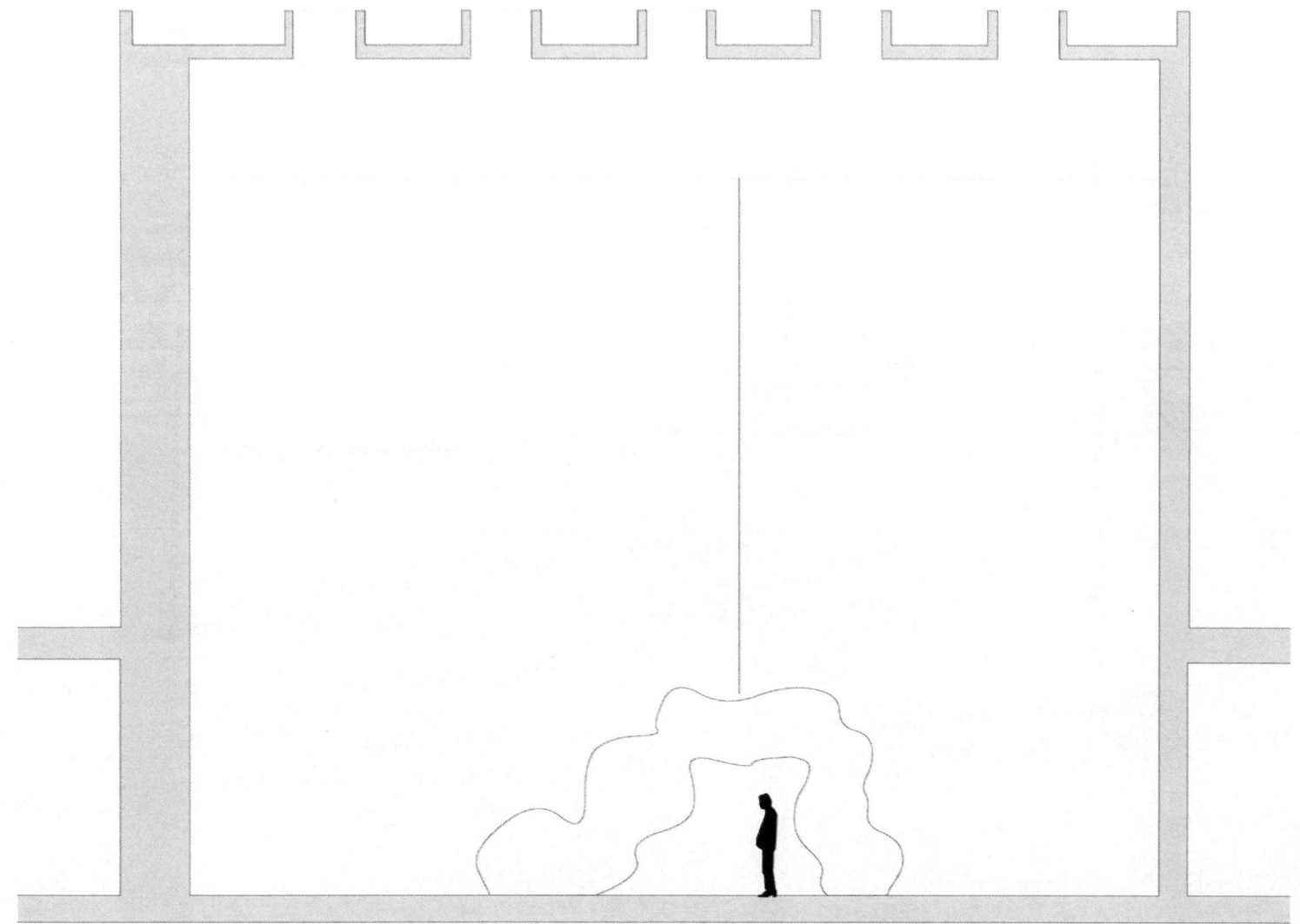

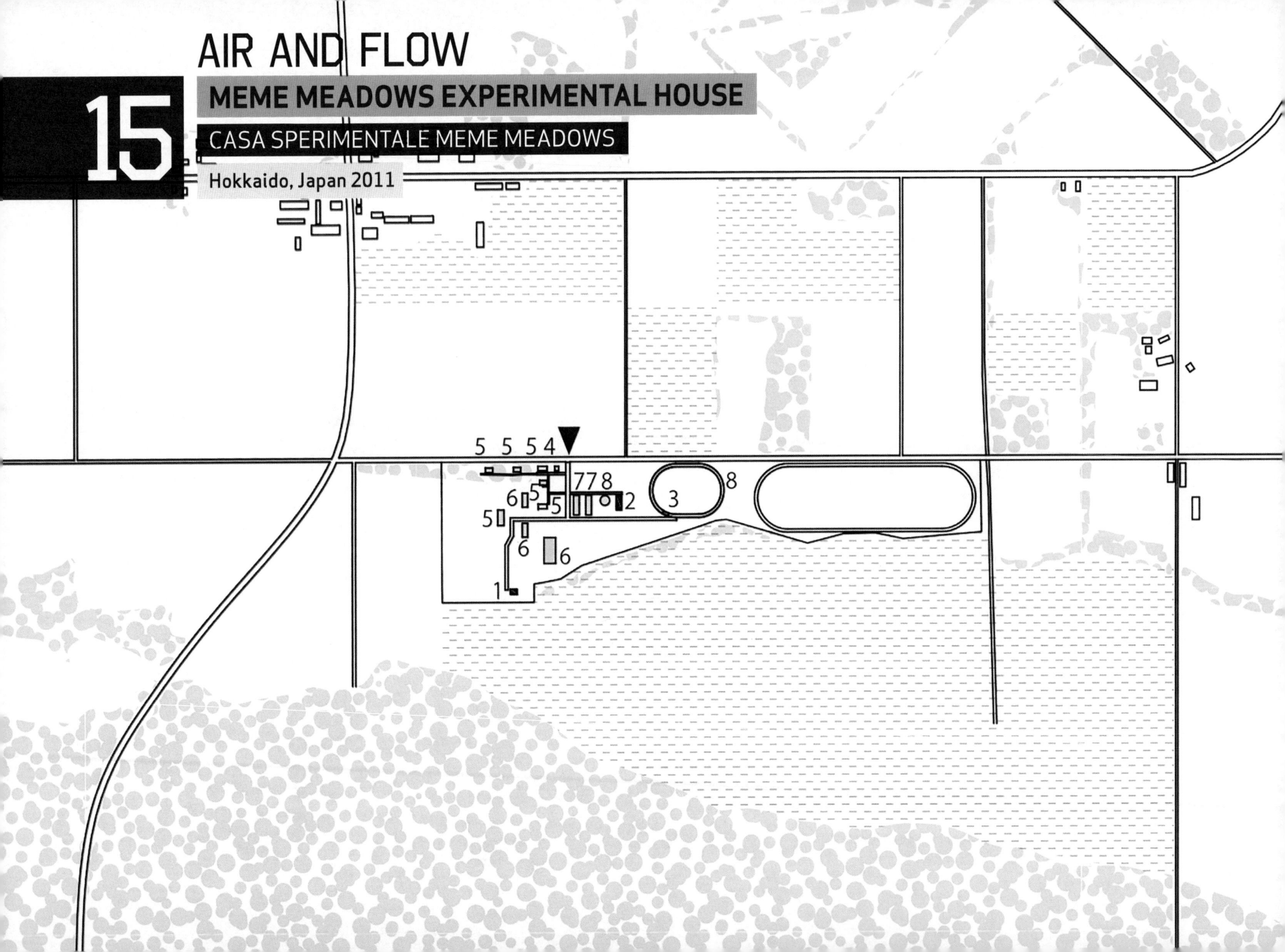

AIR AND FLOW
15 MEME MEADOWS EXPERIMENTAL HOUSE
CASA SPERIMENTALE MEME MEADOWS
Hokkaido, Japan 2011

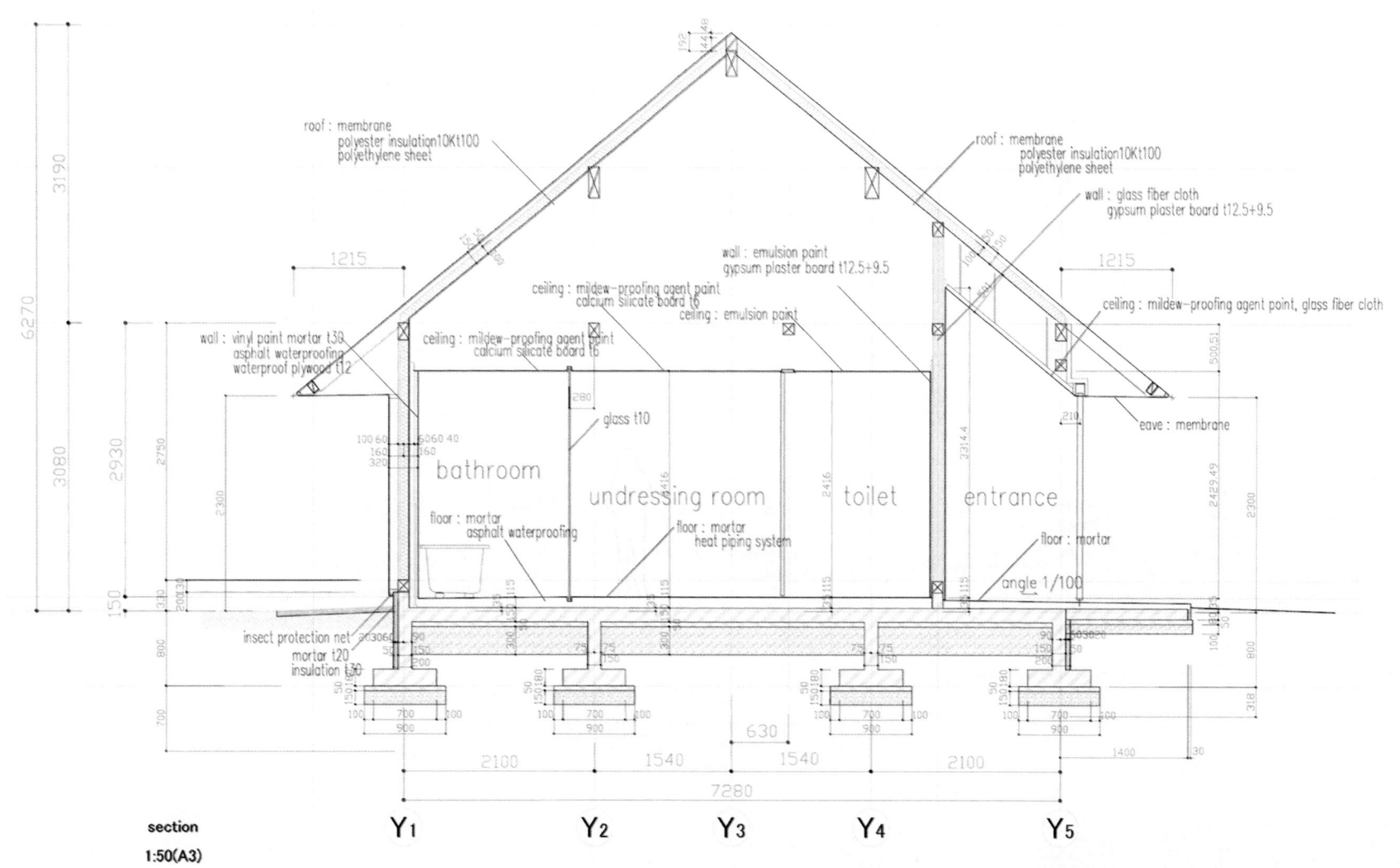

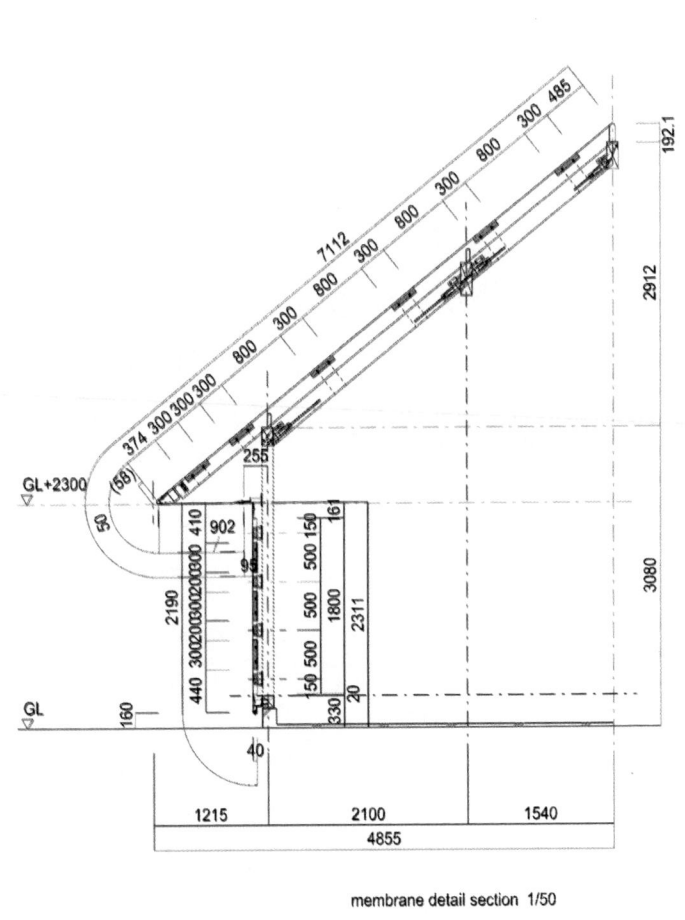

membrane detail section 1/50

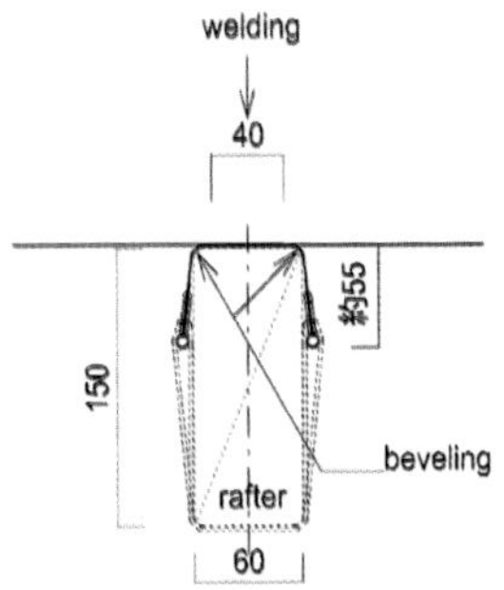

rafte section A 1/5

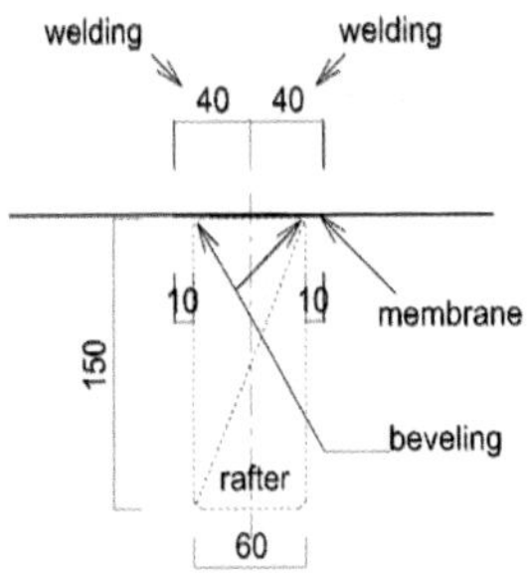

rafter section B 1/5

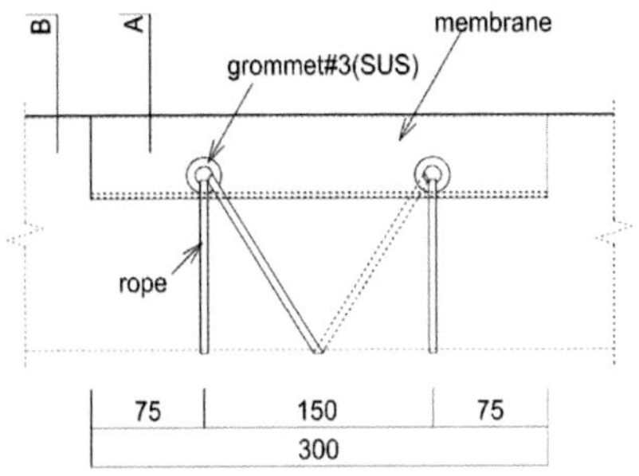

rafter elevation 1/5

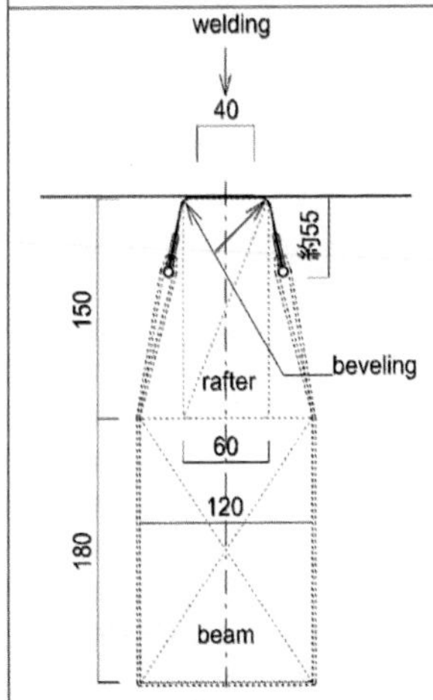

rafter + beam section A 1/5

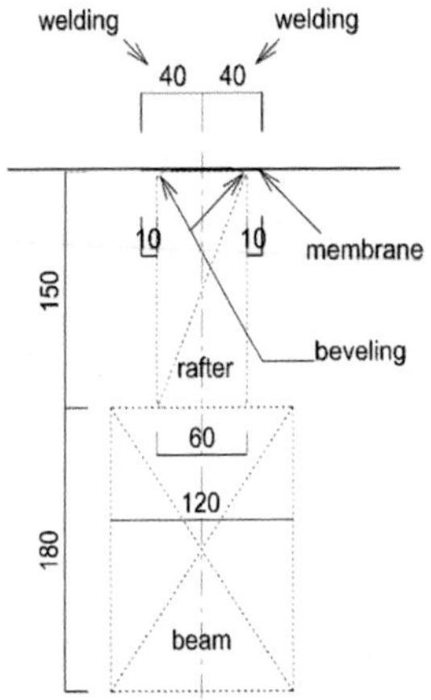

rafter + beam section B 1/5

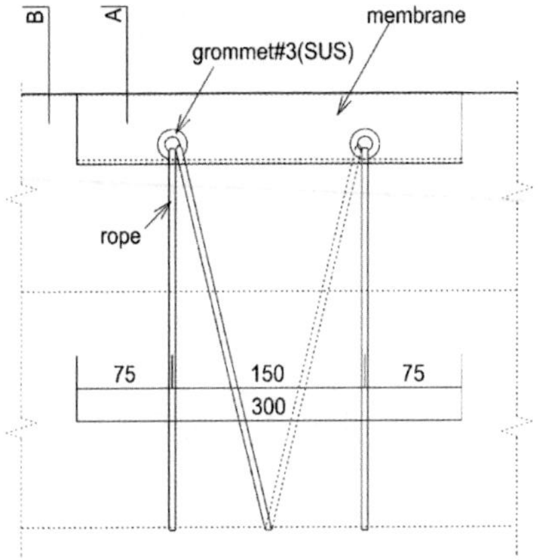

rafter + beam elevation 1/5

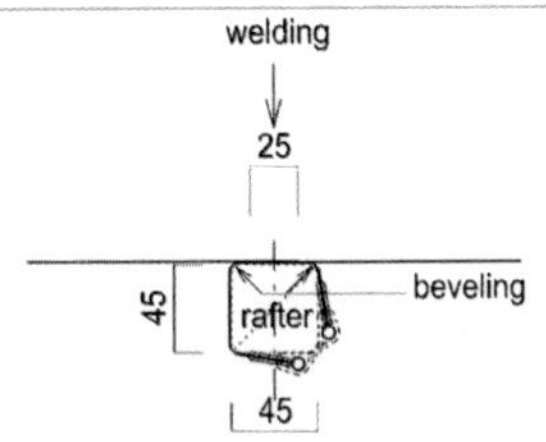

stud section A 1/5

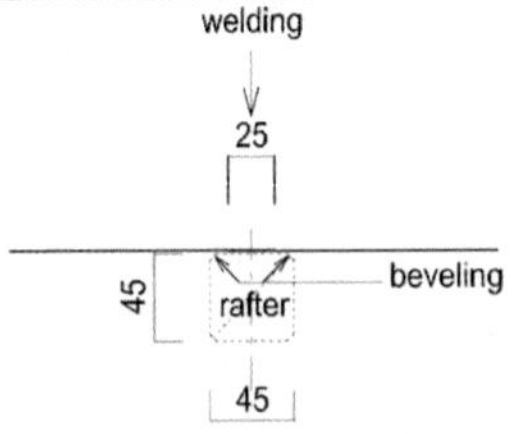

stud section B 1/5

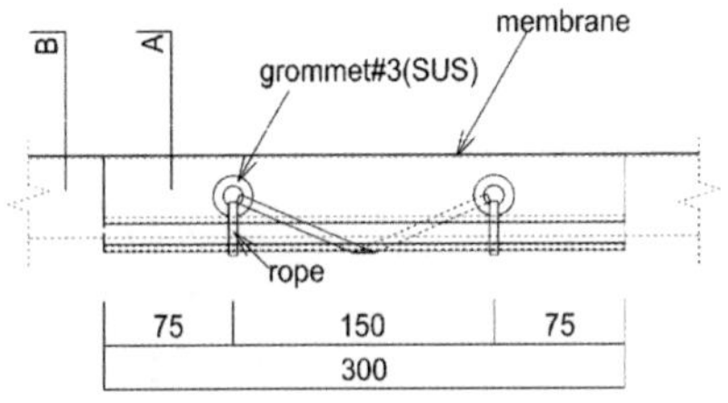

stud elevation 1/5

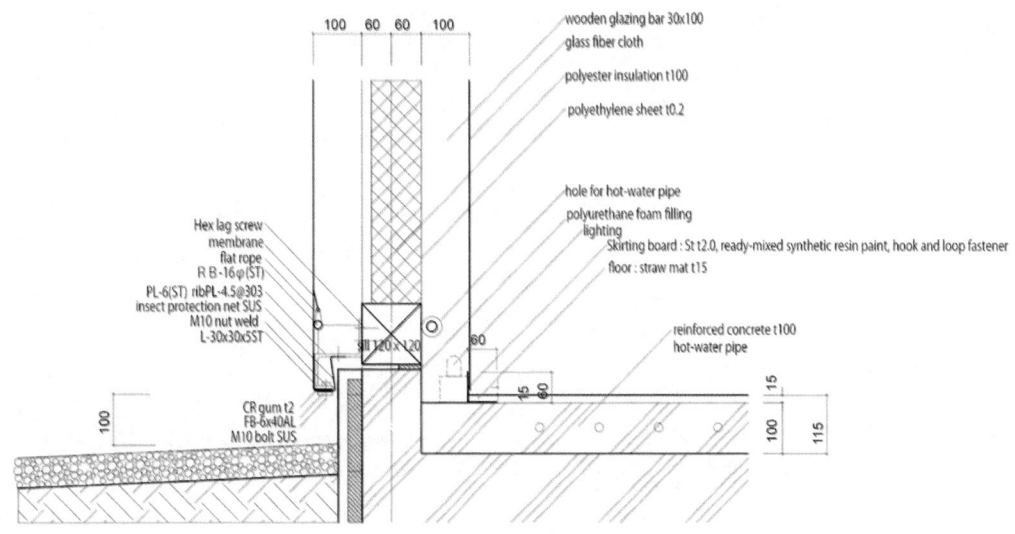

detail section 1/10

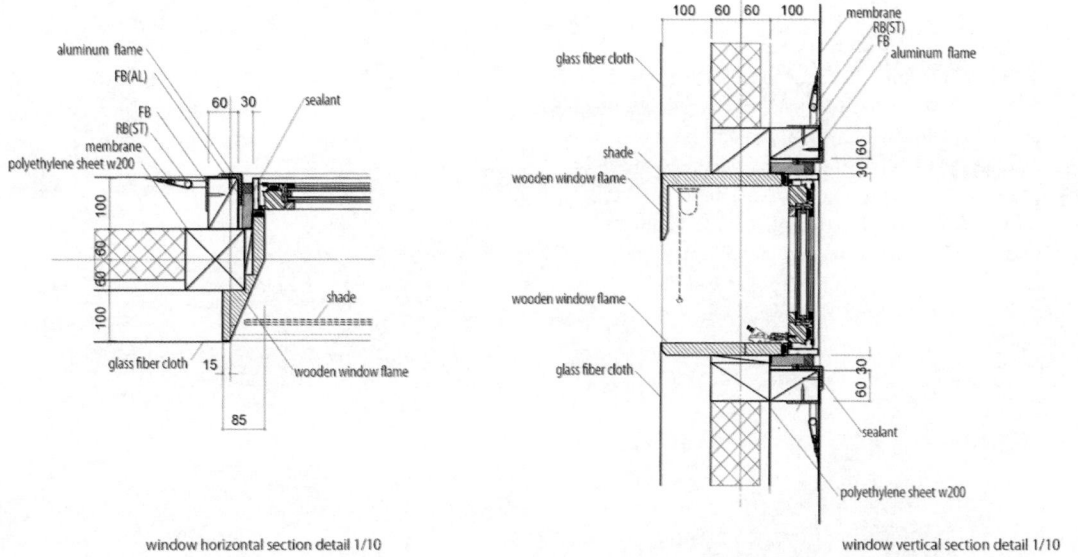

window horizontal section detail 1/10

window vertical section detail 1/10

16
LUCIEN PELLAT-FINET TOKYO MID-TOWN SHOP
NEGOZIO LUCIEN PELLAT-FINET NEL CENTRO DI TOKYO
Akasaka, Minato-ku, Tokyo, Japan (2007)

The collaboration with Lucien Pellat-Finet, a fashion designer named and known as "King of cashmere", started with the request that a space be made using organic materials.
The Frenchman Lucien suggested the concept to be "a Japanese-style gallery" and myself, a Japanese, proposed to express the "softness of cashmere", the charm of the delicate material. While each context was mixed, the project went on as if weaving a piece of cloth, and it came to fruition where one piece of soft skin rose from the floor, as a brand new atmosphere for lucien pellat-finet. To express a soft cloth, I chose structural plywood, a material generally used for architectural structures. By cutting and bringing down these casual materials carefully in order to draw a curve, and placing them equally from the edge, we created a Japanese-touch luxury space. As Lucien Pellat-finet wishes to expand his high-end cashmere line on the street, his collaboration was led to a success by a mixture of luxury and street fashion style.

The soft and organic wood interior of this shop, for a luxury fashion brand, create a warm and relaxing atmosphere in the otherwise chaotic Tokyo Mid-Town high end shopping center

17 PARTICLES
LUCIEN PELLAT-FINET SHINSAIBASHI SHOP
NEGOZIO LUCIEN PELLAT-FINET A SHINSAIBASHI
Nishi-Shinsaibashi Chuo-ku, Osaka (2009)

In the meeting at Shinsaibashi, looking down the street of luxurious brand shops, Lucien asked for a soft and warm space, rather than icy, solid one. In response to his idea, we proposed a plan to realize the softness of Lucien Pellar-Finet cashmere in the architecture. In seeking balance between the cost and the creation of various organic patterns, a 'vegetable wall' was born, which is made of structural plywood with two kinds of width and three types of aluminum connectors. From just beside, it looks that pentagons and parallelogram are repeated and extended further in the interior like a cave, creating a honeycomb-like internal space with lots of different cells. By changing the cutting of sections, each cell in the wall has become practical fittings, like a shelf or box to place the products. Rather than setting in an individual wall or furniture separately in the shop, we wanted to create a single, sequenced and functional wall that covers the entire space. This vegetable wall grows like a liana, from the café in the basement towards the boutique on 1st and 2nd floor and the library on the top floor, and among the 'vines' come out cashmeres like fruits born from the plant. It was a collaboration between fashion and plant-likened architecture. Following the shop in Tokyo MidTown, this time we aimed at 'an organic shape that is tender and warm'. The organic pattern formed on the surface of a plant was used in the architecture to express the softness of Lucien pellat-finet's cashmere. Plywood for structural use is a layer of thinly sliced veneer, and this was combined manually with aluminum connectors specially invented for this project. Thus a soft texture was born in Shinsaibashi, different from typical box-type architectures.

In the collaborative work with Lucien, book director Mr Haba joined so that 'books containing various different worlds' were inserted in the organic texture. The texture, which grew up and spread like plant, bears fruit of information on the top floor and goes off into the cubic fiber glimmering like a cloud.

Since the opening of Tokyo Midtown' shop, Lucien had been dreaming of a boutique that serves champagne, and it was finally realized in Shinsaibashi. The plant-like organic texture in the aboveground floors is also stretched around in the underground, and an unusual space has emerged in which you sense wrapped up by the roots of the plant. Lively conversations from the guests at nights will nurture the organic texture and it will spread further out into Shinsaibashi.

The second shop created for Pellat-Finet, elaborates an honeycomb pattern for the shelves which wraps the entire space of the two floor small project.

18 PARTICLES
SHANG XIA SHOP
NEGOZIO SHANG XIA
Shangai, China (2010)

SHANG XIA is a new brand under the umbrella of Hermes. Its concept was developed to embrace and integrate the essence of a 21st century contemporary Asian aesthetic. Using natural wood and sandstone combined together with high tech fiber a clean, elegant, harmonious and seamless environment was created. The fabric (triaxially folded) that covers the entire interior of the shop was heat-treated and shaped in Japan. It is a material which comes between cloth and plastic, which can retain the softness of natural cloth and strength of shape-memory texture.

19 PARTICLES
CASALGRANDE CERAMIC CLOUD
NUVOLA CASALGRANDE CERAMICHE
Casalgrande, Reggio Emilia, Italy (2010)

Committente/Client
Casalgrandepadana (2010) "Pave your way"

Installation commissioned by Casalgrande Padana to the roundabout at the entrance of the company, entry of all the ceramic district.

Installazione commissionata da Casalgrande Padana per la rotonda davanti all'ingresso dell'azienda, ingresso di tutto il distretto ceramico.

We took the challenge of involving the ceramic tile as an architectural element itself, avoiding its conventional use as a mere cladding. Just after developing with Casalgrande Padana's team the specific detail of how to panel and connect their standard ceramic tiles, we understood the possibilities of how to assembly and organize them creating different structures.
With this unique structure we wanted to avoid creating a monument that stands in the middle of the site: we wanted it to become part of the site. Therefore we decided to create a wall that simply divides the site in two making it a special place with a dual character. Our anti-monumental approach went far enough to decide aligning the direction of the ceramic wall with the road that leads to it so as to make it appear just as a thin vertical line when drivers approach the roundabout and only show its big horizontal scale when driving around it.

Abbiamo colto l'occasione del progetto per usare le lastre ceramiche come elementi puri, evitando di usarlo come rivestimento. Solo dopo aver sviluppato uno specifico dettaglio con il team di Casalgrande Padana, che ci permettesse di connettere le loro lastre standard, abbiamo capito le loro diverse potenzialita' di assemblaggio ed organizzazione. Con questa struttura unica abbiamo voluto evitare di disegnare un monumento che occupasse il centro del sito: volevamo che diventasse parte di esso. Percio' abbiamo deciso di creare un muro che semplicemente dividesse il sito in due luoghi con un carattere duale.
Il nostro approccio anti-monumentale ci ha portato ad allineare il muro alla strada principale in modo che quasi sparisse dalla percezione.

An intricate arrangement of ceramic tiles held together by a tiny and invisible steel structure, play here with light and shadows generating an always different perception of this geometry located at the center of a road roundabout

An intricate arrangement of ceramic tiles held together by a tiny and invisible steel structure, play here with light and shadows generating an always different perception of this geometry located at the center of a road roundabout

20 PARTICLES
GREEN CAST
GREEN CAST
Odawara-shi, Kanagawa Pref., Japan (2011)

The façade of the building is covered with planters made of aluminum die-cast panels, which provides space for facilities.

The 3 (up to 6) aluminum panels, which also form planters, are made in monoblock casting. Each panel is slanted, and its surface appears to be organic, of which cast comes from decayed styrene foam. Equipment such as watering hose, air reservoir for ventilation and downpipes are installed behind the panels so that the façade can accommodate a comprehensive system for the building.

A combination of aluminum panels and vegetation forms this screen facade for a small residential building

PARTICLES
21 XINJIN ZHI MUSEUM
MUSEO XINJIN ZHI
Cheng du, China (2011)

This pavilion is located at the foot of Laojunshan mountain in Xinjin, to usher in the people to the holy place of Taoism, while the building itself shows the essence of Taoism through its space and exhibitions.
The tile used for façade is made of local material and worked on in a traditional method of this region, to pay tribute to Taoism that emphasizes on nature and balance. Tile is hung and floated in the air by wire to be released from its weight (and gain lightness). Clad in breathing façade of particles, the architecture is merged into its surrounding nature.
The façade for the south is divided into top and bottom and staggered in different angles. This idea is to respond to two different levels of the pond in front and the street at the back, and avoid direct confrontation with the massive building in the south. For the east side, a large single tile screen is vertically twisted to correspond with the dynamism of the road in front. The façade for the north side is static and flat, which faces the pedestrians' square. Thus the tile screen transforms itself from face to face, and wraps up the building like a single cloth.
Taking advantage of the varied levels in the architecture's surroundings, the flow is planned to lead people from the front to the back, motion to stillness, like a stroll type of garden. The exhibition space inside is planned spiral moving from darkness to light. From the upper floor a paramount view of Laoujunshan can be enjoyed. Direct sunlight is blocked by the tile, and the interior of the building is covered with gentle light with beautiful particle-like shade.

Traditional roof tiles held by steel cables create the small particles of this organic facade wrapping the museum galleries

PARTICLES
22 FRAC, FONDS REGIONAL D'ART CONTEMPORAIN
FRAC, FONDO REGIONALE D'ARTE CONTEMPORANEA
Marseille, France (2013)

The project of the contemporary art center (FRAC) for the region Provence Alpes Cotes d'Azur (PACA) is the 3D version of the "museum without walls" invented by André Malraux, famous French writer and politician. It is a museum without a museum, a living and moving place, where the art pieces are in a constant movement and join the logic of diffusion and interaction with the visitors.

KKAA thought the FRAC as a signal in the city, which allows a better visibility to contemporary art. The building stands up as a landmark which identity is clearly asserted.

It is composed with two recognizable parts:
The main body along the street Vincent Leblanc contains the exhibition spaces and documentation center

A small tower with auditorium and children's workshop, offers an upper terrace on the main boulevard.

These two clearly identified entities are connected between them by a set of footbridges and are unified by the envelope made by an glass skin, composed with panels with changing opacity. The building explores the theme of the windows and openings on different scales. KKAA wishes to create a particular space of creation and life, which action and effect is bounded to the entire city, as well as the surrounding district and neighborhood (cafe-terrace…).

Small panels made of recycled glass are assembled together to create the light dematerialized facade of the museum building

23 PARTICLES
POLYGONIUM
POLYGONIUM

Kanaya-machi, Takaoka-shi, Toyama, Japan (2008)

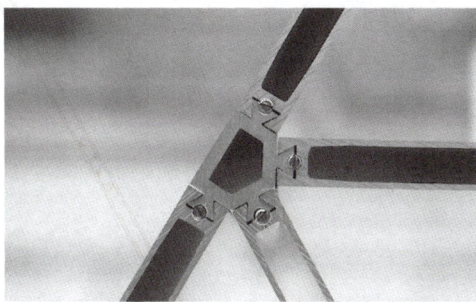 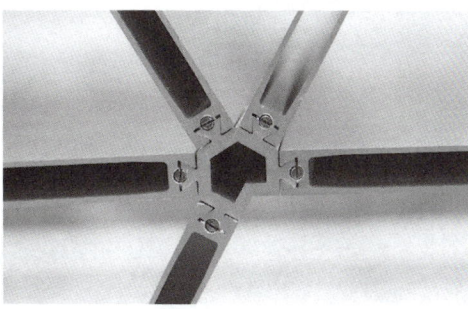  

This is a modular furniture system, made by a truss structure with extruded aluminum. We got our hint from a game named "Card Castle", a game of assembling edge-to-edge into triangle figures. Such a simply jointed triangulated structure transfer force axially, which means each peace can be thin and light, and the entire construction is capable of making long spans.

The triangles are consisted of boards and joints. There are 5 kinds of joints, which fit all configurations, and fixes the connection by driving a pin in the center hole of the joint. Assembly and disassembly is completed in an amazingly short time, because this pin is able to disconnect only by hammering on the side of the board.

One side of the triangle is 40cm; the depth of shelf is 60cm, and one side is made by two boards easy packing and transport, with the dimension of w20cm×d60cm×t10mm, hollow construction. The connected boards create a triangle with 40cm sides, able to withstand loads up to 100kg. As this aluminum block has its joint as rigid connection, it is possible to create a beam floating in the air, although it is also "masonry" construction. So, the aluminum triangle system has an interesting construction that is somewhere between masonry and trusses.

We have been designing a residence by using this system. Not just for making a shelf in a residence, this system is also strong enough to build a residence, which is easy to assemble and disassemble.

Small panels made of recycled glass are assembled together to create the light dematerialized facade of the museum building

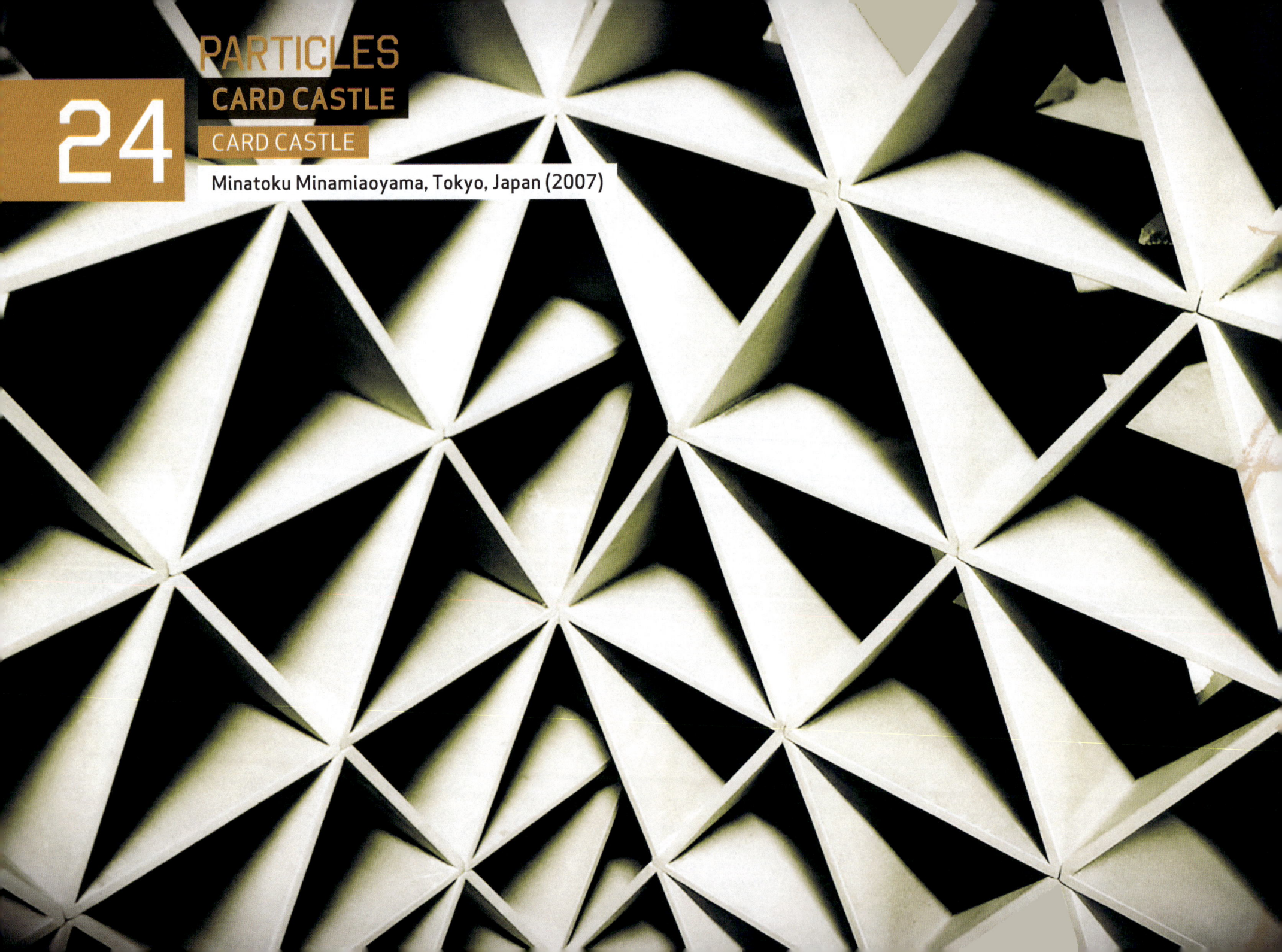

24 PARTICLES
CARD CASTLE
CARD CASTLE
Minatoku Minamiaoyama, Tokyo, Japan (2007)

The stone of Pietra Serena enlightens us with the beauty of "Principles". Although the stone is a heavy substance, the greenish gray color and the neutral surface gives us the feeling that the stone is extremely transparent. This stone honors a unique transparency to this "prinicple" This is probably why Michelangelo had favored this stone. In a period where glass could not be used massively and freely, he thought of utilizing the transparency of this stone to convey the "principles" of architecture to the people. Using this transparent stone, I thought of expressing one "principle" myself.
That is the principle of the triangle. By assembling 3 stone boards with the same dimensions, a stable triangular shape is created. By building the triangular units upon another, we are even able to formulate a massive world. It is because the triangle is stable that we are able to create a world in this form. I thought about conveying the beauty of this principle by using the specific material called Pietra Serena. In order to accomplish this, the Pietra Serena had to be made as thin as possible. By making the stone thin allows the transparency to appeal, becoming closer to the abstract state of principles.
For this experimental project, we have built a stone plates pavilion which truss structural system is like a card castle. We used a stone which used to be greatly appreciated by Michelangelo and Brunelleschi: the pietra serena.
The modular construction system consists in piling up triangular blocks, each block being constituted by 3 squared stone plates (dimensions 25cm x 25cm x t1cm) glued together on the edges.

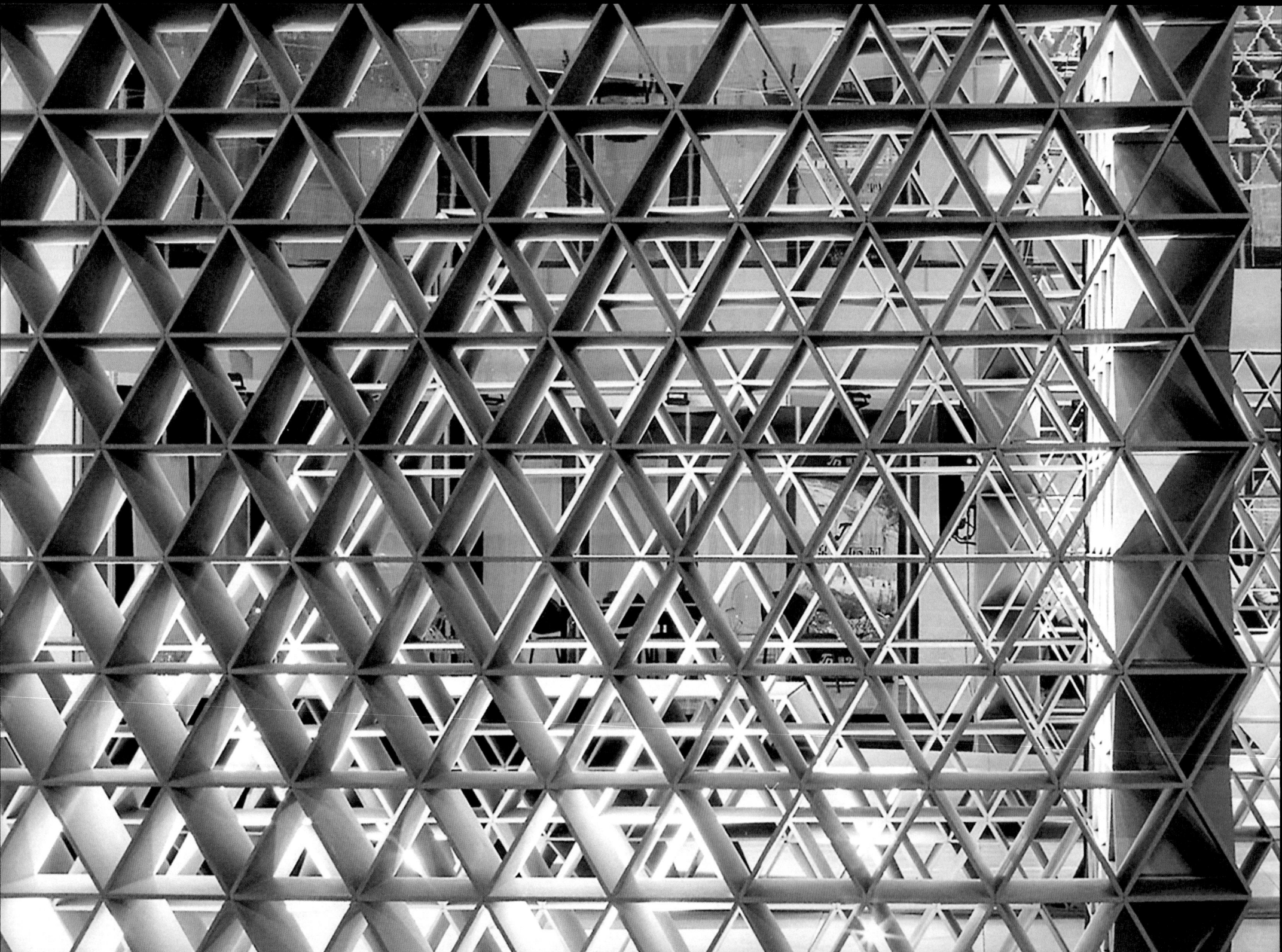

25 PARTICLES
UMBRELLA HOUSE
CASA UMBRELLA
La Triennale Di Milano, Italy (2008)

This project started under the condition of suggesting a new kind of a 'temporary house'. What we planed considering the ease of construction and building was to utilize materials, which are commonly distributed in markets. The product we have selected, an 'umbrella', has been developed and improved to be light weight, easy to carry by folding, and above all, in effectively keeps off the rain. We thought that we can produce a new product, a new kind of architecture by putting them up in three dimensional way.

This "Casa Umbrella" is composed of each triangle on a regular icosahedron replaced by an umbrella. A triangle created by the bones by an umbrella is utilized as a truss structure, and every single detail is adapting the detail of a common umbrella. The connection detail of the umbrellas is the water cut-off fasteners used for a diving suit, therefore you can produce a new space in an open space, by simply opening the umbrella, fastening the zipper. The size of the umbrella is defined based on the intended spaces to be created- for example, a few umbrellas can produce a small roof or a partition, while 15 umbrellas can create a shelter.

The material of the umbrella surface is a polyester non-woven fabric called 'Tyvek' produced by DuPont, which has an outstanding quality in water proofing and moisture proofing that is easy to sew as it also goes well together with zipper. In a rainy day, it becomes a rain shelter. In a fine day, it becomes a small arbor by opening a zipper to bring in a natural light and a gentle breeze. "Casa Umbrella" becomes to be a 'temporary house' of new days.

Casa=umbrella in Japanese, this small experimental house for an exhibition in Milan is made by custom made umbrella realized with a Japanese craftsman

26 PARTICLES
NAGAOKA CITY HALL "AORE"
MUNICIPIO "AORE" A NAGAOKA
Otedori, Nagaoka-shi, Niigata, Japan (2012)

With the growth of cities and their scale, public buildings of 20th Century were likely to be driven away to the suburbs, often as isolated concrete boxes in parking lots. We wanted to reverse this flow with Nagaoka Aore. We moved the city hall back to the center of the town and revived a real "heart of town," which is located in a walking distance from anywhere, working along with people's everyday life. This is exactly like the city hall historically nurtured in Europe, and embodies the idea of compact city in the environment-oriented age. We adopted the traditional method of "tataki," and "nakadoma," which is to function as a meeting point for the community, is no longer the mere concrete box – the space is gently surrounded by placid structure, finished with wood and solar panels.

The public space pervades this town hall building, bringing a sense of community to an otherwise cold bureaucratic function. The building has been very successful since its opening and the covered plaza and other public spaces are always busy with community activities

PARTICLES
LUCIEN PELLAT-FINET TOKYO MID-TOWN SHOP
NEGOZIO LUCIEN PELLAT-FINET NEL CENTRO DI TOKYO

16

Akasaka, Minato-ku, Tokyo, Japan (2007)

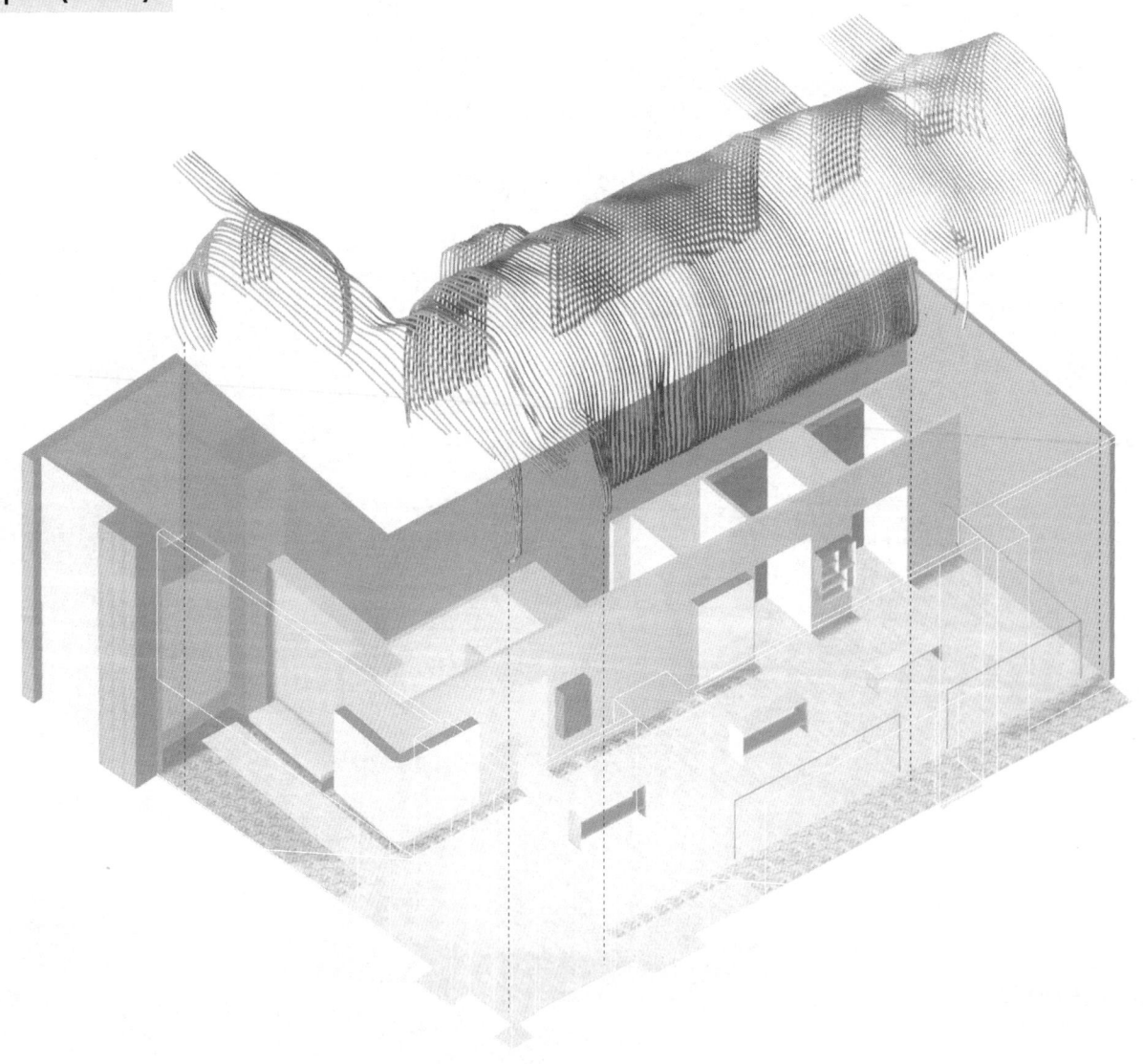

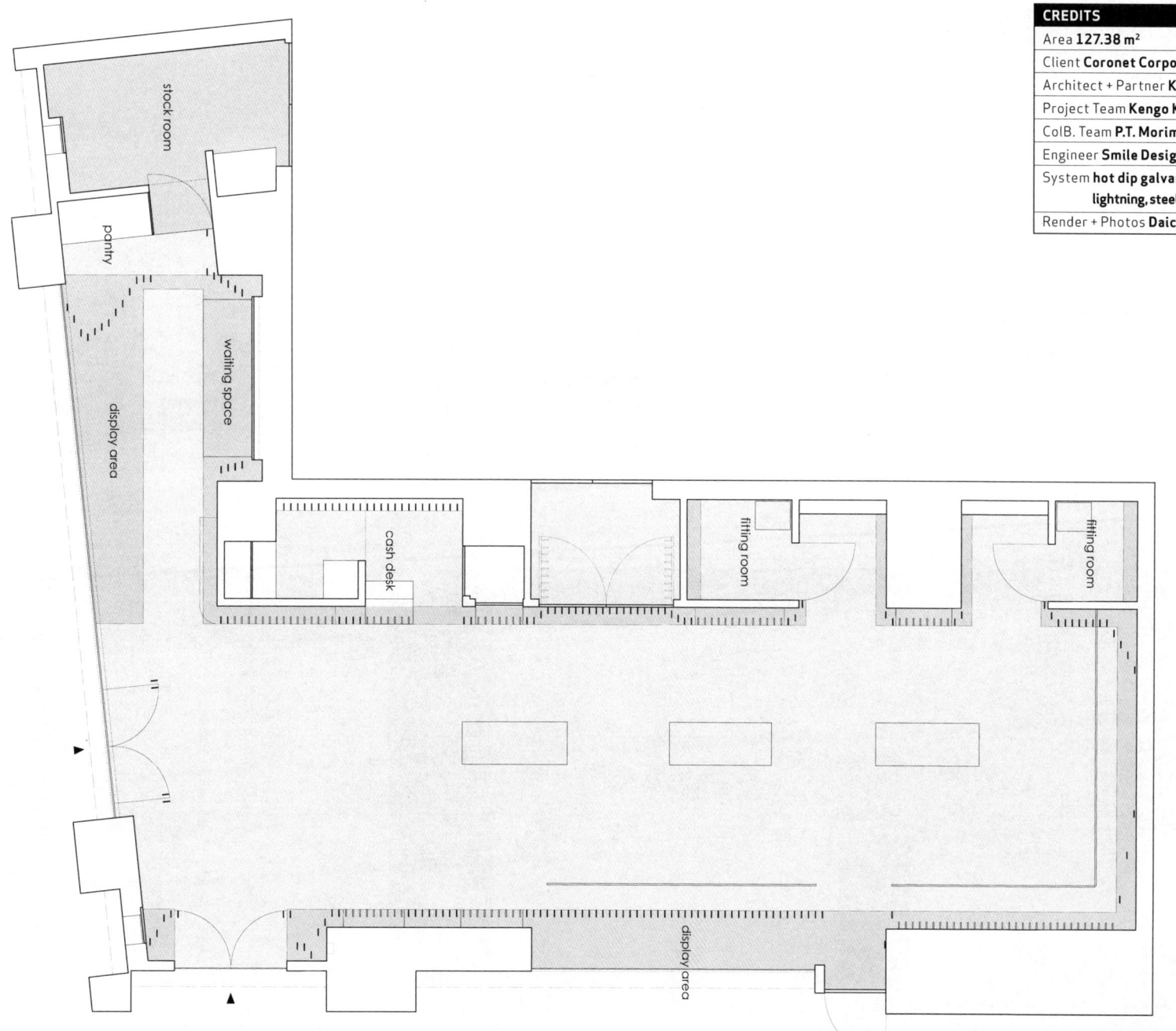

CREDITS	
Area	**127.38 m²**
Client	**Coronet Corporation**
Architect + Partner	**Kengo Kuma & Associates**
Project Team	**Kengo Kuma, Kazuhiko Miyazawa**
ColB. Team	**P.T. Morimura & Associates, LTD.**
Engineer	**Smile Design**
System	**hot dip galvanizing, baking white paint, indirect lightning, steel plate bended, Japanese larch sheet, lightning**
Render + Photos	**Daici Ano**

PARTICLES

17 LUCIEN PELLAT-FINET SHINSAIBASHI SHOP
NEGOZIO LUCIEN PELLAT-FINET A SHINSAIBASHI

Nishi-Shinsaibashi Chuo-ku, Osaka (2009)

CREDITS
Area	**133m²**
Client	**Coronet Corporation**
Architect + Partner	**Kengo Kuma & Associates**
Project Team	**Kengo Kuma, P.T.Morimura & Associates, LTD.**
ColB. Team	**Smile Design Co., Ltd**
Engineer	**Ejiri Structural Engineers**
Render + Photos	**Daici Ano**

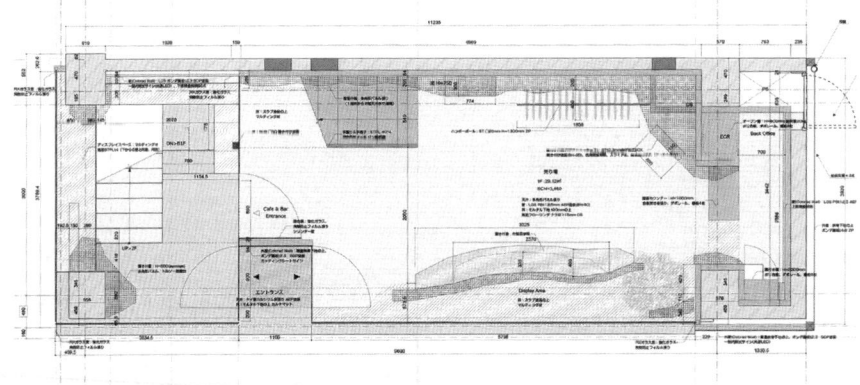

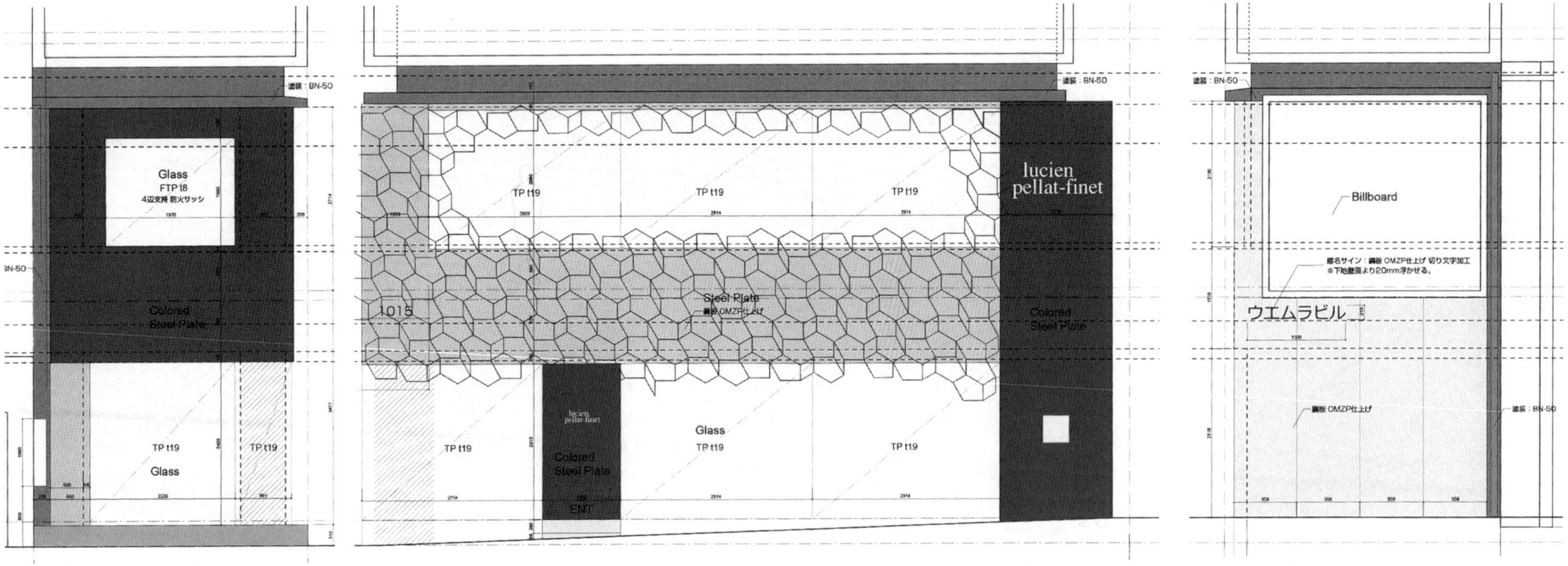

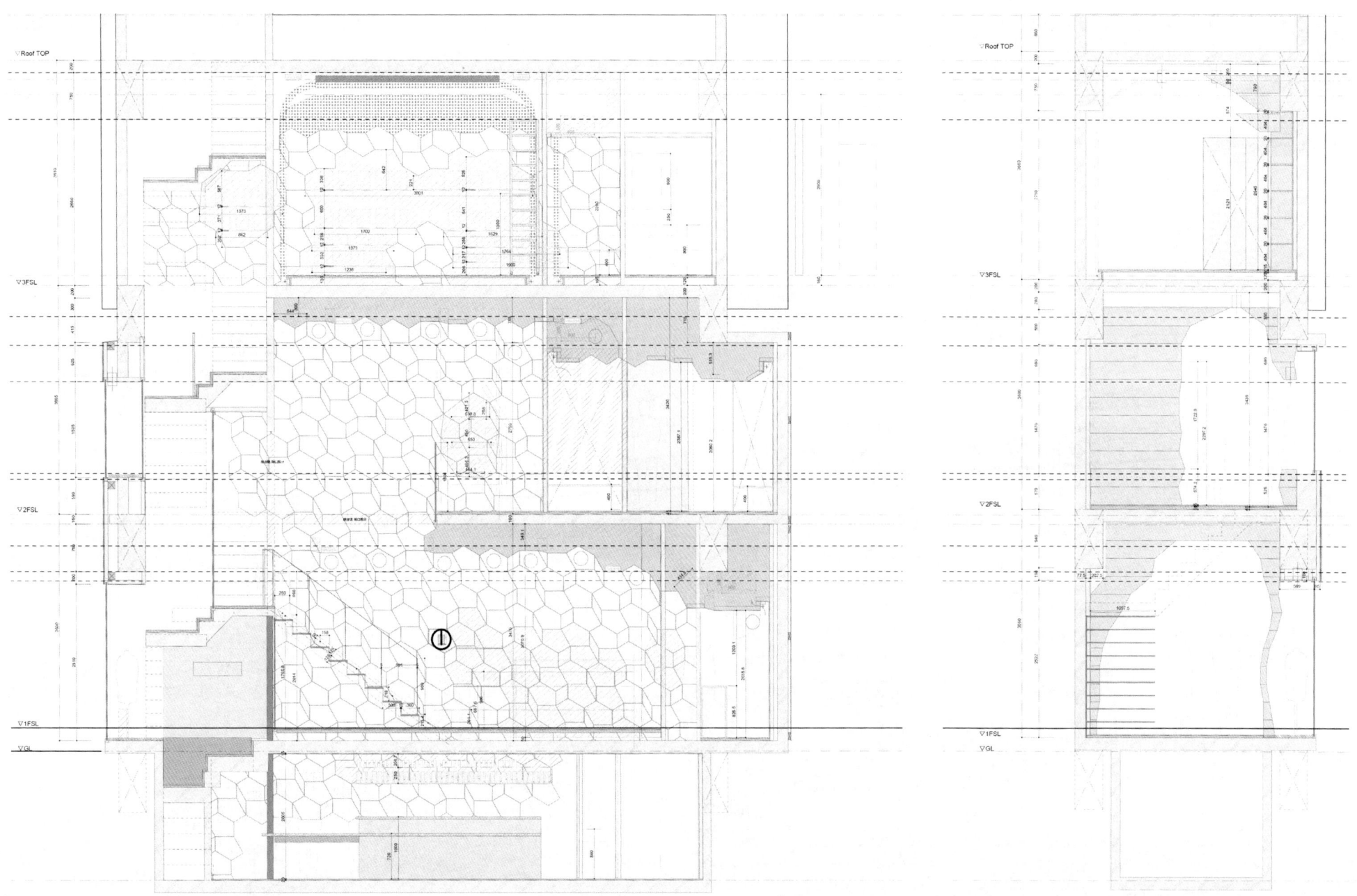

18 PARTICLES
SHANG XIA SHOP
NEGOZIO SHANG XIA
Shangai, China (2010)

CREDITS	
Area	**126m²**
Client	**Shang xia**
Architect + Partner	**Kengo Kuma & Associates**
Project Team	**Kengo Kuma, Koizumi Lighting Technology Corp**
ColB. Team	**NOMURA (Beijing) Co., Ltd.**
Engineer	**Ejiri Structural Engineers**
Render + Photos	**Daici Ano**

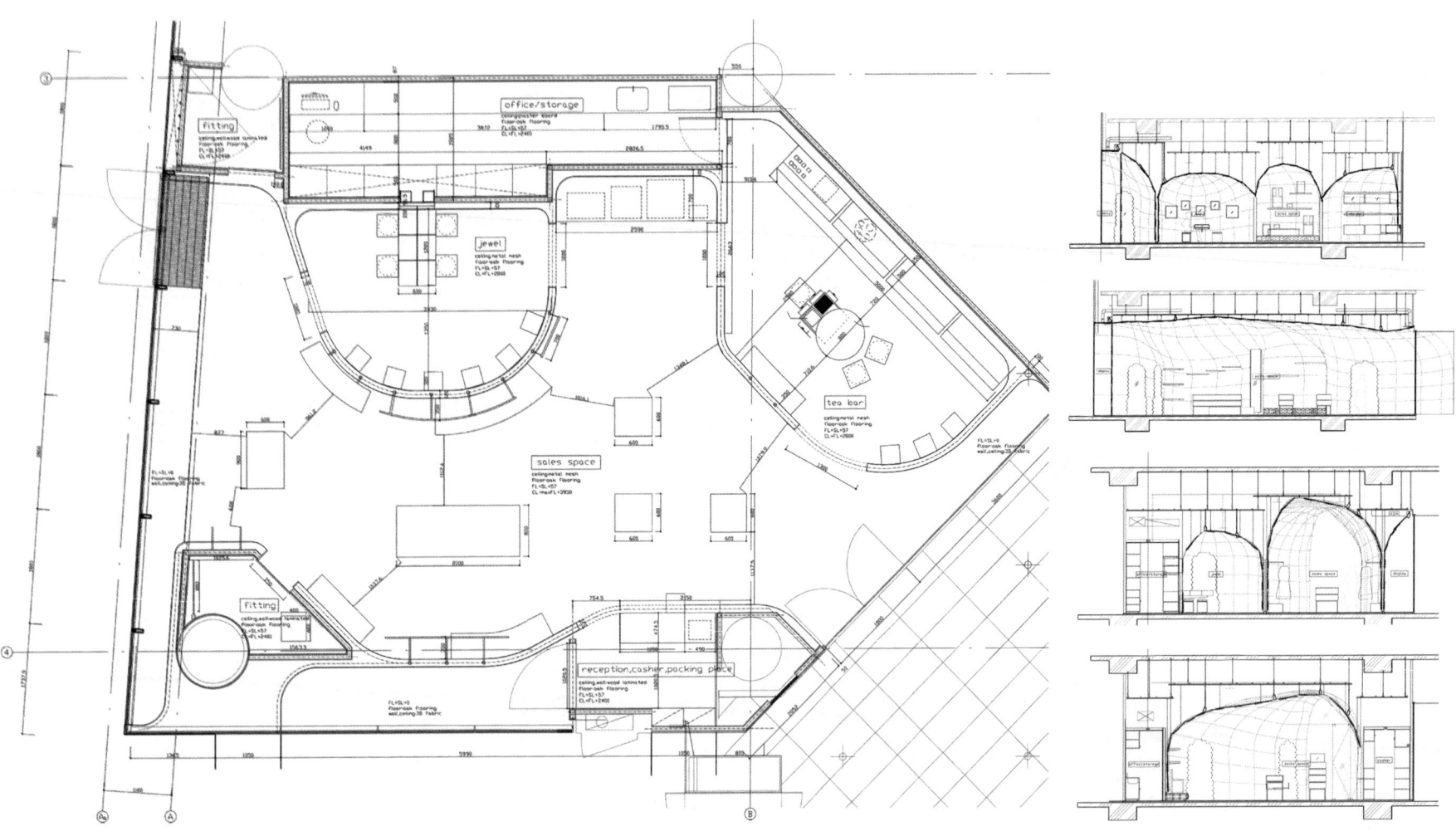

PARTICLES

19 CASALGRANDE CERAMIC CLOUD
NUVOLA CASALGRANDE CERAMICHE

Casalgrande, Reggio Emilia, Italy (2010)

CREDITS	
Area	2697 mq
Client	Casalgrande Padana spa
Architect + Partner	Kengo Kuma & Associates
Project Team	Kengo Kuma + Javier Villar Ruiz + Ryuya Umezawa
ColB. Team	Alfonso Acocella (Università di Ferrara) + Luigi Alini (Università di Catania) + Enrico Rombi (CCDP Reggio Emilia) + Angelo Silingardi (CCDP Reggio Emilia) + Mauro Filippini (Casalgrande Padana spa)
Engineer	Ejiri Structural Enjineers + Enrico Rombi (CCDP Reggio Emilia) + Alberto Zen (CCDP Reggio Emilia) + Luigi Massa (Casalgrande Padana)

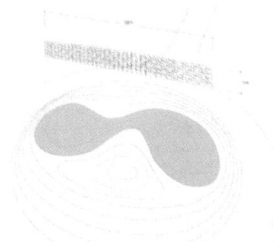
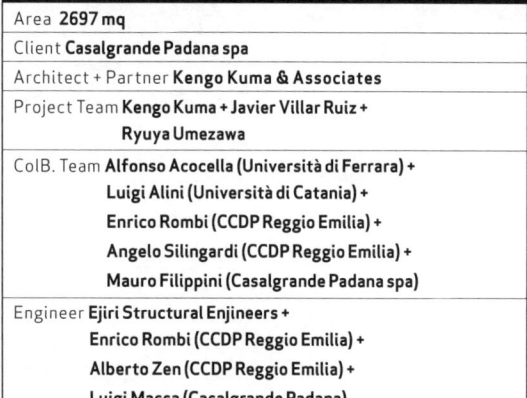
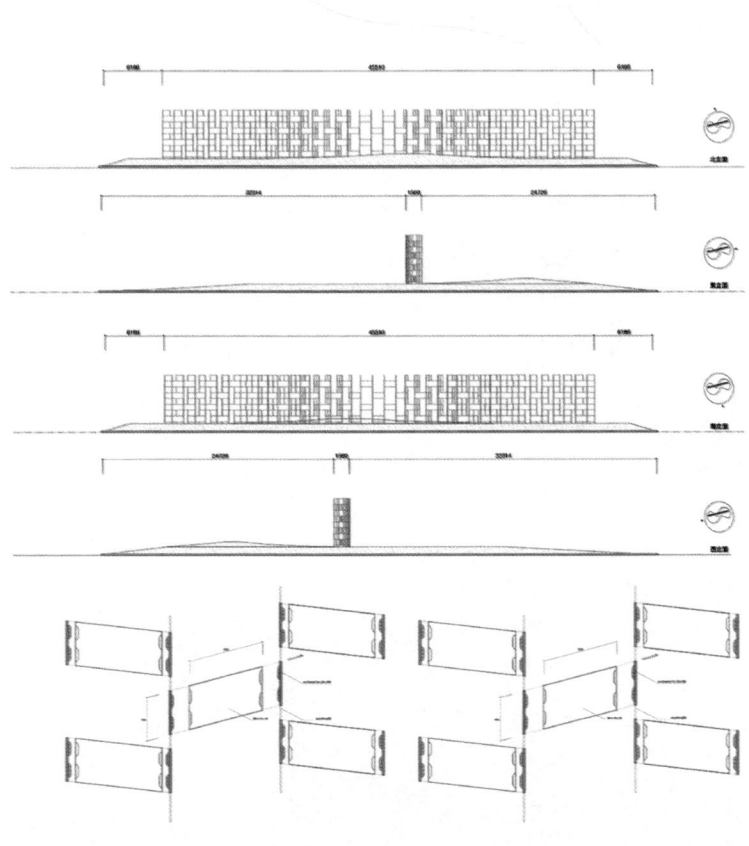
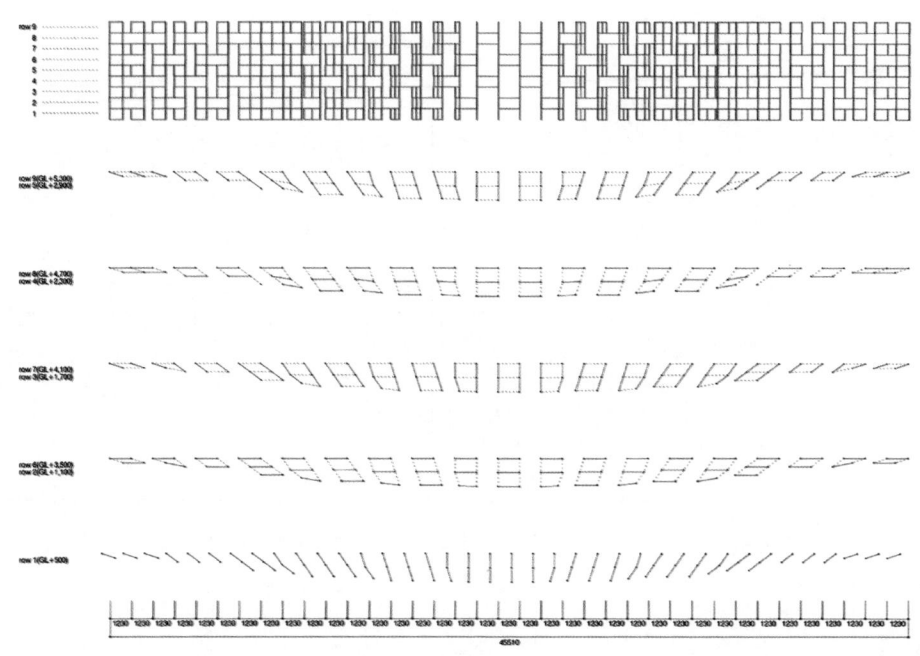

PARTICLES

20 GREEN CAST

GREEN CAST

Odawara-shi, Kanagawa Pref., Japan (2011)

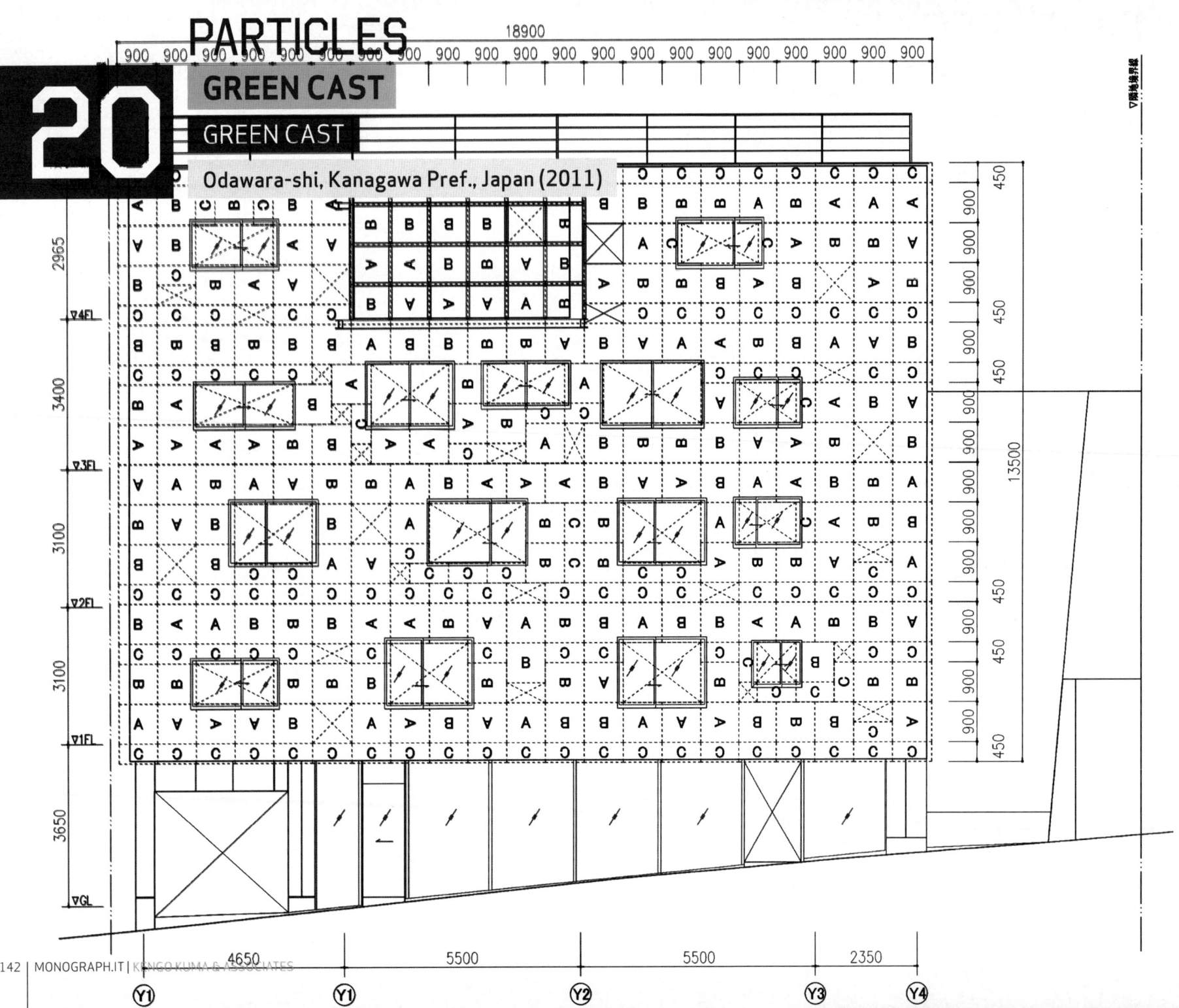

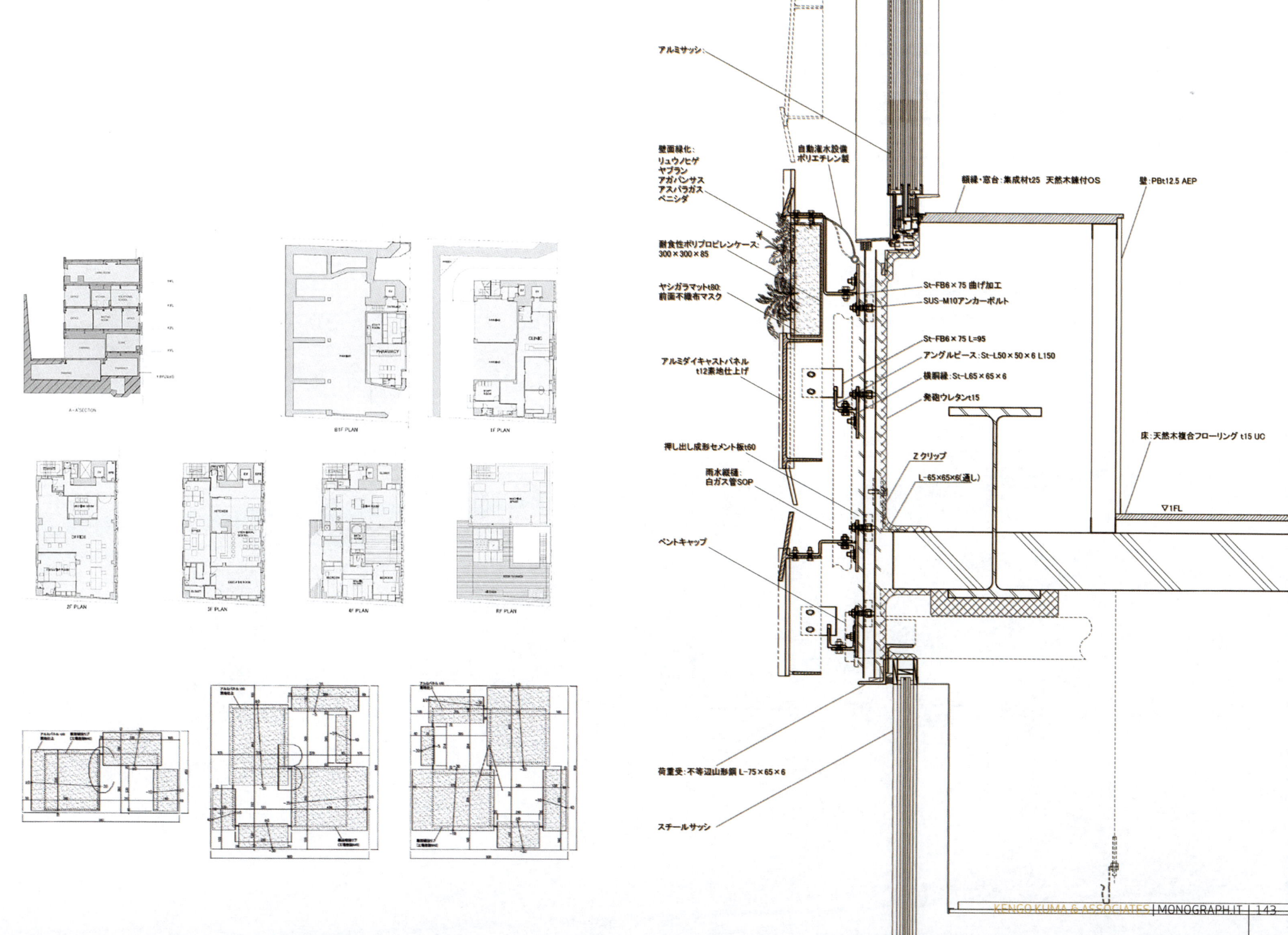

PARTICLES
21 XINJIN ZHI MUSEUM
MUSEO XINJIN ZHI
Cheng du, China (2011)

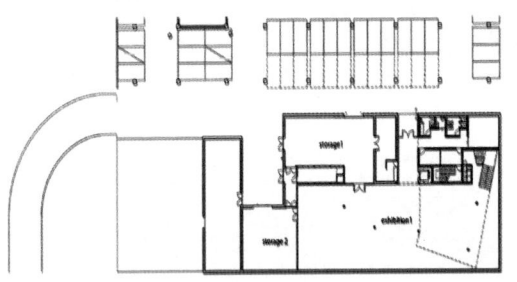

BF
1/400

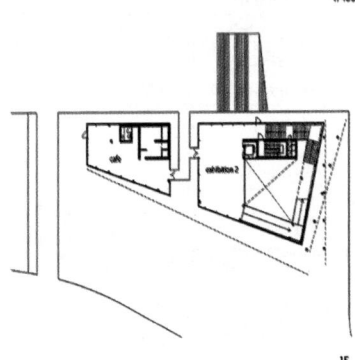

1F

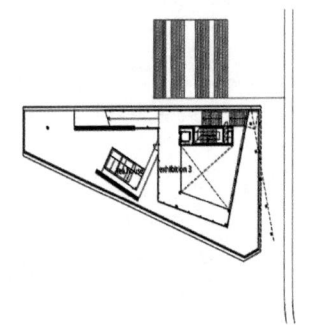

2F

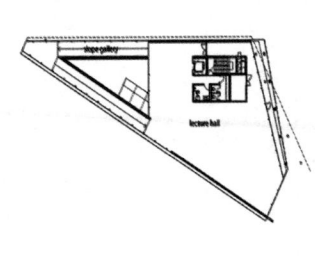

3F

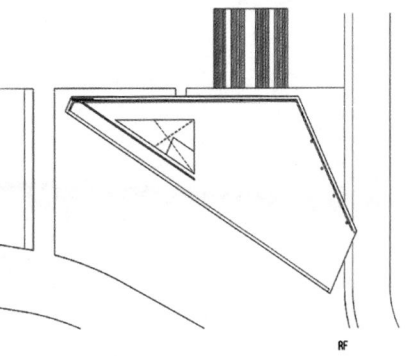

RF

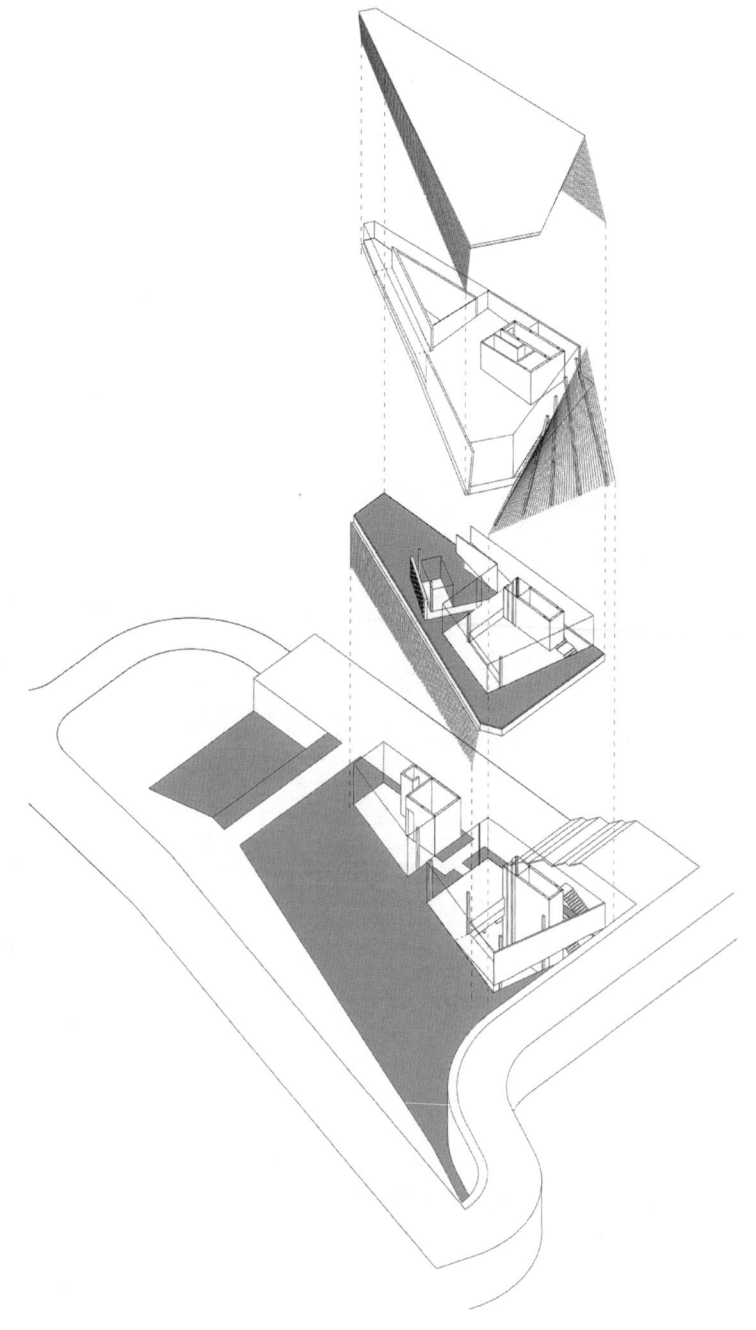

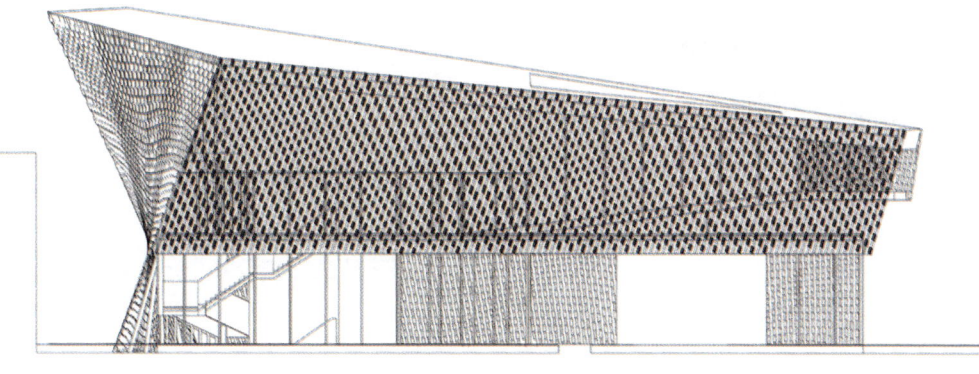
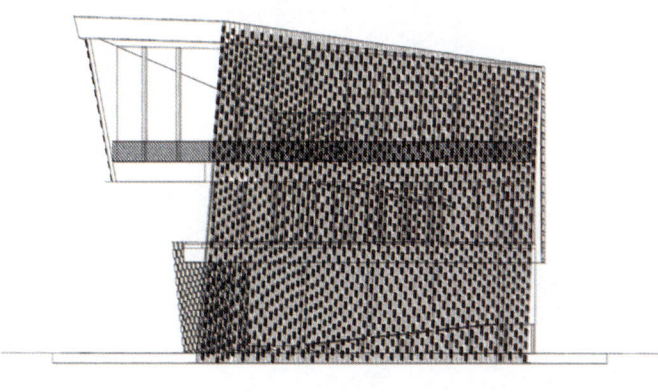
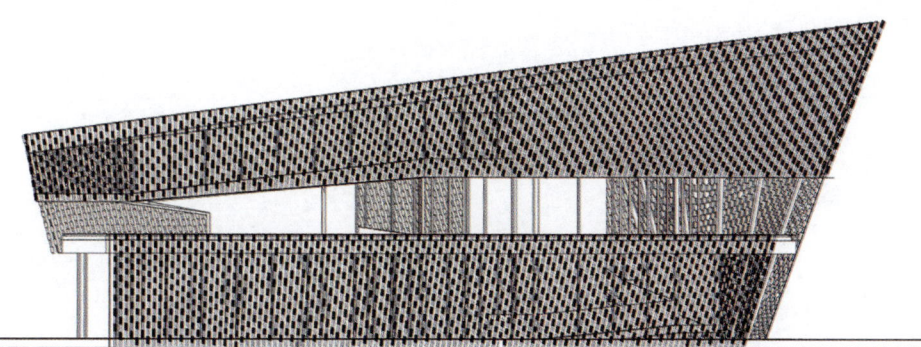

CREDITS	
Area	**2,580m²**
Client	**Fantasia group**
Architect + Partner	**Kengo Kuma & Associates**
Engineer	**Oak Structural Design Office + P.T.Morimura & Associates, LTD**
System	**Reinforced concrete, partly steel flame**

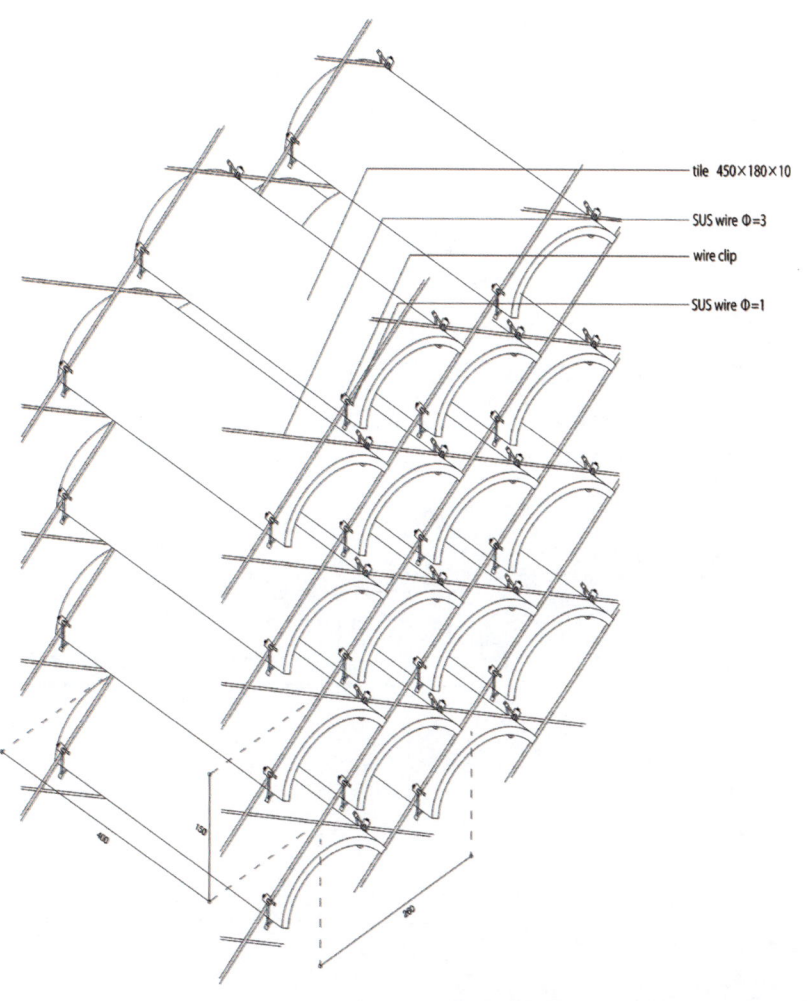

tile 450×180×10
SUS wire Φ=3
wire clip
SUS wire Φ=1

PARTICLES

FRAC, FONDS REGIONAL D'ART CONTEMPORAIN
FRAC, FONDO REGIONALE D'ARTE CONTEMPORANEA
Marseille, France (2013)

1. ENTRY
2. CAFE
3. REFLECTING POOL
4. RECEPTION
5. SHOP
6. EXHIBITION 1
7. ATELIER
8. DELIVERY
9. CONFERENCE
10. FOYER
11. SCULPTURE GARDEN
12. EXHIBITION 2
13. EXHIBITION PREPARATION ROOM
14. URBAN TERRACE
15. RESOURCE CENTRE
16. CHILDREN WORKSHOP
17. OFFICE
18. EXHIBITION 3
19. ROOF

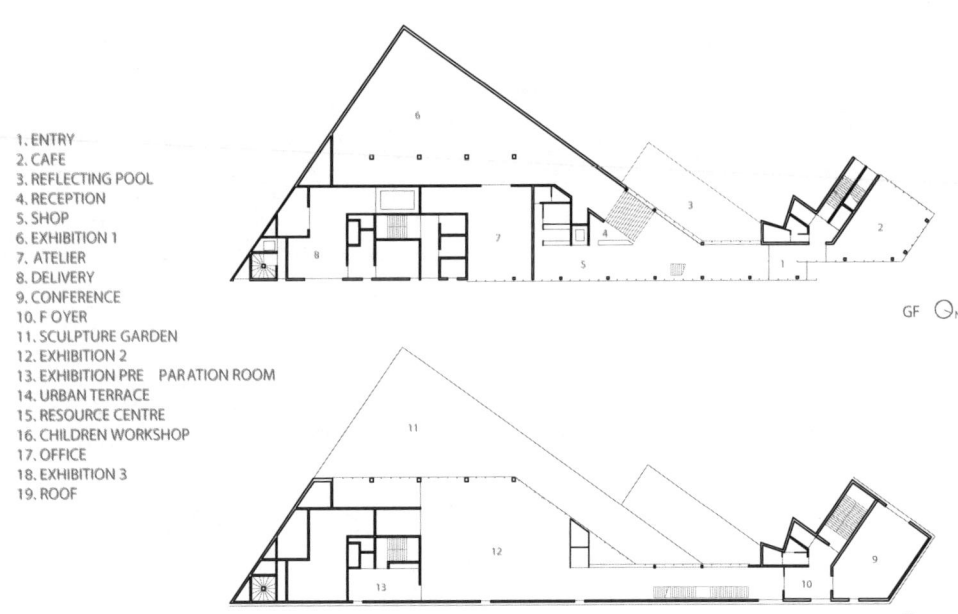
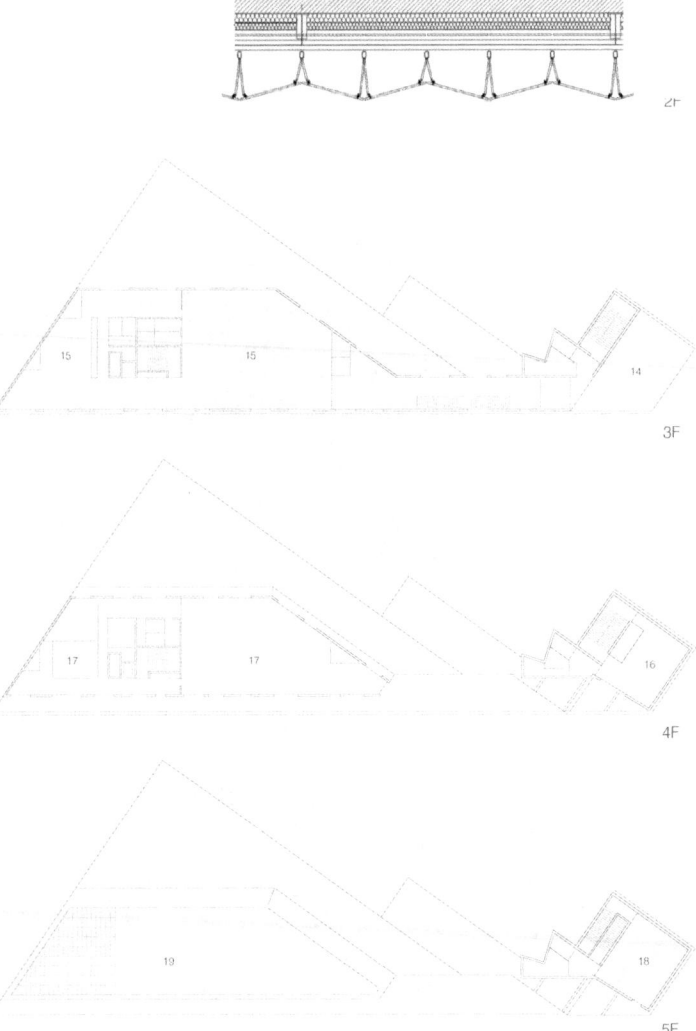

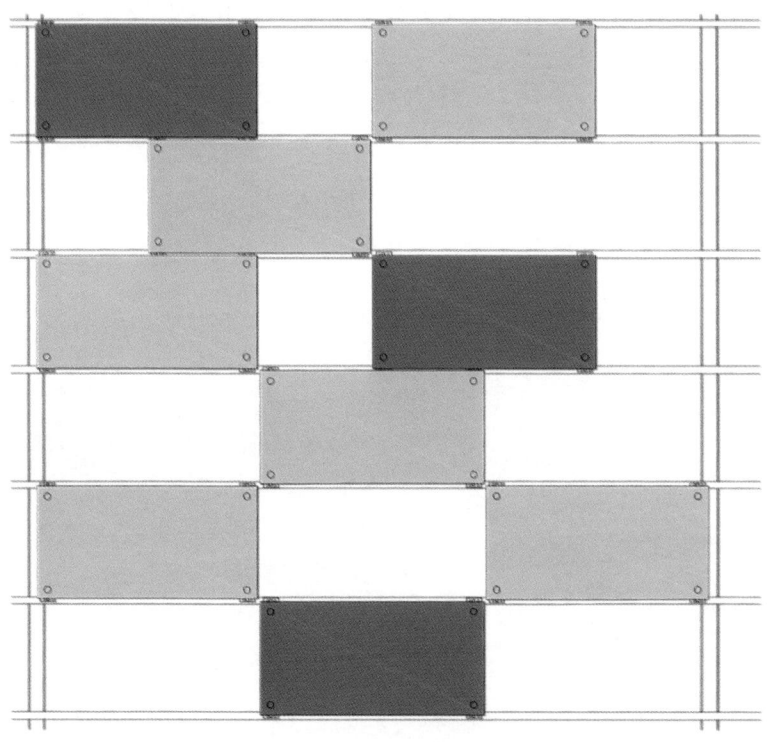

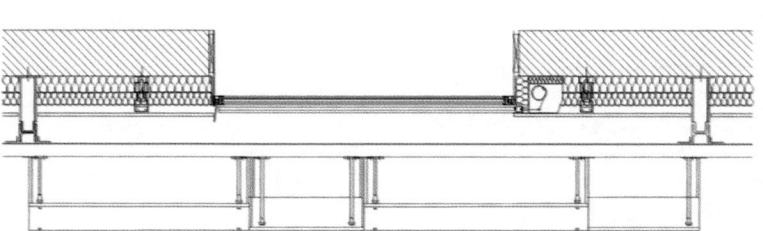

CREDITS	
Area	**5.757m²**
Budget	**17,5 M€ HT / 21,5 M€ TTC**
Architect + Partner	**Kengo Kuma & Associates + Toury et Vallet**
Project Team	**Kengo Kuma + Yuki Ikeguchi + Nicolas Moreau, Louise Lemoine + Félicien Duval + Shinku Noda + Jun Shibata +**
ColB. Team	**Jean-Daniel Boyé, Frank Anderle, Loïc Lequertier, Pascal Ferrera**
Engineer	**CEBAT ingénierie**
System	**Reinforced concrete, partly steel flame**

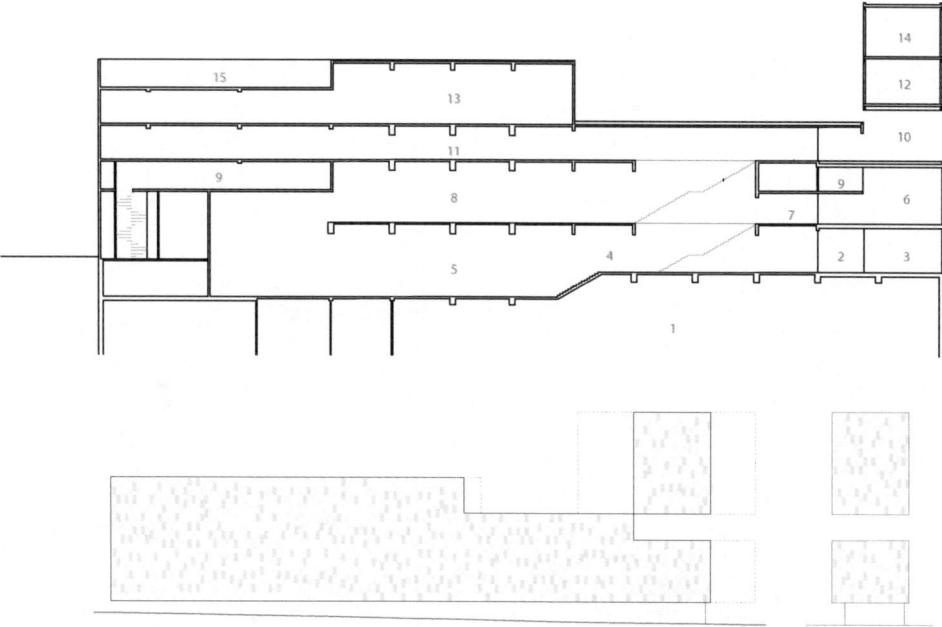

KENGO KUMA & ASSOCIATES | MONOGRAPH.IT | 147

PARTICLES
POLYGONIUM
POLYGONIUM

23

Kanaya-machi, Takaoka-shi, Toyama, Japan (2008)

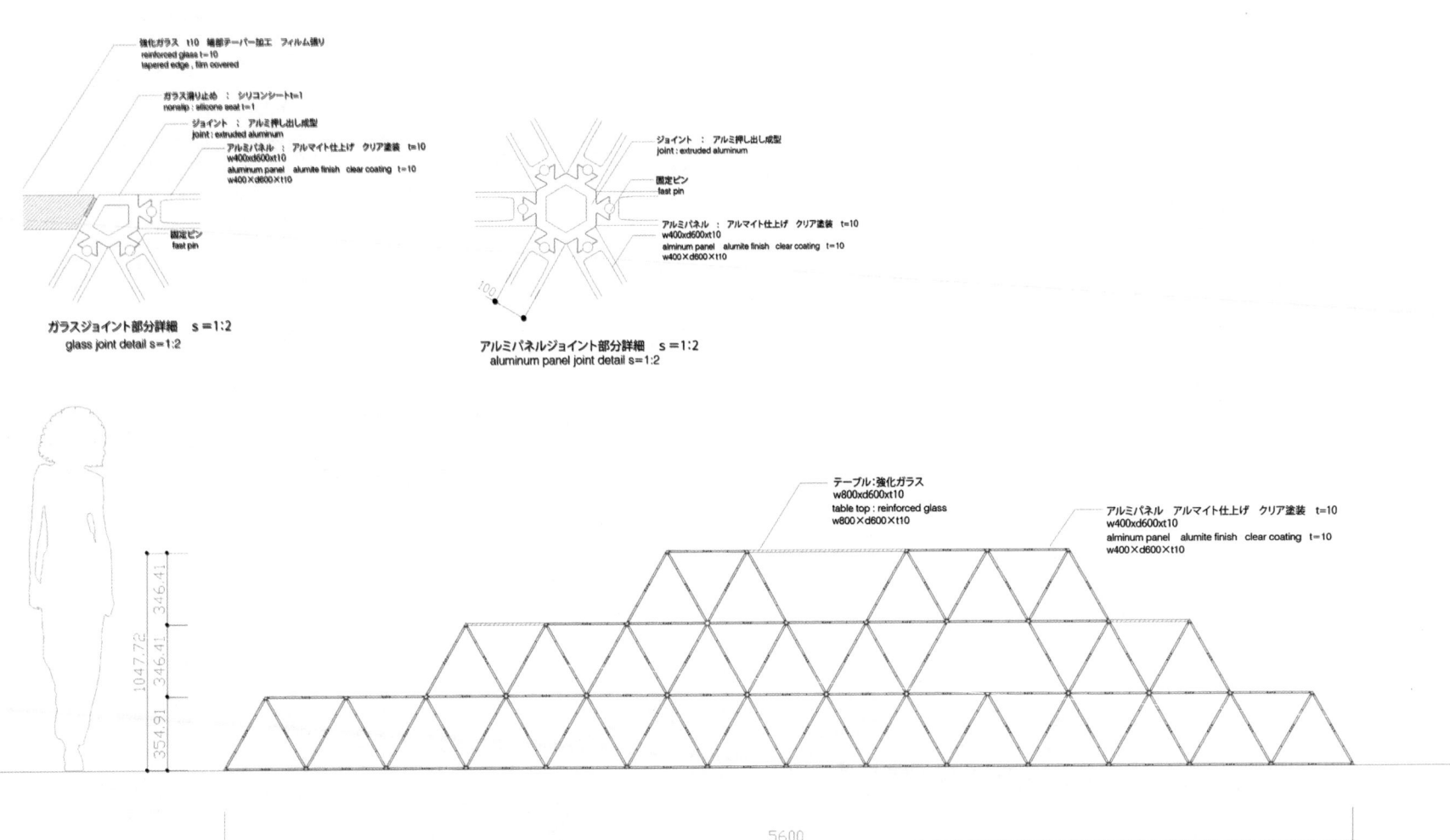

24 PARTICLES
CARD CASTLE
CARD CASTLE

Minatoku Minamiaoyama, Tokyo, Japan (2007)

CREDITS	
Contest	Verona MARMOMACC 2007
Area	104sqm
Client	Il Casone spa
Architect + Partner	Kengo Kuma & Associates
Project Team	Kengo Kuma + Javier Villar Ruiz + Ryota Torao
ColB. Team	Targetti Sankey + Il Casone
Engineer	Ejiri structural engineers
System	Piling up triangular blocks and glued together on the edges (dimensions 25cm x 25cm x t1cm)
Render + Photos	Toni Garbasso + Peppe Maisto

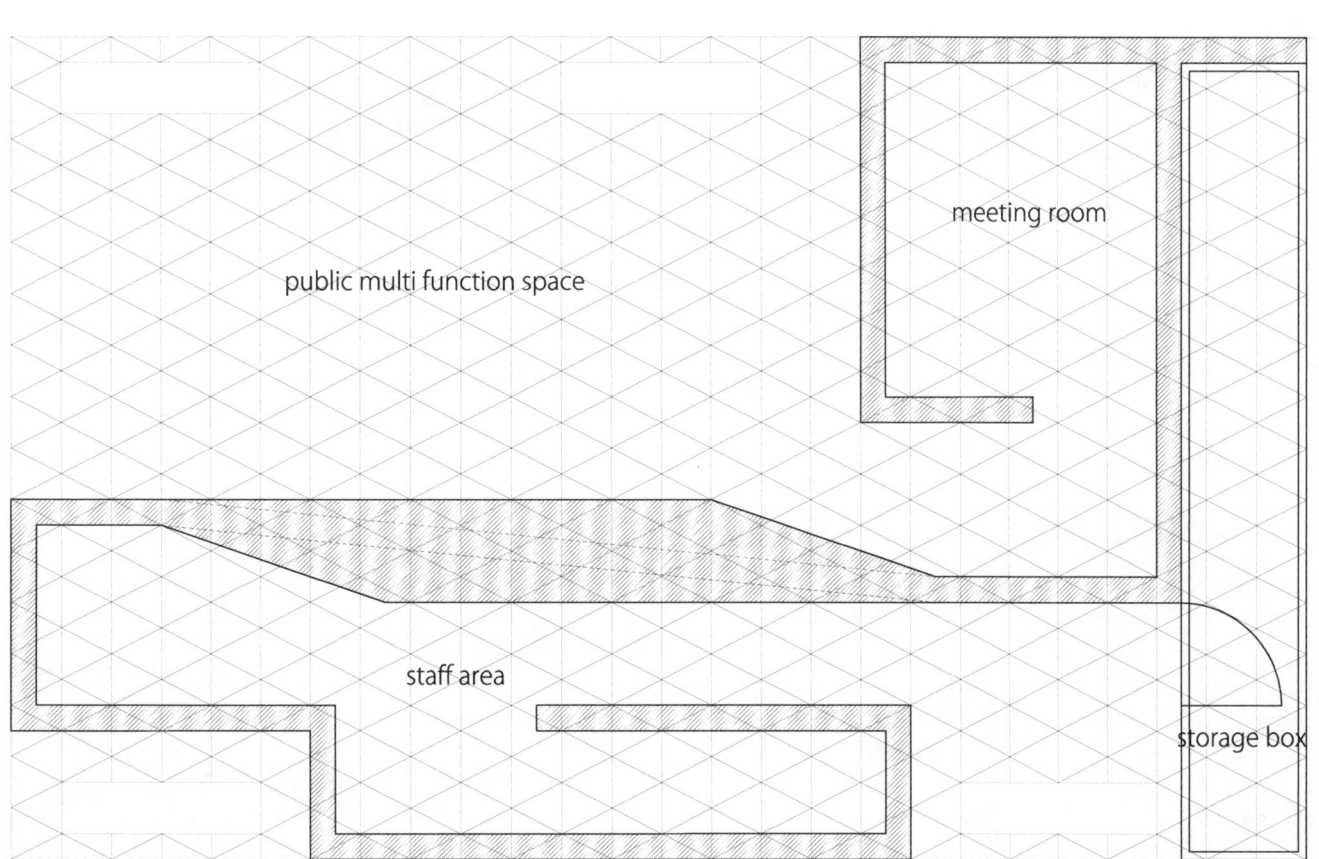

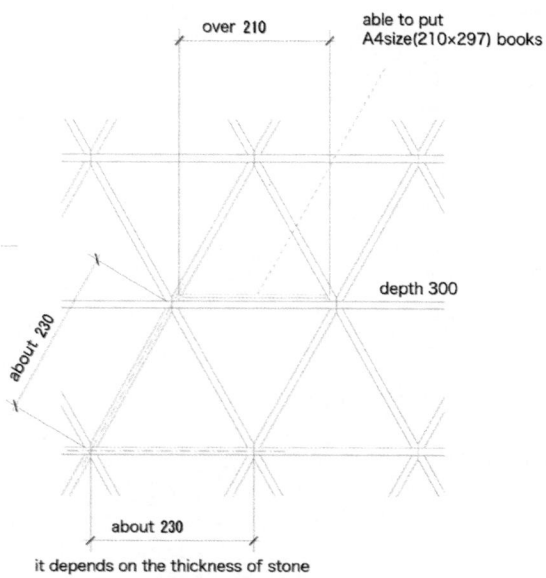

PARTICLES

POLYGONIUM

23

POLYGONIUM

Kanaya-machi, Takaoka-shi, Toyama, Japan (2008)

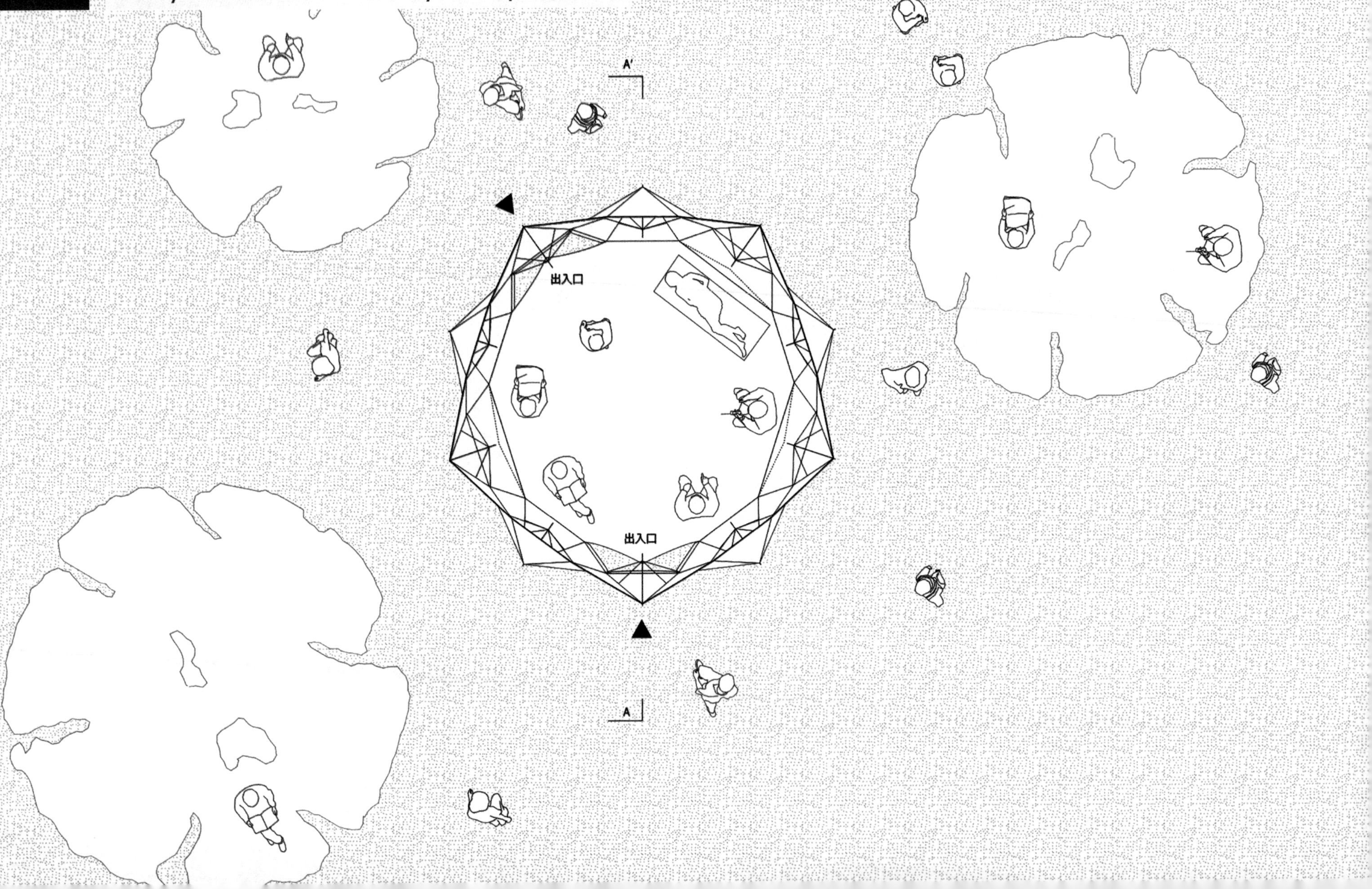

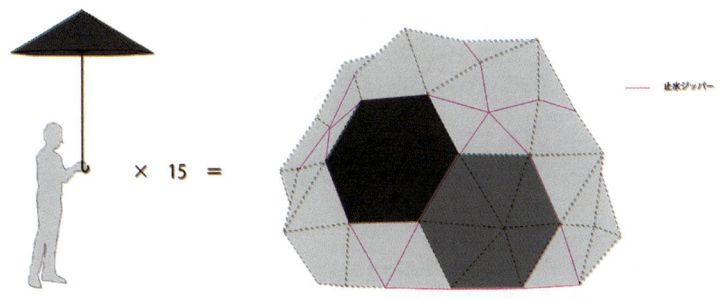
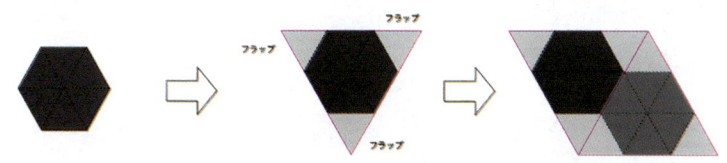
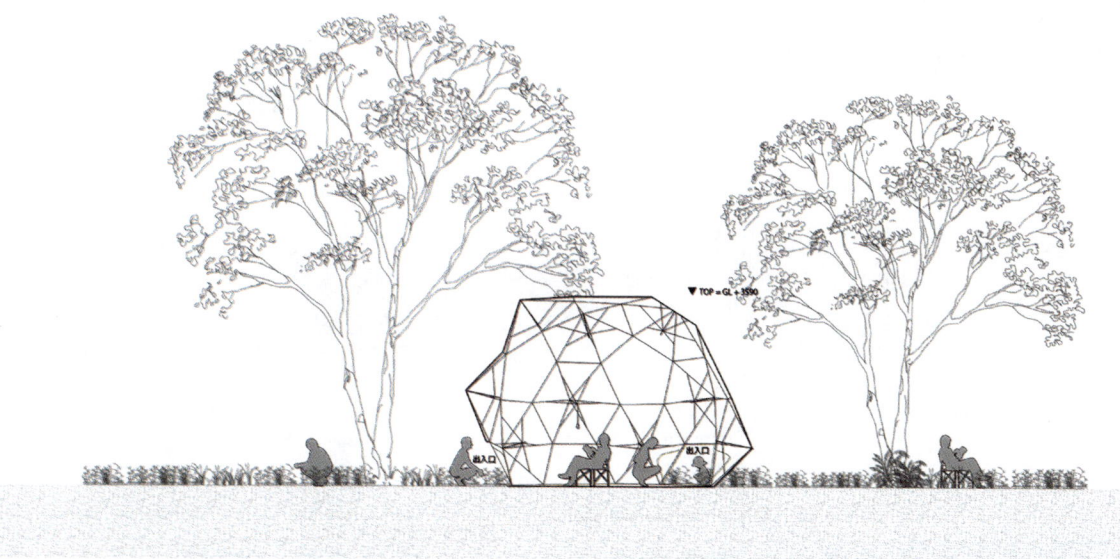

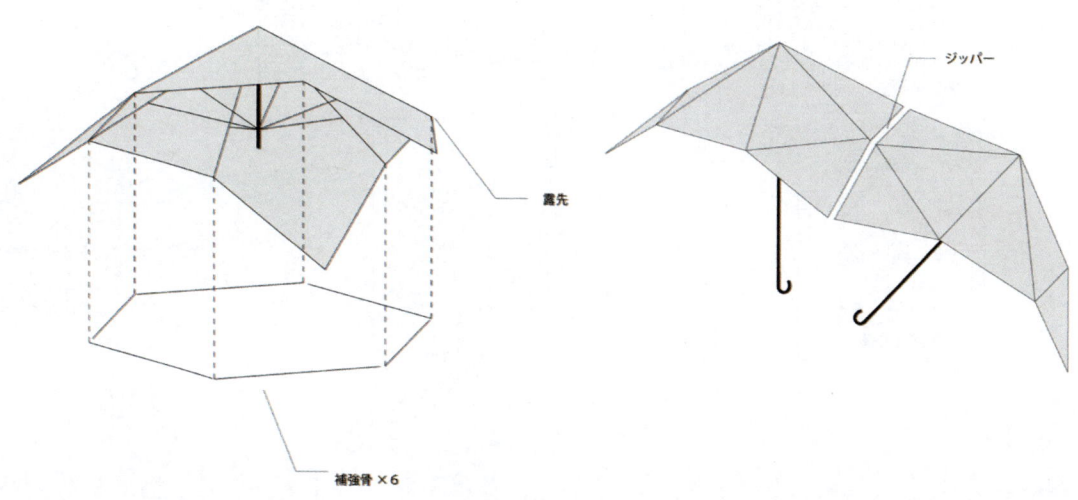

PARTICLES
26 NAGAOKA CITY HALL "AORE"
MUNICIPIO "AORE" A NAGAOKA
Otedori, Nagaoka-shi, Niigata, Japan (2012)

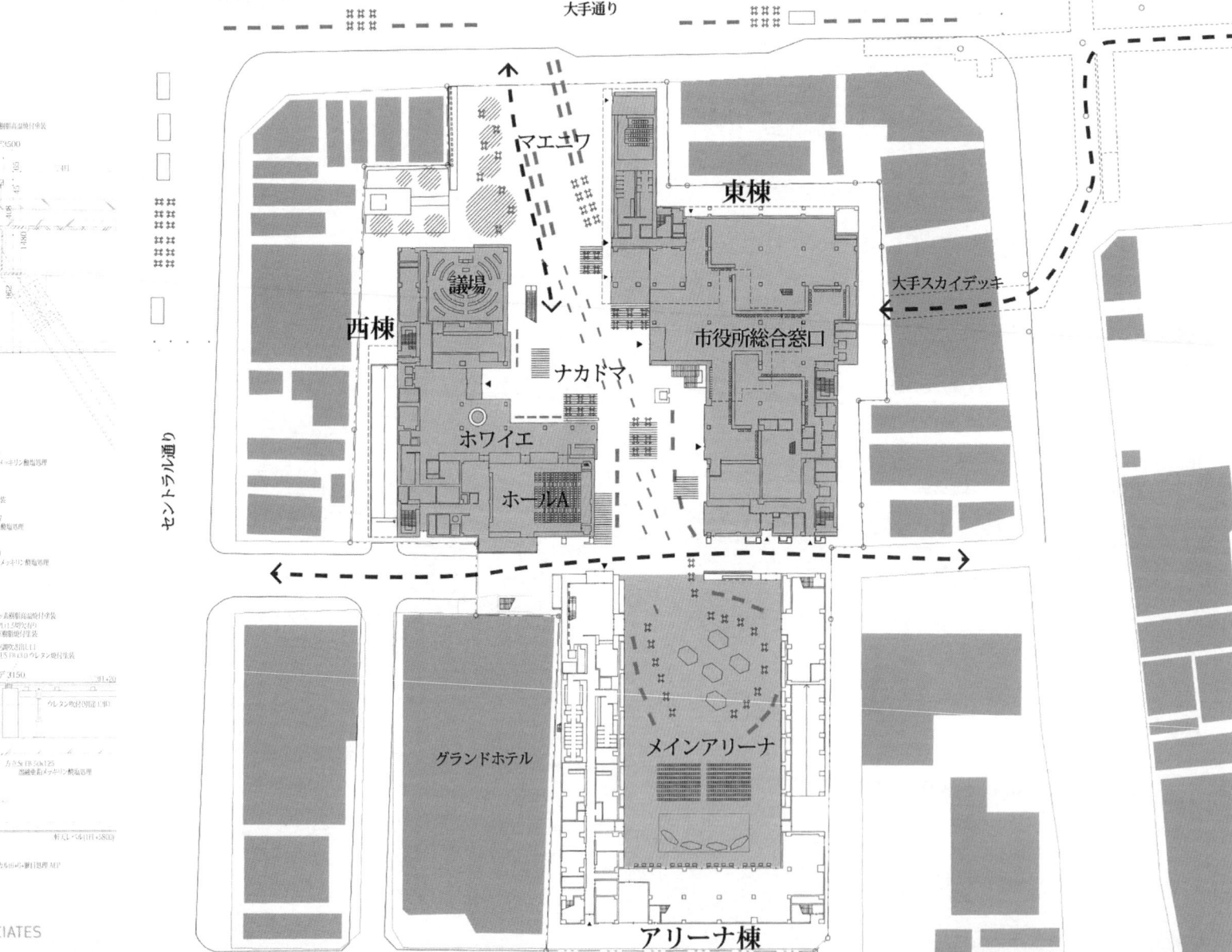

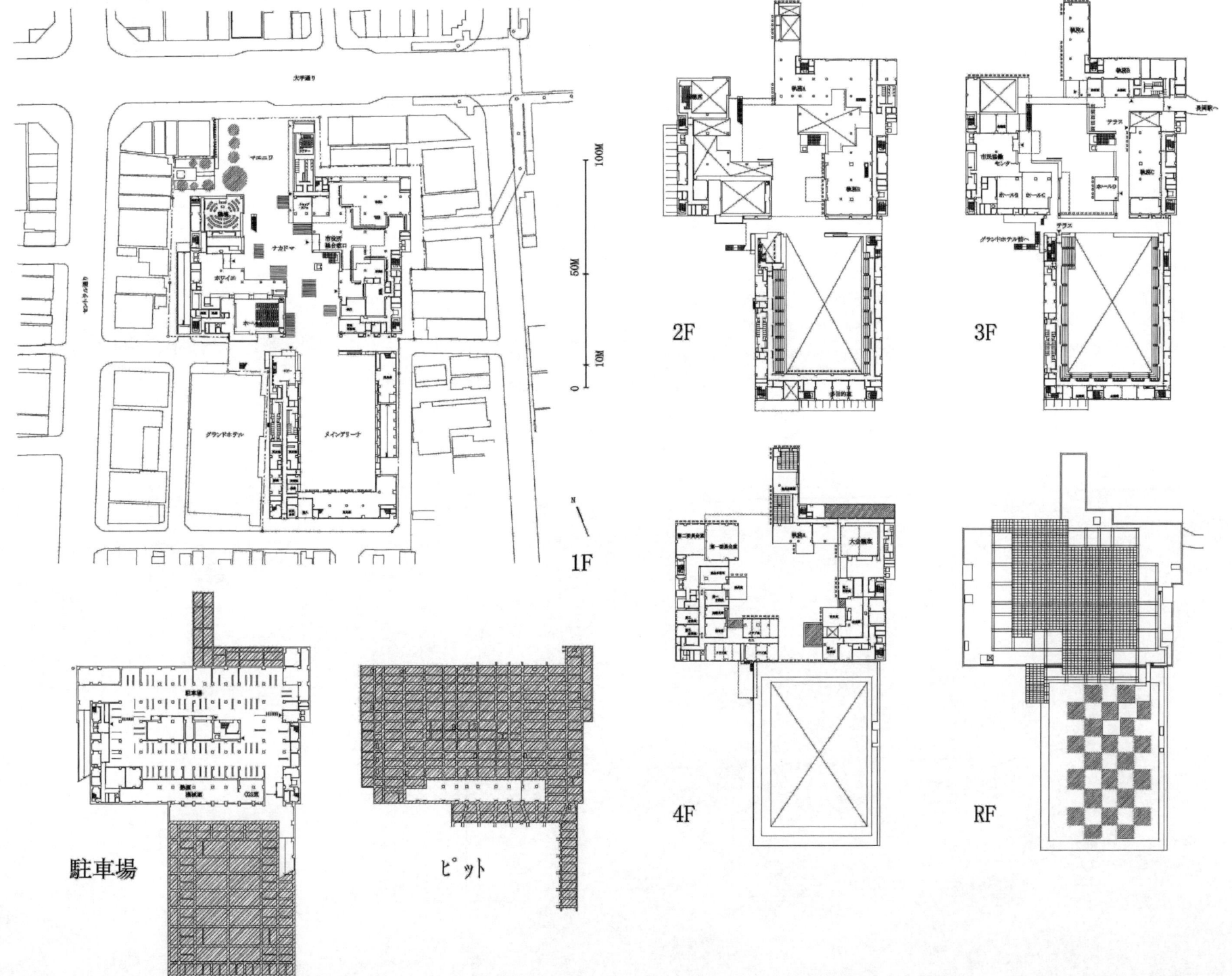

27 FOLDING
PAPER SNAKE
PAPER SNAKE
Anyang, Republic of South Korea (2005)

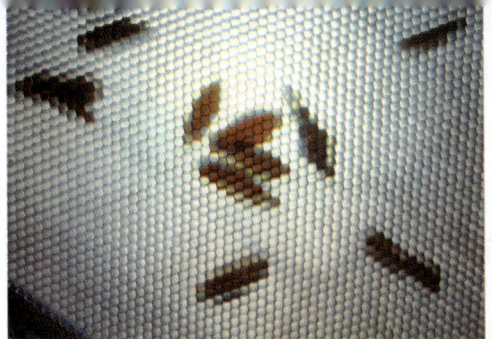

We were asked by the City of Anyang (a city in the periphery of Seoul) to design a resting space in between the trees from where to look down to the valley and its river. The visitors of this Public Art Project will walk around the forests discovering different works by international artists and architects. Our pavilion is located in a privileged position where paths meet and from where to enjoy great views. We wanted to create an architecture that could wind among the trees and follow the topography of the site. Nature told us where to best locate the resting spaces.

So as to obtain a structural material as light and transparent as possible we developed, together with our engineer, a 47mm thick 'sandwich panel' composed by a Paper Honeycomb core glued and pressed between two sheets of FRP sheets.

The porosity of these structural surfaces lets the natural light and shadows pass through. The pavilion becomes a sensitive receiver of the surrounding nature responding to its weather changing conditions. It is an architecture that belongs now to the site.

28 FOLDING
Y-HUTTE HOUSE
CASA Y-HUTTE
Minami Aoyama, Minato-ku, Tokyo, Japan (2008)

A villa with wood as theme. A tentative modern version of Laugier's 'Primitive Hut', reproducing a dense space surrounded by trees, deep in the woods. Just like branches that reach for the sky, a number of wooden joists stretches toward heaven. Three surfaces lean over on each other to form a roof. Floor plan under the roof is also triangular: everything is based on triangles. The triangle is what I found at the end of my pursuit of deviation from Cartesian Grid-a quadrangular world that rules today's cities and architecture.

I reflected upon how a hut in a forest should be. A quadrilateral plan drawn on a perpendicular Cartesian coordinate system would restrict the direction and would be too artificial and constructive in the natural forest. I am more interested in an architecture that is "close to nature". So I came up with a form structured by resting three panels on each other to produce a triangular pyramid and cutting its corners. A large single-space is created by the three panels.

The panels, functioning as both roof and wall, are held by wooden ribs at 300mm pitch, and these ribs give an effect of diffusing light just like the branches and leaves of a tree. The slanted panels meet together in a tree-like manner, giving it an impression of top branches of trees tied together. This effect is the reason why Flank Lloyd Wright and Buckminster Fuller preferred triangular to rectangular form for its quality of resembling nature. The plan becomes a hexagon, and when each edge is given different elements; dining set, fire place, piano, kitchen counter, bed, writing table, the elements are adjoined in obtuse angles and dispersed in the space creating a loosely partitioned room.

As a heating device, an "Ondor-type (Korean floor heater)" floor heating system is introduced. Hot air is sent under the space between the doubled-floor, and vented through the slit opened near the window to prevent condensation.

In summer, air conditioning is limited to ventilation considering the cool climate. The titled panels and high ceiling enables ventilation through natural gravity. In addition, the sky lights are positioned corresponding to the dominant wind which cools down and thus creating effective ventilation.

This hut, designed through the investigation of the form, "close to nature", somehow resembles Laugier's "Primitive Hut" and ancient pit dwellings.

29 FOLDING
WOOD BERG HOUSE
CASA WOOD BERG
Japan (2008)

This residence in the center of Tokyo is screened to the outside with folding planes made of small timber louvers, creating privacy and generating a soft light atmosphere

30 FOLDING CHIKUGO
CHICUGO
Fukuoka, Japan (2013)

We redefined roof, one of the main elements in architectural vocabulary, as an assembly of small slopes. The museum is firmly rooted in the local community and is open to the environment in many respects. We also applied a variety of materials into the roof and the wall, as part of our attempt at "community-forming." This village-like museum with "scattered roofs" is harmonized with its surrounding traditional hamlet. For structure, number of rigid triangles are piled up, which work to gain transparency and openness to the building.

The folding planes generating the geometry of the building, makes the museum to touch the ground only in the corners creating an open and dynamic architecture.

KENGO KUMA & ASSOCIATES | MONOGRAPH.IT | 167

31 FOLDING
MUSEUM AT THE CHINA ACADEMY OF ART
MUSEO DELL'ACCADEMIA D'ARTE CINESE
Hangzhou, China (2014)

The China Central Academy of Fine Arts in Beijing and China Academy of Art in Xiangshan are taking a major role In art education. In the Central Academy of Fine Arts, the museum designed by Arata Isozaki has recently been completed, being the answer to the modern campus thronged with buildings in the city in Beijing. On the other hand, we are planning to build a new type of university museum in harmony with mountains with small tea gardens in a beautiful natural environment within the suburbs of Hangzhou. As a result of studies in which an arrangement was made that no slopes would be cut of modified and that the architecture would be configured to closely relate to mountain slopes, a lozenge shaped pattern naturally appeared in a contour line. The lozenge appeared not only in plan but also in elevation and in three dimensions as well. I finally understood that the mountains as a topographical existence appear as triangles in elevation. The diagram of lozenges generates a fluid exhibition space with linear and alternating floor levels and with the partially external spaces which appear in between. Clay tiles and stones in the old house in the district are to be gathered as reusable materials, and the details to build a three dimensional body with these materials are now being investigated. This methodology proposes the idea that rather than gardens being put in contrast to architecture, the soil of the tea gardens is actually transformed into the architecture.

FOLDING
SUSA INTERNATIONAL STATION
STAZIONE INTERNAZIONALE DI SUSA
Susa, Italy (2012)

32

Susa is a small city located in the middle of a valley within the Italian Alps, near the border with France. A long time ago, this strategic position made the Susa valley an important gateway between the two countries, however, over the decades, with the growing hegemony of air transportation, it has become just another valley.

A renewed interest in the development of the high-speed trains is now giving the Susa valley another chance to recover its strategic role. Susa's position in particular is pivotal as it will be right in the axe of the future high-speed line linking Turin and Lyon. Although its moderate size, this station represents an important milestone for this ambitious railway project, and at the same time brings to the whole local territory opportunities until now unimaginable.

The valley of Susa is already a heavily "infra-structuralized" territory where roads, technical facilities and a regional railway have a strong presence. Our project wants to think beyond the building itself and wishes to recover the nearby "asphalted" areas by transforming them into new public spaces. Public spaces not only serving the station itself, but becoming the pedestrian connection between other public facilities, spaces and parks along the river that have until now been isolated. By doing this we hope to enhance the site and the whole territory.

The station is conceived so as to become an extension of its surrounding spaces. The building rises from the ground as an exterior spiraled promenade that achieves all-around views of the valley… a panoramic balcony where locals, tourists and connecting travelers can all be reminded and enjoy the beauty of the surrounding alpine landscape.

Our aim is to avoid the new station becoming a stranger within the valley. With the design recalling the surrounding mountains and not prioritizing any of its facades, the station has the intention to tie and merge within the surrounding alpine environment. Reinterpreted in a contemporary way, the characteristic nature of the building's many metallic flakes establishes a textural dialogue with the local traditional stone-slab roof architecture.

The Susa International station being not only an inter-exchanger between the regional railway and the new high-speed trains, it will incorporate additional programs and activities that will serve the whole valley. To mention a few, a multi-functional hall, a regional museum, f&b facilities. We have taken the chance to locate all these activities on the upper levels creating a generous covered piazza on the ground level bringing comfortable conditions to the station's accesses considering the temperamental weather conditions of the region. Altogether these elements allow the architecture to establish a direct and intuitive connection between the station itself, its new surrounding public spaces and further afield.

The surfaces generating the building grow from ground to roof into a spiral-like structure, generating a natural mix of public spaces and the station building.

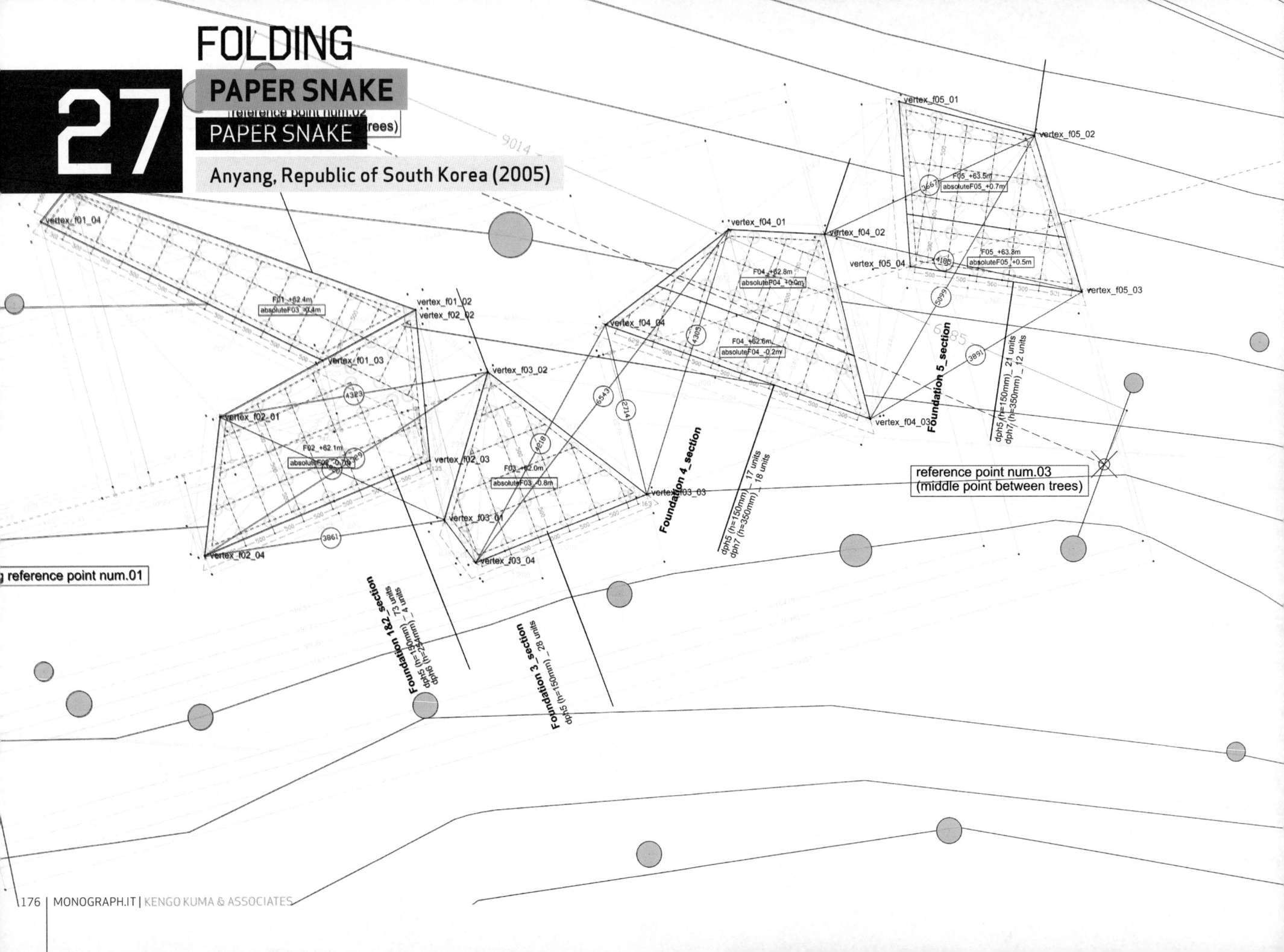

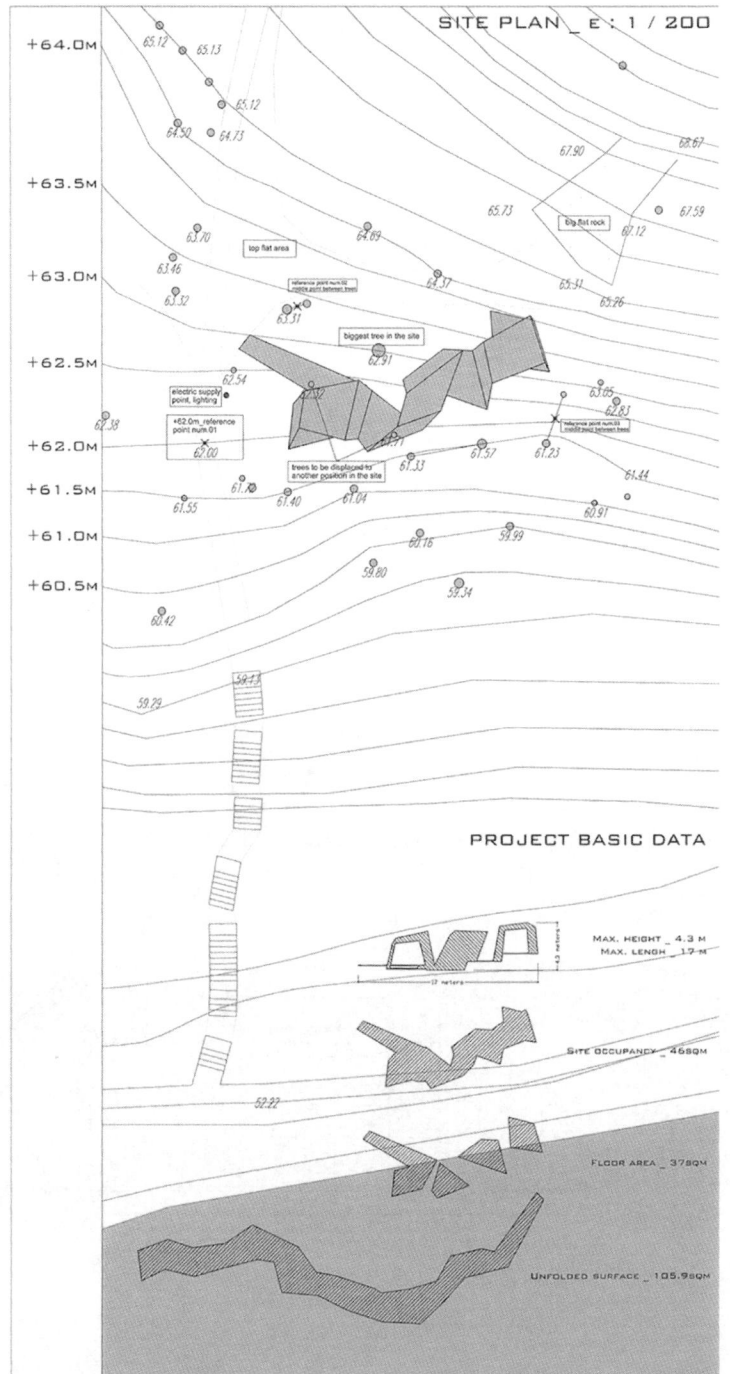

CREDITS	
Contest	**APAP2005 _ Anyang Public Art Project 2005**
Area	**46 sqm**
Budget	**10.000 USD**
Client	**City of Anyang for APAP2005 event**
Architect + Partner	**Kengo Kuma & Associates**
Engineer	**Ejiri Structural Engineers**

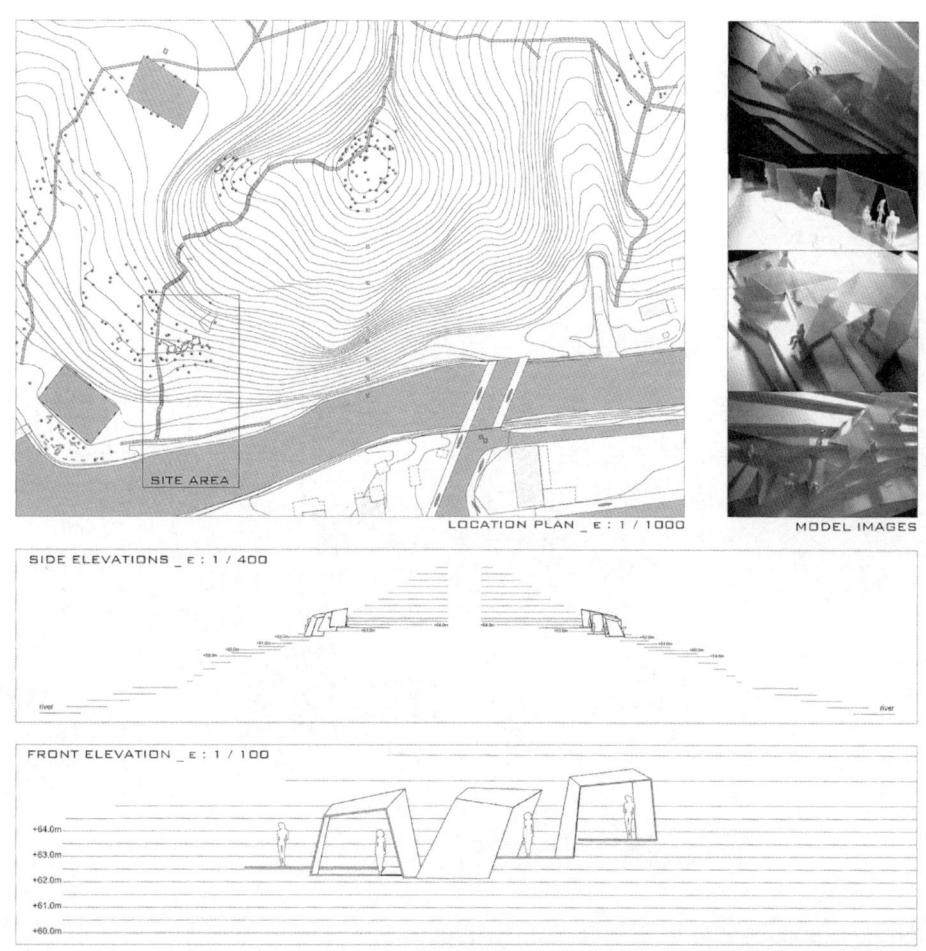

FOLDING

28 Y-HUTTE HOUSE
CASA Y-HUTTE

Minami Aoyama, Minato-ku, Tokyo, Japan (2008)

CREDITS	
Area	**90.51 m²**
Project Team	**Kengo Kuma & Associates + Masamichi Hirabayashi, Taiko Kasai**
ColB. Team	**Structural Design Office Ejiri**, structural; **P.T. Morimura & Associates, Ltd.**, mechanical
Engineer	**Dai'ichi Kensetsu Ltd.**
System	**timber**
Render + Photos	**Yuji Takeuchi**

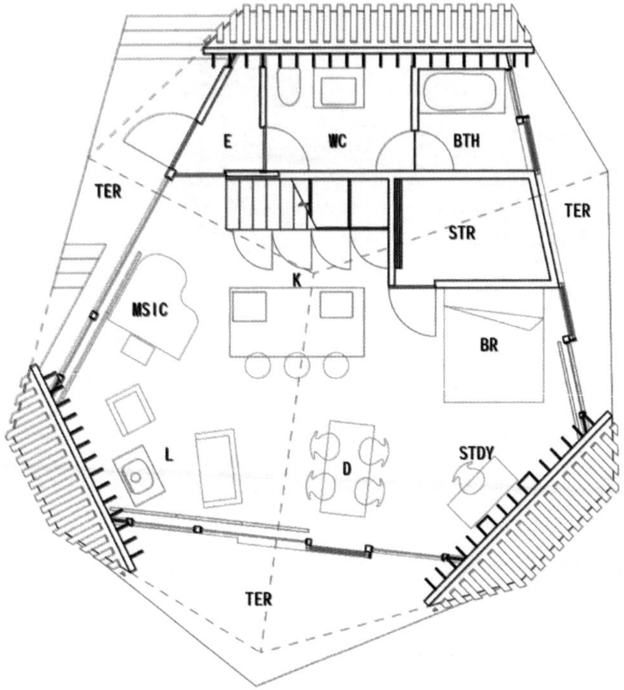

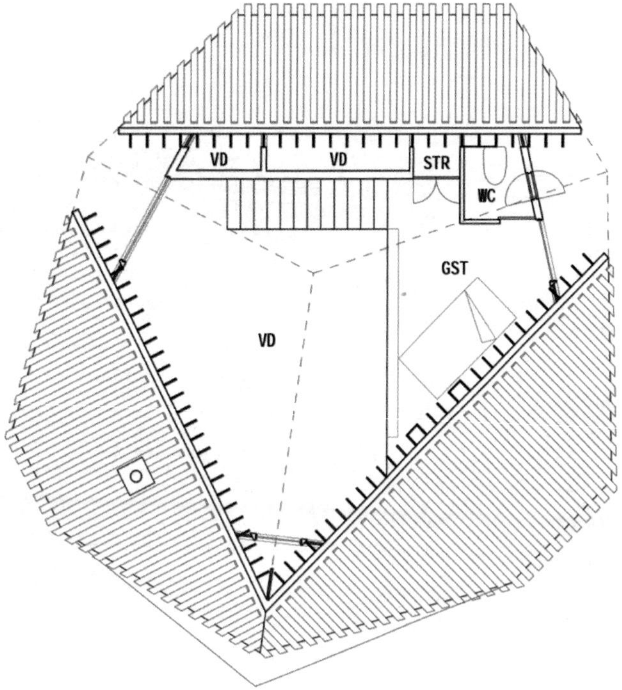

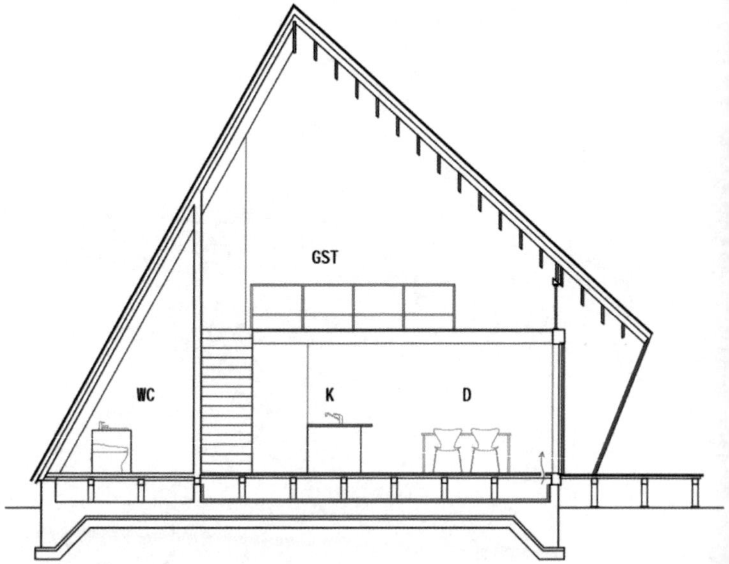

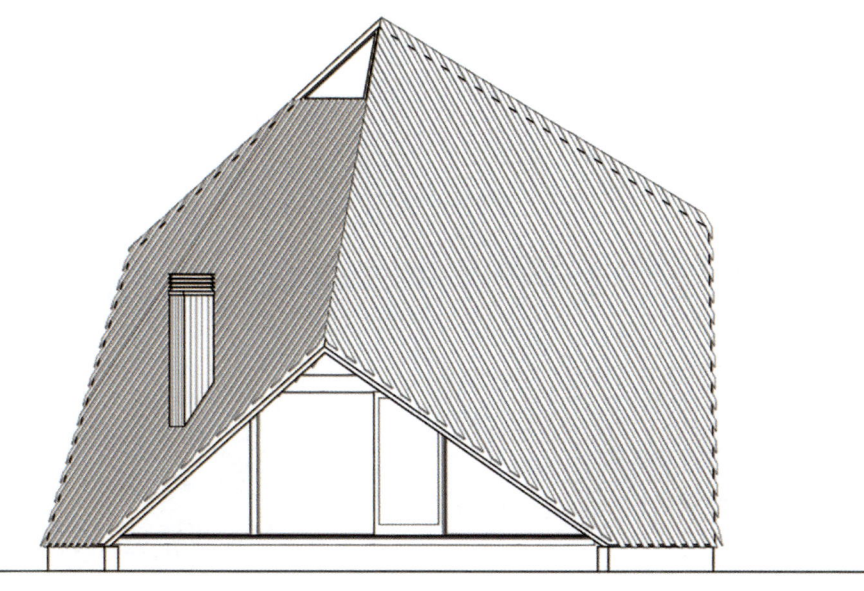
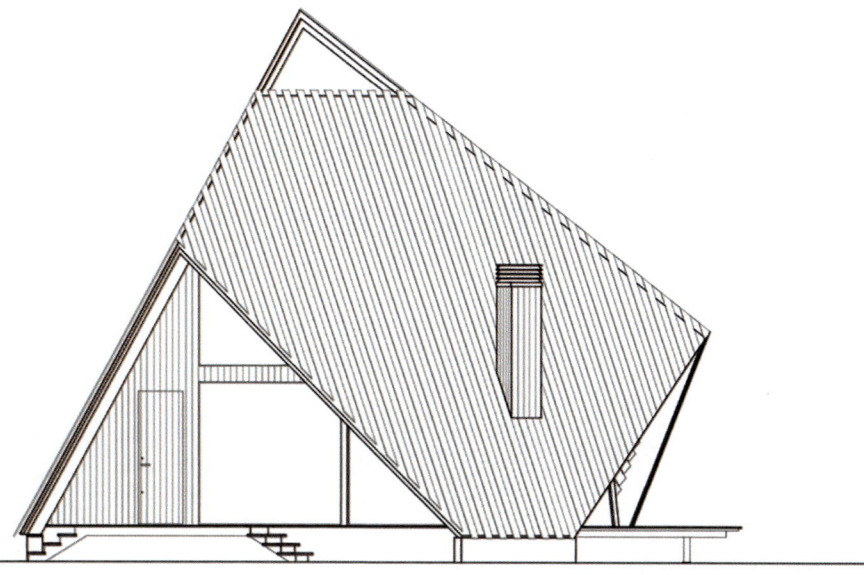
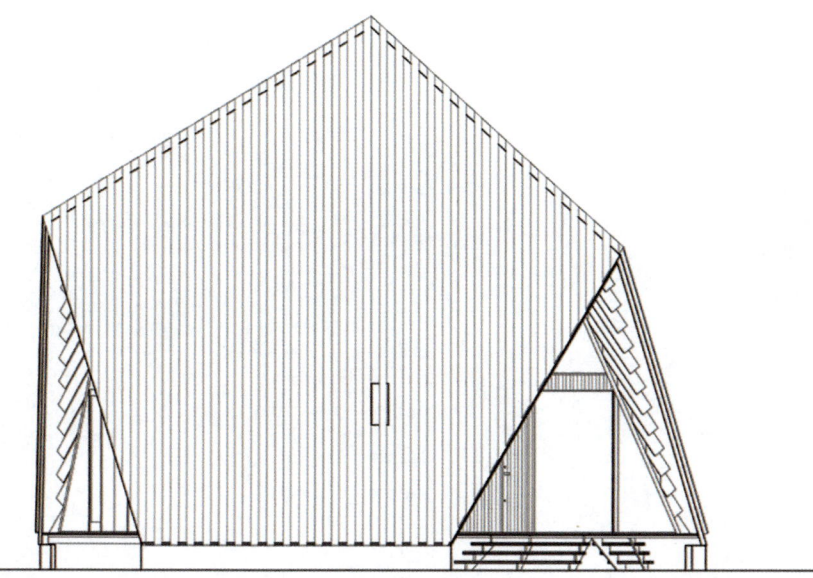
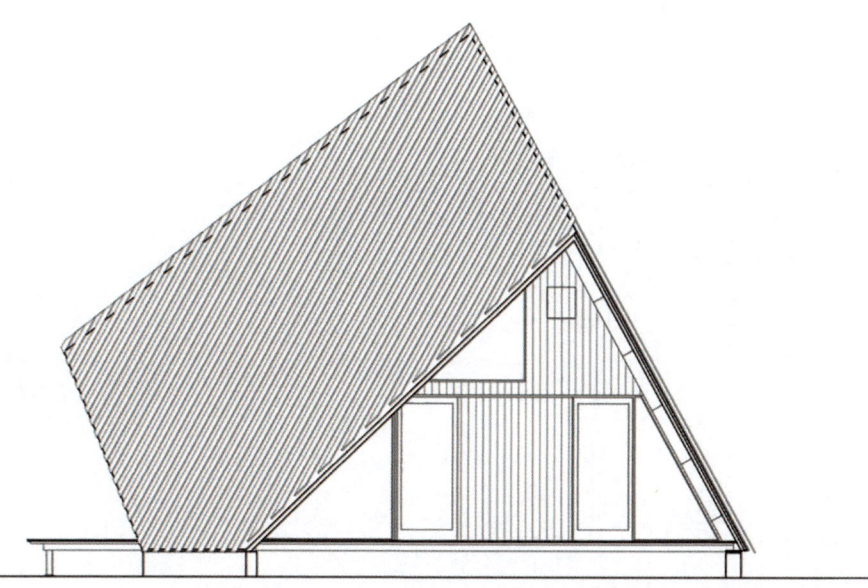

KENGO KUMA & ASSOCIATES | MONOGRAPH.IT | 179

29 FOLDING
WOOD BERG HOUSE
CASA WOOD BERG
Japan (2008)

B1F plan

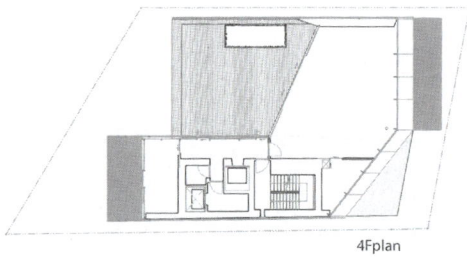
4F plan

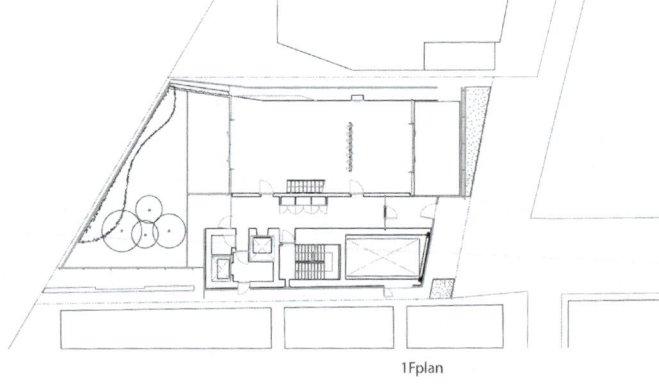
1F plan

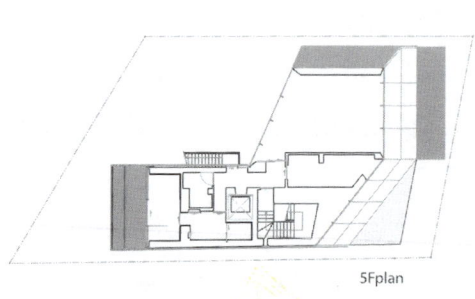
5F plan

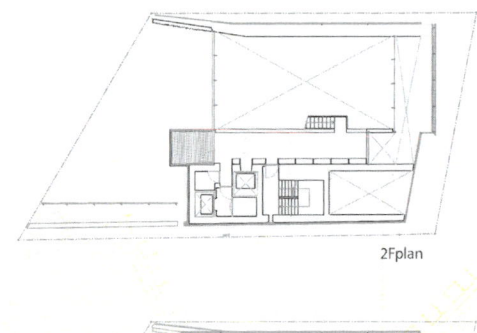
2F plan

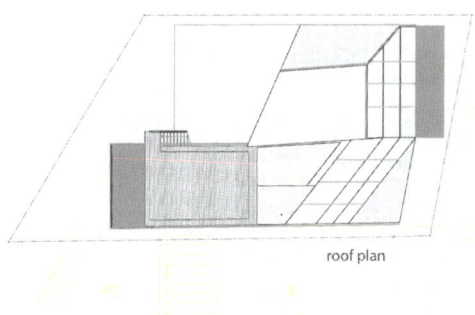
roof plan

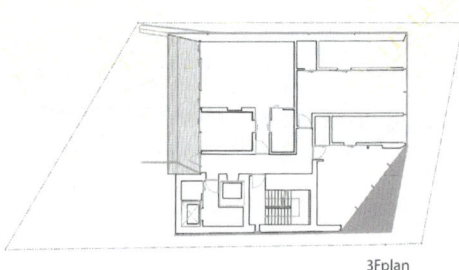
3F plan

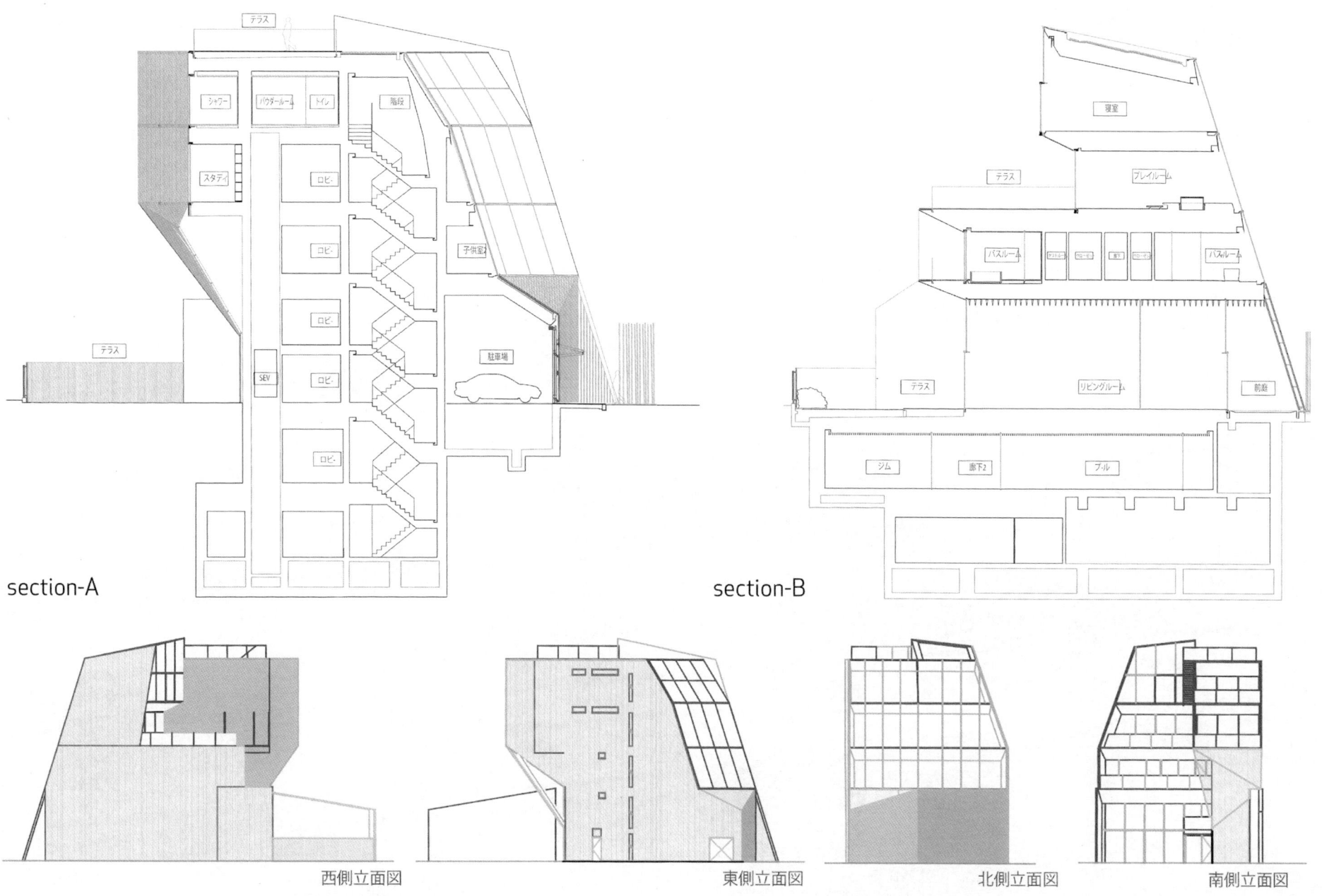

30 FOLDING
CHIKUGO
CHICUGO
Fukuoka, Japan (2013)

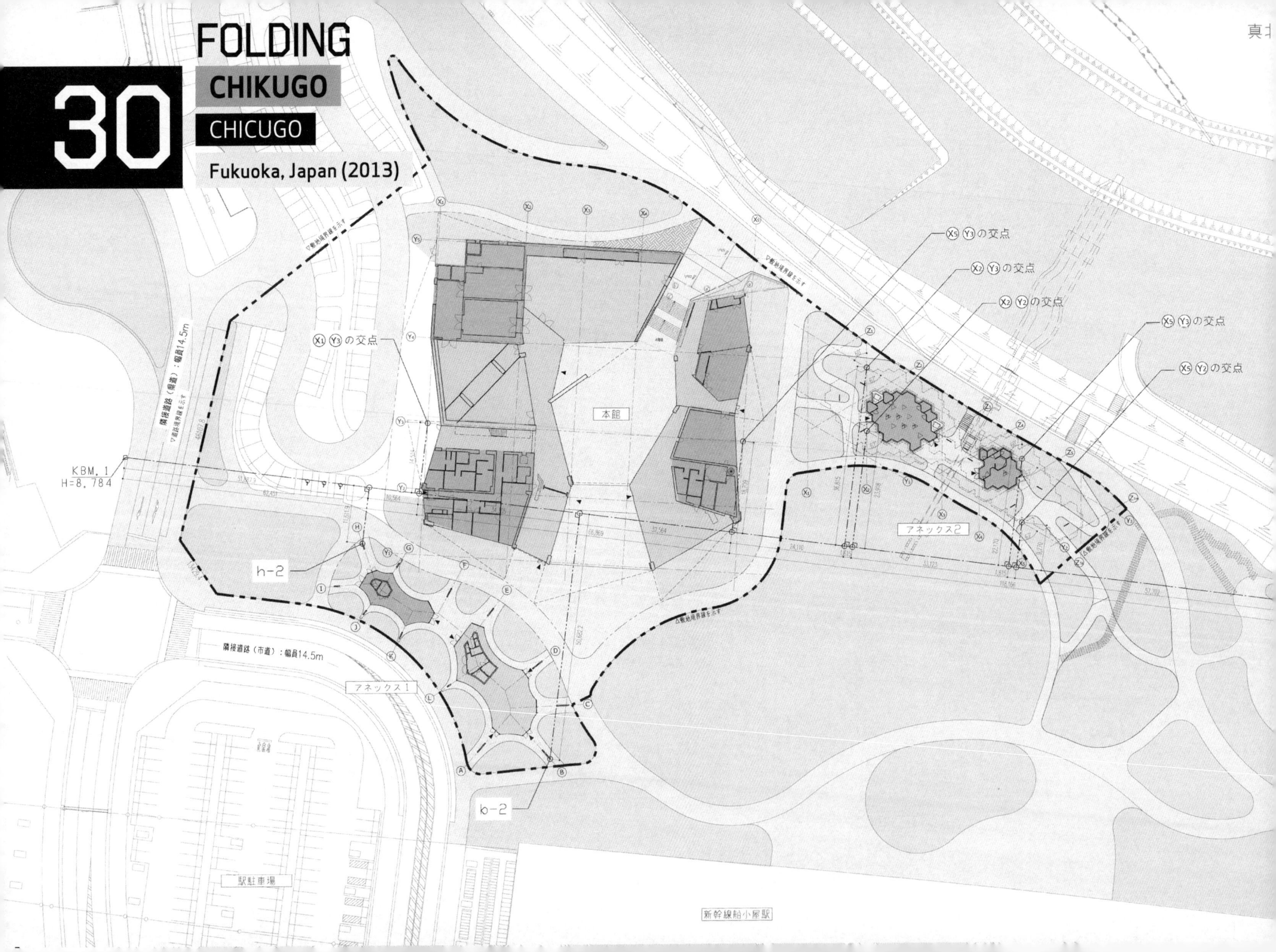

FOLDING

31 MUSEUM AT THE CHINA ACADEMY OF ART

MUSEO DELL'ACCADEMIA D'ARTE CINESE

Hangzhou, China (2014)

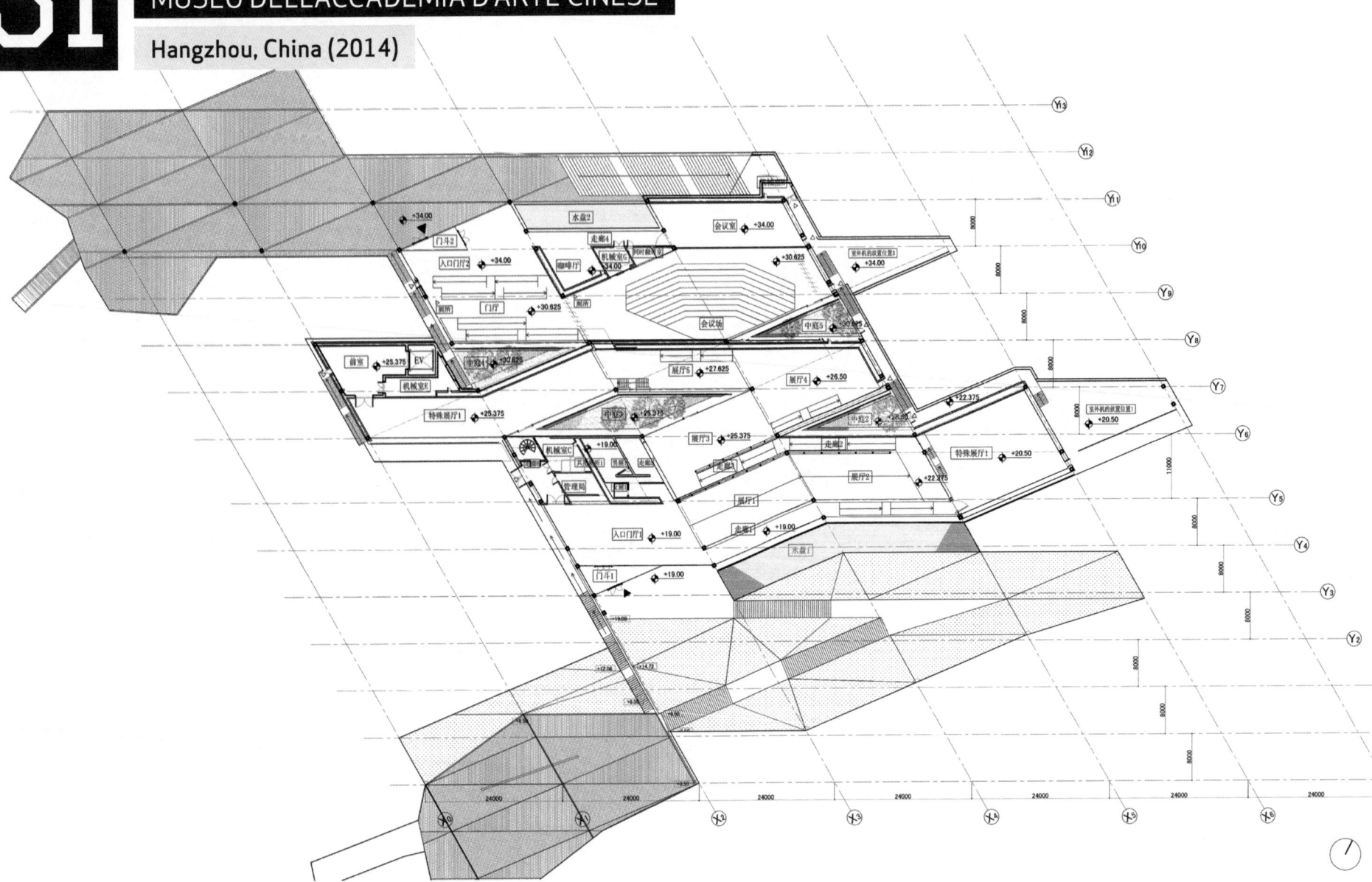

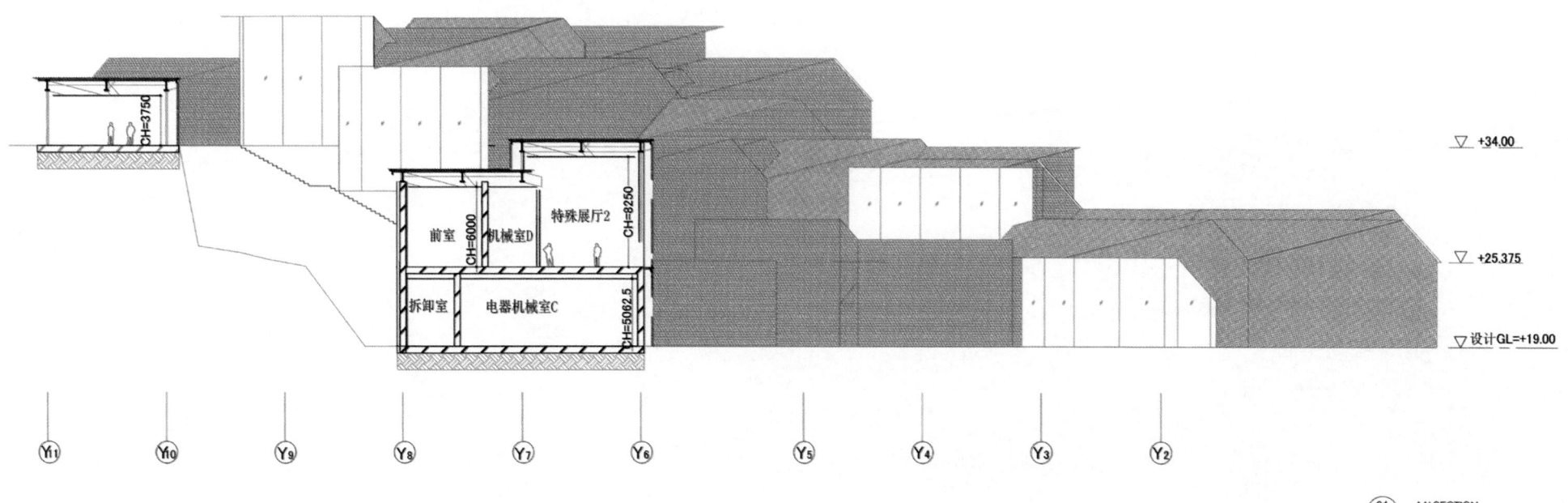

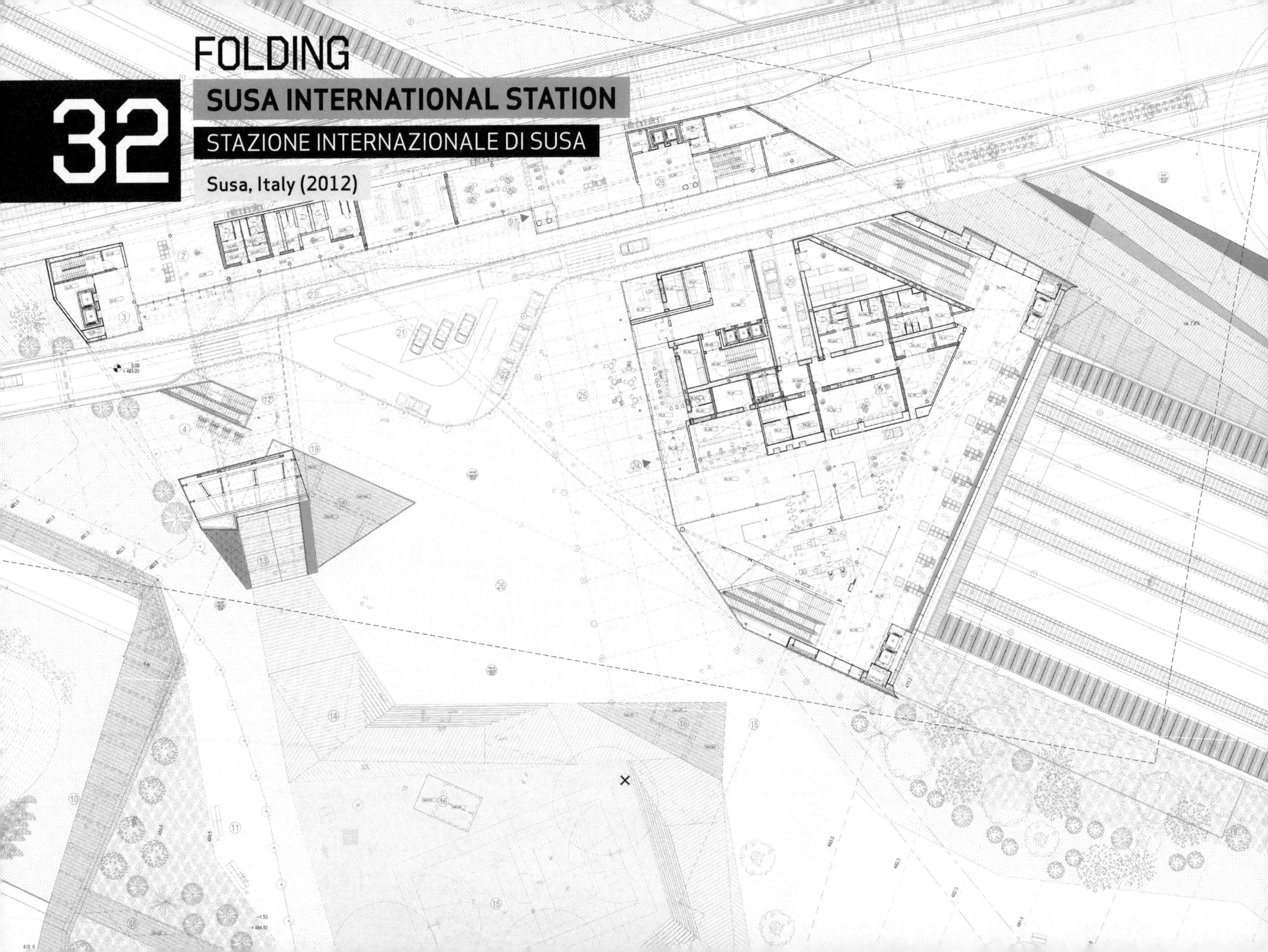

32 FOLDING
SUSA INTERNATIONAL STATION
STAZIONE INTERNAZIONALE DI SUSA
Susa, Italy (2012)

ROOF
33 | KURE CITY ONDO CIVIC CENTER
CENTRO CIVICO KURE CITY ONDO
Minami Ondo, Hiroshima, Japan (2007)

When we visited the site for the first time, we were fascinated by the landscape of the Inland Sea of Japan. Our theme in architecture was to abstract this characteristic view of this area, which consists of roofs and tiles, and to incorporate it into the building. We made an attempt to bring in the structure of the landscape to the detail of the roof, by abstracting and fractionalizing the sight into particles. However, it was not 'copying and pasting' of the scenery around it. We aimed at an architecture that gently floats up to the surface, while blending in with the environment. Although the scale of the Civic Centre is different from the houses around it, they still share the particles – roof-tiles – which form the buildings, and this is one of the strong points of Japanese tiled roof. The roof itself can be massive, but having the same particles as other buildings can remove its sense of pressure. So from the very beginning we emphasized on using authentic tiles. Authentic tile (plain rectangular tile and hollow semi circular tile are used alternately) is distinct as a particle (grain), and when used as louver, the space between tiles could be obscured. Starting with the planning of the whole volume has been customarily the order of designing, but we worked in the opposite way – deciding on the detail first.

In the Civic Centre cohabits the branch of the city hall, community centre and library. Each facility has its own complicated function, but we envisaged that such difference could be accommodated under the same roof. Like a wide wrapping cloth, it allows flexibility – roof does not merely cover what comes beneath it, but can work on its own as a solid or porous facet. Louvers used in this architecture have two roles – the one is with the tiles as a border, and the other is as a membrane of the building – I had long thought that only roof and floor would be enough for a building, but by applying louvers this way, even 'wall' could gain a certain kind of expression.

Using the local materials of the site comes at the centre of our attitude towards design. I would call it agricultural approach. Rather than pursuing one's original style as an architect, you actually visit the place and follow what grows out of it. Architecture should not be cut off from the ground, like a building designed and transported from elsewhere that has no relation to the site. Our aim is to create architecture that confronts and fuses into the earth.

The site looks down the calm Inland Sea of Japan and has a water conduit within. Its landscape consists of the ridgeline of the mountains and islands faced with the surface of the sea. For materials, the unit system of traditional tile-roofing (plain rectangular tile and hollow semicircular tile are used alternately) technique was applied to the louvers to stress plasticity. In the external wall the use of wood weight in the siding boards was partially omitted so that it could accent three-dimensional expression.

Roof is o a major recurring theme in KKAA architecture, Here a two folds roof becomes the main element of the building. becomes roof and facade at once.

ROOF
34 NEZU MUSEUM
MUSEO NEZU
Minato-ku, Tokyo, Japan (2012)

It is an attempt to design a museum as an urban design, rather than a single building. The avenue of Omotesando, where high-end brand shops and boutiques are jostling one another, begins with the wood of Meiji Jingu Shrine, and concludes in the south end with Nezu museum abundant in green. In the vast site exceeding 20,000m² was the private residence of Nezu family. The museum has an excellent collection of Japanese and oriental antiques, and with its verdurous Japanese garden and tea rooms, the museum has gained great popularity since its opening in 1914. On the occasion of the renewal, we thought of designing a dumbbell-shaped town which embraces two forests at both ends. The old and decrepit storehouse and exhibition house were replaced by new buildings, while the 'new' building added in 1990 was half-renovated as house for storage and management.

We wanted the new museum to be linked naturally with its surroundings by the shade from the gentle slope of the roof, located between the busy commercial area and the wood. Layered tiled roof with lowered eaves inherit the original image of the museum and harmonize the new building and the garden. We intended to merge the edge of such linear element to the wood. The end of the rood is a steel plate treated in phosphoric acid to be thinned to its maximum, so that the tile would match the refined works of art in the museum, erasing theme park-like sense of unreality that the tiles tend to have. Phosphoric acid-treatment is also applied to the steel plate panel in the exterior wall, as the material can assimilate to the shade.

The building is not fenced in from the city. Rather, it is open to it through the bamboo thicket, an attempt for a museum as an urban design. People go along the bamboo under the deep eave, like a passage from the lively town to the forest of beauty. Just like 'Roji' approach for tea room, visitors need to make turns to change their mood and end the flow from Meiji Shrine and Omotesando (literally means a main approach to shrine and temples).

Inside the museum is softly wrapped in coral gray from Qingdao, a stone which has a similar expression to the bamboo, and integrated into the garden under the big shade of the roof. Interior is structured also with layered thin roofs of bamboo 'neritsuke' (thinly shaved bamboo is stuck to plywood) and people savor the beauty of all.

In the garden the café was renewed as well, while preserving its stone wall and fire place from the old Nezu residence, another spot for the visitors to enjoy the nature of the garden. Thus, this museum is a device that reunites the city and the forest.

KENGO KUMA & ASSOCIATES

The sculptures are positioned here in front of the glazed facade. This creates a natural and always changing background for the exhibits.

KENGO KUMA & ASSOCIATES | MONOGRAPH.IT | 195

35 ROOF
ASAKUSA - CULTURAL AND TOURIST INFORMATION CENTER
ASAKUSA - CENTRO DI INFORMAZIONI CULTURALI E TURISTICHE

Tokyo, Japan (2009)

In the corner premise of just 326Ð across Kaminari-mon Gate, the building was required to accommodate plural programs such as tourist information center, conference room, multi-purpose hall and an exhibition space.

The center extends Asakusa's lively neighborhood vertically and piles up roofs that wrap different activities underneath, creating a "new section" which had not existed in conventional layered architecture. Equipments are stored in the diagonally shaped spaces born between the roof and the floor, and by this treatment we could secure large air volume despite its just average height for high-and medium-rise buildings. Furthermore, the roofs not only divide the structure into 8 one-storied houses but also determine the role of each floor. First and second floor has an atrium and in-door stairs, creating a sequence from which you can feel the slope of the two roofs. On 6th floor, taking advantage of the slanted roof, we were able to set up a terraced floor with which the entire room can function as a theater. As angles of the roofs inclined toward Kaminari-mon and the heights from the ground vary from floor to floor, each floor relates differently to the outside, giving a unique character to each space.

Lozengeone of the seven roof creating the building is used here as a conference room

The cafe terrace on the top floors offers a view into the historical area of Asakusa in Tokyo

36 ROOF
TEIKYO ELEMENTARY SCHOOL
SCUOLA ELEMENTARE TEIKYO

Tama-shi, Tokyo, Japan (2014)

We aimed at a wooden schoolhouse of our age. The building consists of a big roofing and materiality of wood for interior and exterior.

By changing its length and height of eave, roof can create multiformity to respond to its environment and different programs. In this building, we designed a big roof to run through the entire building, differentiating expressions on each side – a relaxed face toward south where abundant green of Tama hill expands – and subtle appearance to the north facing public housing standing in lines. We also changed its form accordingly to the volume of each classroom. As the result, it has grown to a building that looks like 12 different-sectioned terraced houses being arranged in a row.

Composition of the space emphasizes the atmosphere of the terraced (1-storied) house created by the roof. While the structure is 3-storied, the atrium connects the sections of the special room and the open space on 2nd and 3rd floors, so that you can feel the slope of the roof on every floor. Further, in the center of the building situates the Media Center that skips three stories as a measure to avoid segregation within the building.

We used cedar for the material of the exterior, as an attempt to recover a wooden schoolhouse in the midst of the big city. We also applied three different lining method for the wall, according to the location and function of the parts in the building – siding work, louvers and Yamato-bari (wood panels arranged with its side slightly layered onto the next one – forming as a whole regular unevenness) so that the building can hold various expressions. Cedar is treated in heat to secure durability. We also utilized the plasticity of trees. We set up a huge wall of a recycled material made from chips of straw, rush and poplar, which can work as a notice board. As there is more freedom in the design of interior for schools, we managed to achieve this environmentally-friendly plan that can enhance the warmth of natural materials.

Big roofing is also good for environment as a efficient building facility. Using the wide roof toward the south, we installed there a device to gather heat. In this solar system, the air warmed under the roof circulates and vents from under the floor during winter. The roof also gathers rainwater. The water flows through the vertical drainpipe to the water conduit in the south, and it nurtures a biotope in front of the science room.

the use of soft materials for the interiors and the effort to maximize spatial connections between the classrooms and the common spaces, make this school a unique place for children to learn in an open environment.

37 ROOF
KIDS ACADEMY TAIYOGAOKA HOIKUEN
ACADEMIA PER BAMBINI TAIYOGAOKA HOIKUEN
Taiyogaoka, Kanazawa-shi, Ishikawa Prefecture, Japan (2013)

We wanted to build a nursery school close to the ground. The building is wood-structured, single-story, and its exterior wall is covered with trees and plants. The floor is sloped to follow the landscape underneath, so that the structure can be further lowered, nearer to the ground. We wanted to assimilate the architecture with the earth, as if they have merged into each other. To fit the size and action of the children, we also designed the building to stand as low as we could. Inside, there are lots of small niche-like "caves." We are sure that the kids have found a place of their own.

38 ROOF
GARDEN TERRACE MIYAZAKI
TERRAZZA - GIARDINO MIYAZAKI
Shimohara-cho, Miyazaki, Japan (2012)

A big folding canopy makes the entrance of the hotel with a wood louvers screen

The hotel was built at a vast site near JR Miyazaki station, where a factory once stood. Around it houses and aparrments spread in no particular order. Facilities of the hotel - guest rooms, banquet room and restaurants are arranged to circle the courtyard. Loosely sloped roof came out as the result of each function underneath. It wraps the entire building - two-storied structure under the deep eaves. Bamboo is planted and water is laid out in and out of the hotel and its courtyard, providing calm and tranquil environment that stretches even to the residential area.

39 ROOF
GLASS/WOOD HOUSE
CASA GLASS/WOOD
New Canaan, Connecticut, USA (2012)

This is a project in Connecticut (US) to repair a residence designed by John Black Leigh, and add a new house to the site. New Canaan is known as a town where many houses from the 1950s by such architects as Philip Johnson and Marcel Breuer still remain, and the one we worked on was the residence for Joe Black Leigh (built in 1956), also a friend of Philip Johnson. Our aim was to inherit the spirit of its beautiful glass architecture, or in other words, the spirit of New Canaan.

The existing building was a symmetric glass box of Palladian villa architecture, standing solitarily in a forest. We built a new house to make this glass box orthogonal and formed an L-shaped terrain, as an attempt to create a kind of "intimacy" in the forest. Philip Johnson's house stands alone, so we proposed the L-shaped plan in which the new building hitched on the old one, in order to present a new relation between the nature and the architecture. L-shaped plan is considered the prototype of the staggering layout in traditional Japanese architecture, which allows two axes to cross, frame varied spaces, create a sense of floating in the corners, and allow one to change consciousness by turning.

As an attempt to make the architecture "intimate," we adopted a type of mixed structure in the new house, where a wooden joisted roof comes over pillars of flat steel bars in 3 inches × 6 inches. In addition, we slightly shifted the position of the pillar at the corners to further enhance transparency and accelerate the moving of consciousness in this part. We gave a major change also in the existing house, by getting rid of the symmetry and covering the exterior with wooden louvers, so that the architecture would gain more "intimacy."

Thus, we worked to realize an "intimate transparency" or "mild transparency" to take over the isolated transparency of the 1950s.

Two thin flat surfaces, roof and floor, are the two elements of this house extension, aimed at maximizing the immersion into the surrounding nature

ROOF
MACDONALD PUBLIC FACILITY COMPLEX
COMPLESSO PUBBLICO MACDONALD

40

Paris 19th district, France (2014)

The creation of a public equipments complex within the warehouse Macdonald allows to realize the link between existing architecture and architecture to come, revealing the needs and developments of a changing society. It is also the pretext of the connexion between traditional processes and contemporary needs.

Existing warehouse's architect, Marcel Forest, described it as a base, convenient to the reception of future extensions.

This one will be realized by a light metallic structure, a support of a big linear roof sheltering an ensemble of public services.

This big roof put on the existing base, participates in the development of an architectural heritage by adapting it to contemporary functional needs.

By its dimensions, its situation and its size, the existing building and its extension is to be looked as and considered on a territorial scale, offering a horizon, proposing an infrastructure.

The territory becomes therefore support of the new project; the existing offers the base whereas the roof serves as an unifying element, sheltering a succession of spaces and functions.

Urban and landscaped insertion

The project is located in a strategic position, at the start of the 600m long existing warehouse, between the viaduct of railroad networks and the boulevards Maréchaux, in the center of a zone in full urban restructuration connected to the city and its surrounding by new tramway lines. The insertion of the project answers three imperatives:

- The urban reglementation
- The will to create a strong and contemporary architectural image
- The will to join the context in a just balance, responding to the obligation of preservation of the North facade

The architectural intervention is made of a game of horizontal which strengthens the expression of the existing building.

The unity and the homogeneity of the place are looked for to avoid the expression of the programmatic accumulation.

The rhythm of the facade, sequenced, is given by a succession of metallic vertical elements.

The continuity of the architectural vocabulary of the various equipments confers to give to the building a unity which joins on the scale of the whole masterplan designed by OMA.

The relation between inside and outside is handled through the use of filter. It composes, defines and distinguishes facades and is therefore decline through 2 different types: on the outside dark grey metallic louvers that dialogue with the context marked by its industrial past, on the inside a double glass skin, made of an alternation of glass panels and of a metallic membrane which spreads the light.

The depth of the filter is investigated in its multiple dimensions. Space and light are therefore amplified.

The succession of the courtyards organized in terrace on different levels allows the needed separation between the junior schoolyard and the high school courtyard. The sequence of the outside spaces is materialized by the implementation of vegetable strips: these are also similar in a way to a filter and bound the space without creating real borders.

ROOF

33 KURE CITY ONDO CIVIC CENTER
CENTRO CIVICO KURE CITY ONDO
Minami Ondo, Hiroshima, Japan (2007)

CREDITS	
Area	**4642.91m²**
Architect + Partner	**Kengo Kuma & Associates**
ColB. Team	**Konoike/Nikko JV, Rokko Electricity, Kinden, Sannyo Kucho Kogyo**
Engineer	**Oak Structural Engineering + Morimura & Associates**
System	**Steel Structure**
Render + Photos	**Mitsumasa Fujitsuka**

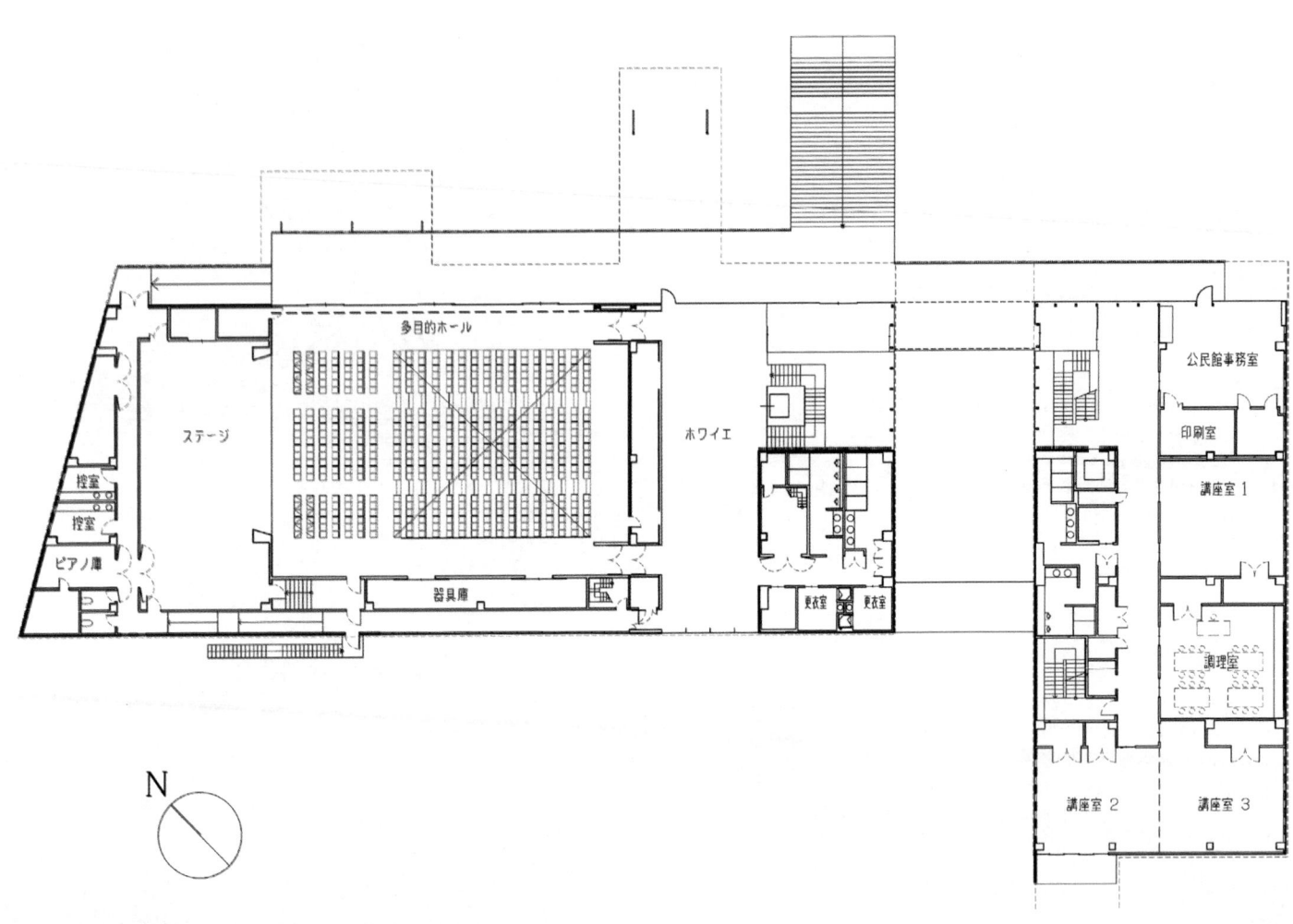

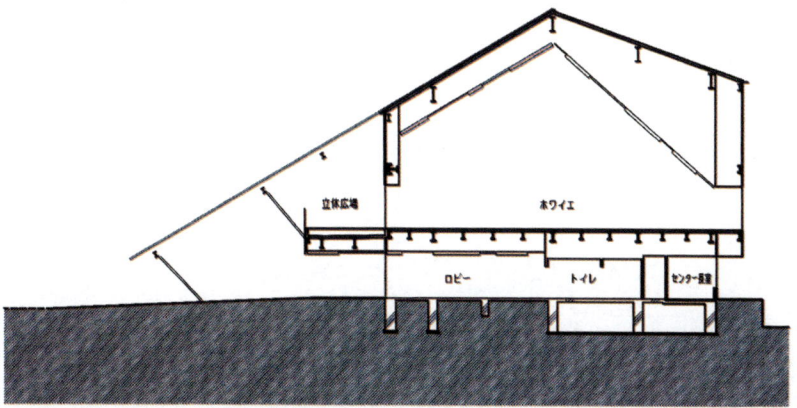
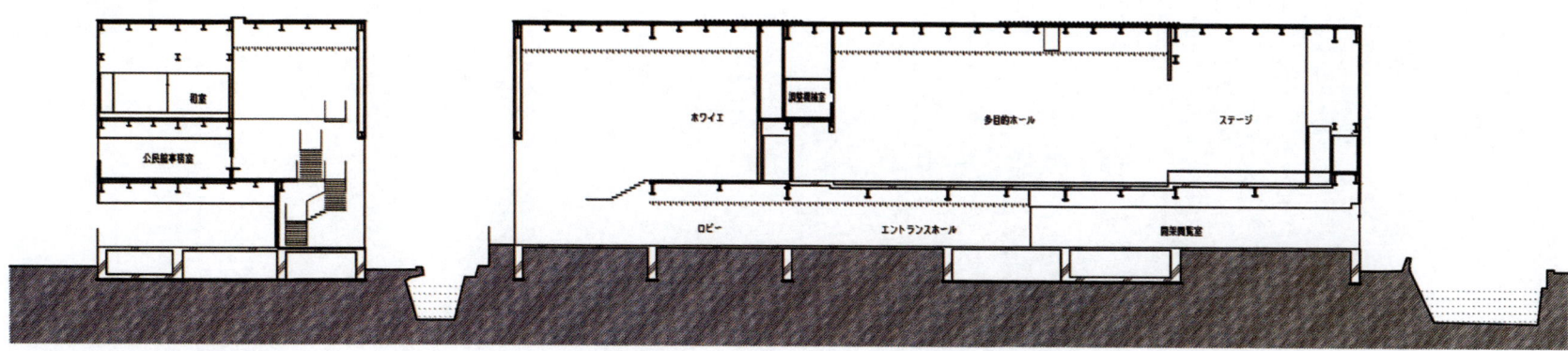

34 ROOF
NEZU MUSEUM
MUSEO NEZU
Minato-ku, Tokyo, Japan (2012)

CREDITS	
Area	**4,014.08m²**
Client	**Nezu Museum**
Architect + Partner	**Kengo Kuma & Associates**
ColB. Team	**Panasonic Electric Works Co., Ltd.**
Engineer	**SHIMIZU CORPORATION**
Render + Photos	**FUJITSUKA Mitsumasa**

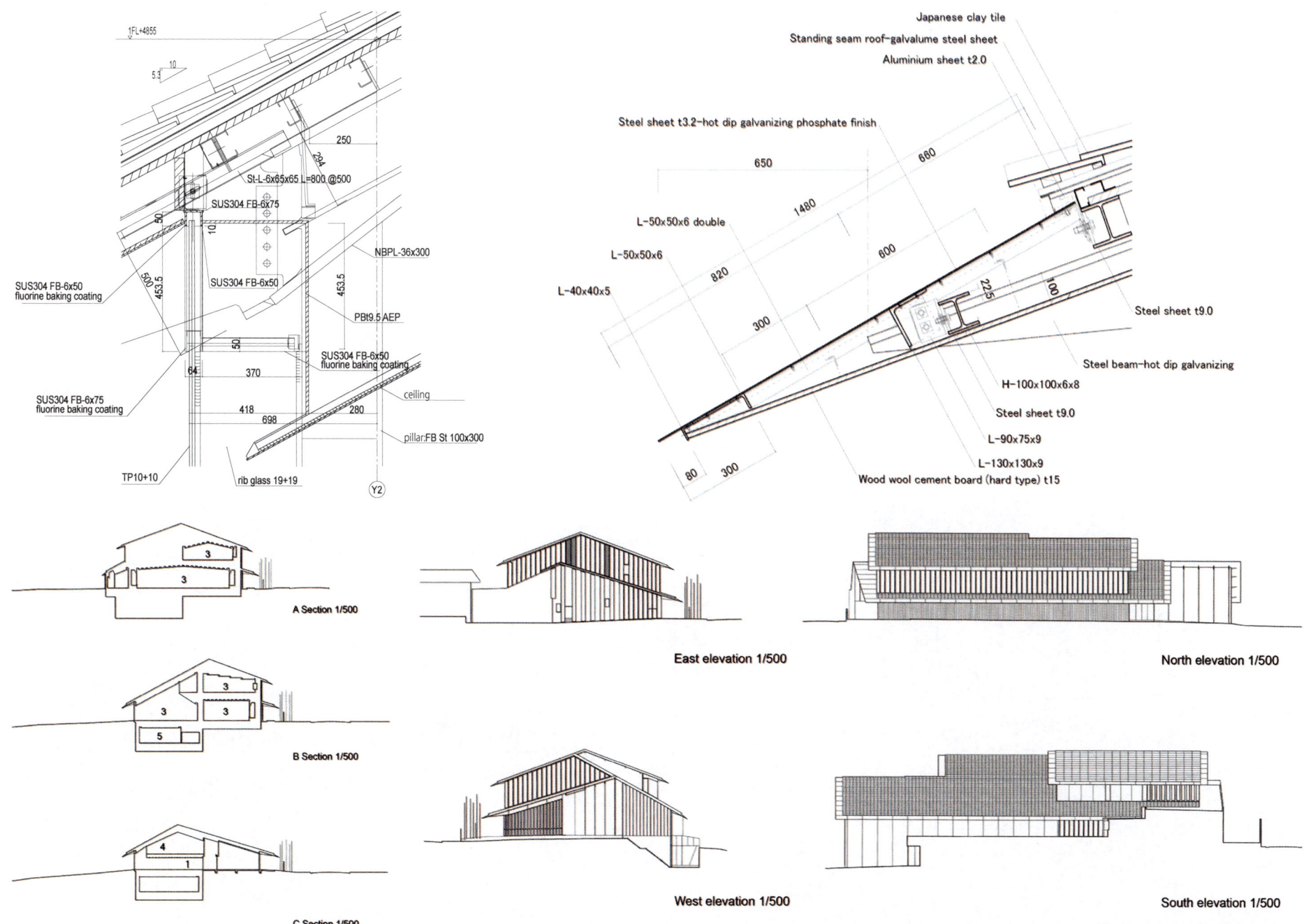

ROOF

35 ASAKUSA - CULTURAL AND TOURIST INFORMATION CENTER
ASAKUSA - CENTRO DI INFORMAZIONI CULTURALI E TURISTICHE
Tokyo, Japan (2009)

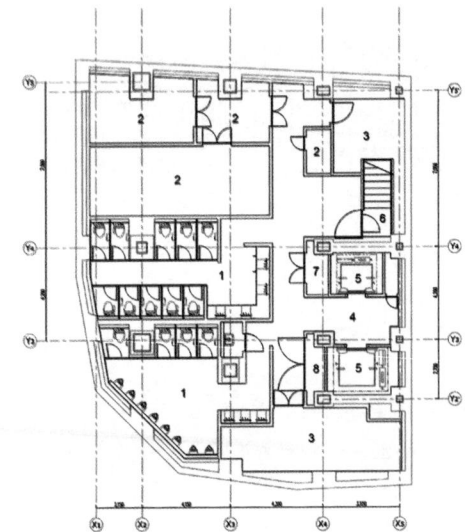

B1F Plan S=1:150

1. TOILET
2. MACHINE ROOM
3. STORAGE
4. EV HALL
5. EV
6. STAIRS A
7. DS
8. EPS

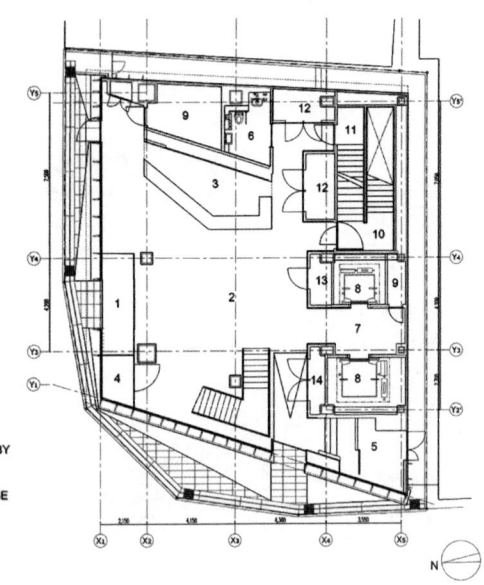

1F Plan S=1:150

1. WINDBRAKE ROOM
2. INFORMATION LOBBY
3. INFORMATION
4. DISPLAY SPACE
5. FOREIGN EXCHANGE
6. TOILET
7. EV HALL
8. EV
9. STORAGE
10. STAIRS A
11. STAIRS B
12. MACHINE SPACE
13. PS
14. EPS

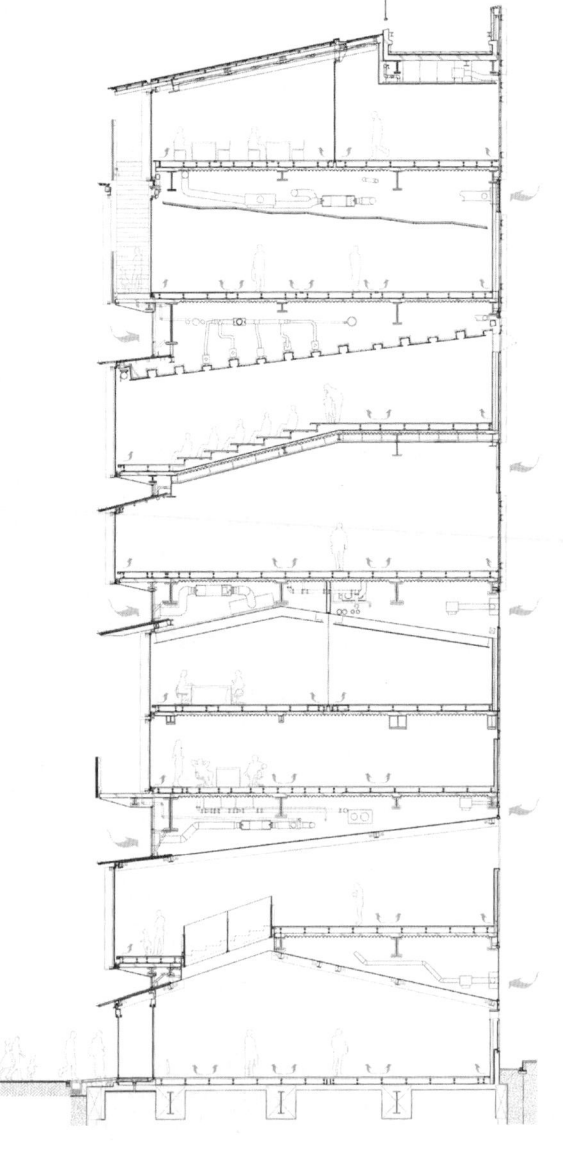

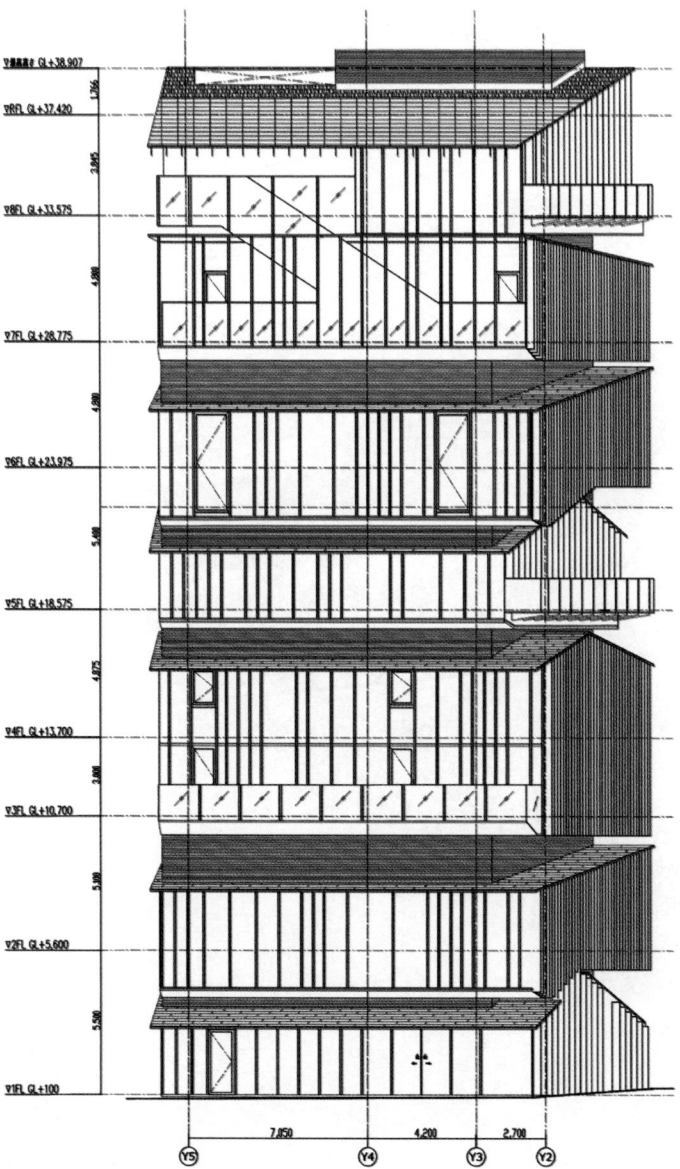

North Elevation S=1:200

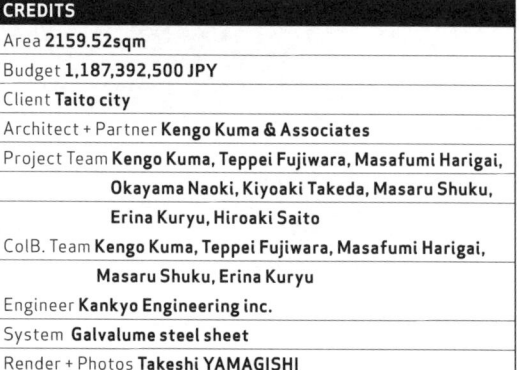

CREDITS	
Area	**2159.52sqm**
Budget	**1,187,392,500 JPY**
Client	**Taito city**
Architect + Partner	**Kengo Kuma & Associates**
Project Team	**Kengo Kuma, Teppei Fujiwara, Masafumi Harigai, Okayama Naoki, Kiyoaki Takeda, Masaru Shuku, Erina Kuryu, Hiroaki Saito**
ColB. Team	**Kengo Kuma, Teppei Fujiwara, Masafumi Harigai, Masaru Shuku, Erina Kuryu**
Engineer	**Kankyo Engineering inc.**
System	**Galvalume steel sheet**
Render + Photos	**Takeshi YAMAGISHI**

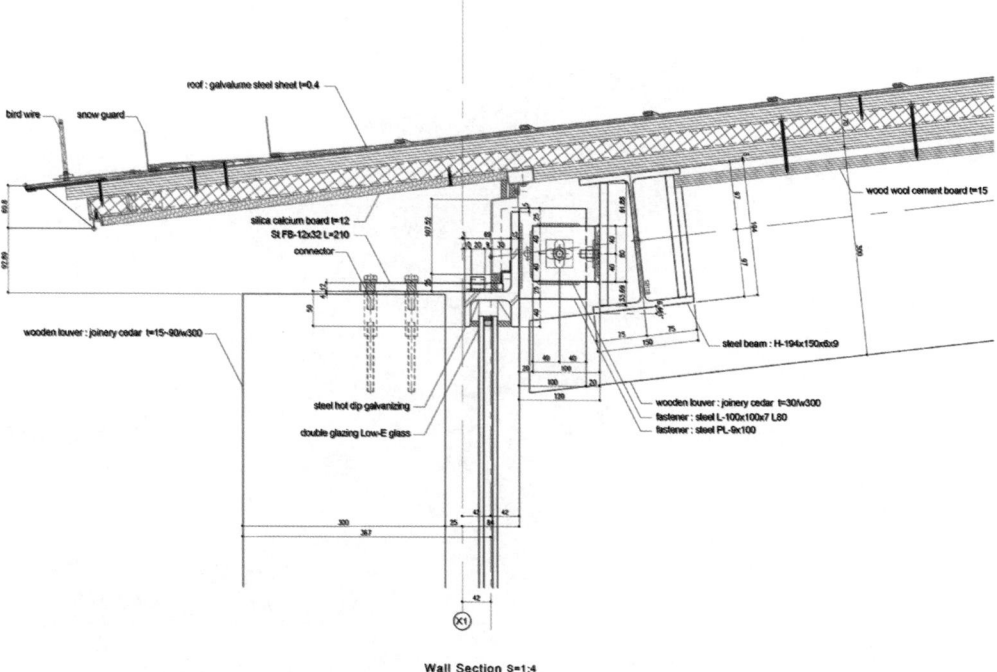

Wall Section S=1:4

36 ROOF
TEIKYO ELEMENTARY SCHOOL
SCUOLA ELEMENTARE TEIKYO
Tama-shi, Tokyo, Japan (2014)

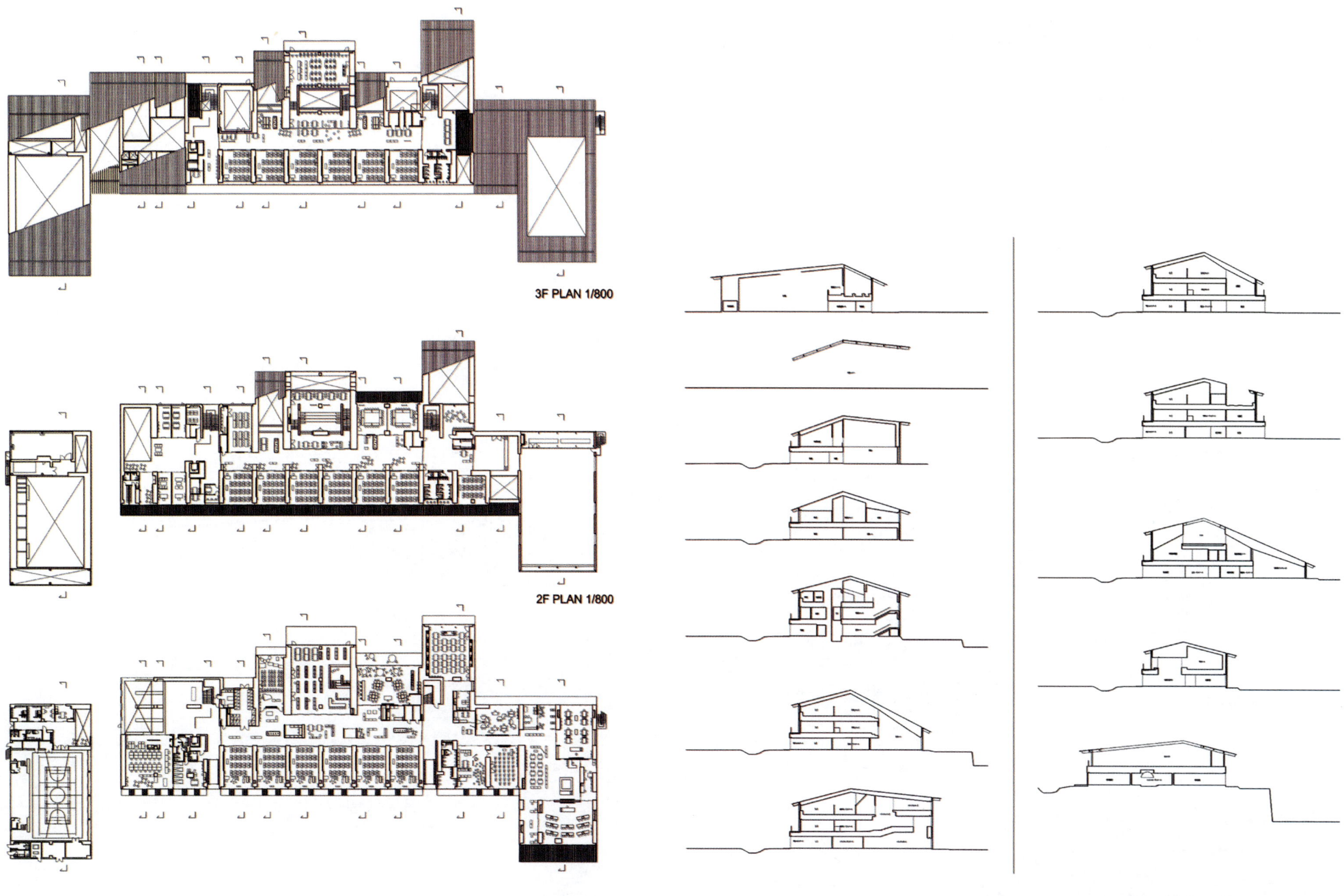

ROOF

37 KIDS ACADEMY TAIYOGAOKA HOIKUEN
ACADEMIA PER BAMBINI TAIYOGAOKA HOIKUEN
Taiyogaoka, Kanazawa-shi, Ishikawa Prefecture, Japan (2013)

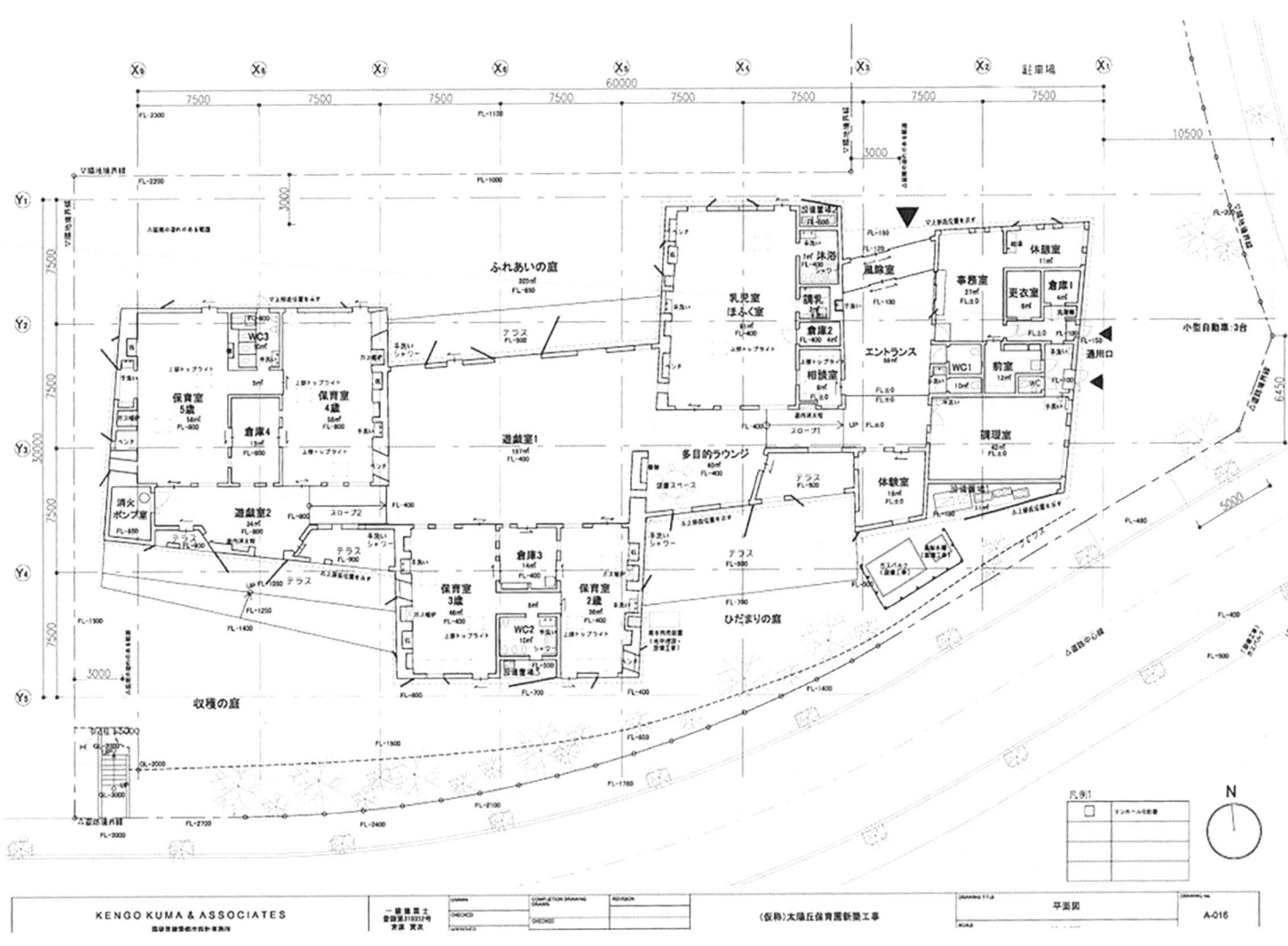

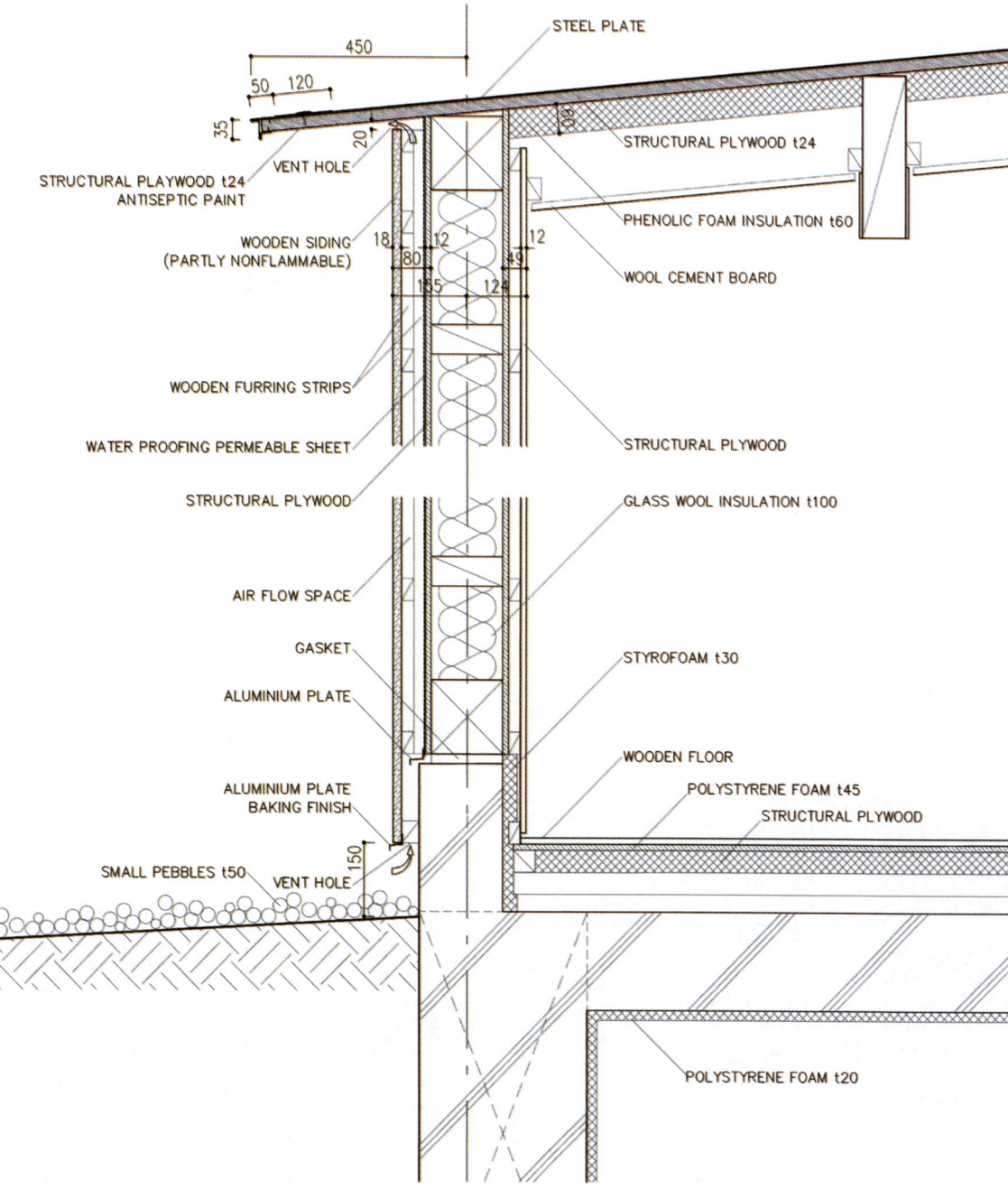

CREDITS	
Area	**992.63m²**
Client	**Social Welfare Organization CHUOUFUKUSHIKAI**
Architect + Partner	**Kengo Kuma & Associates**
Engineer	**Ejiri Structural Engineers**
System	**steel plate + wooden siding**

38 ROOF
GARDEN TERRACE MIYAZAKI
TERRAZZA - GIARDINO MIYAZAKI
Shimohara-cho, Miyazaki, Japan (2012)

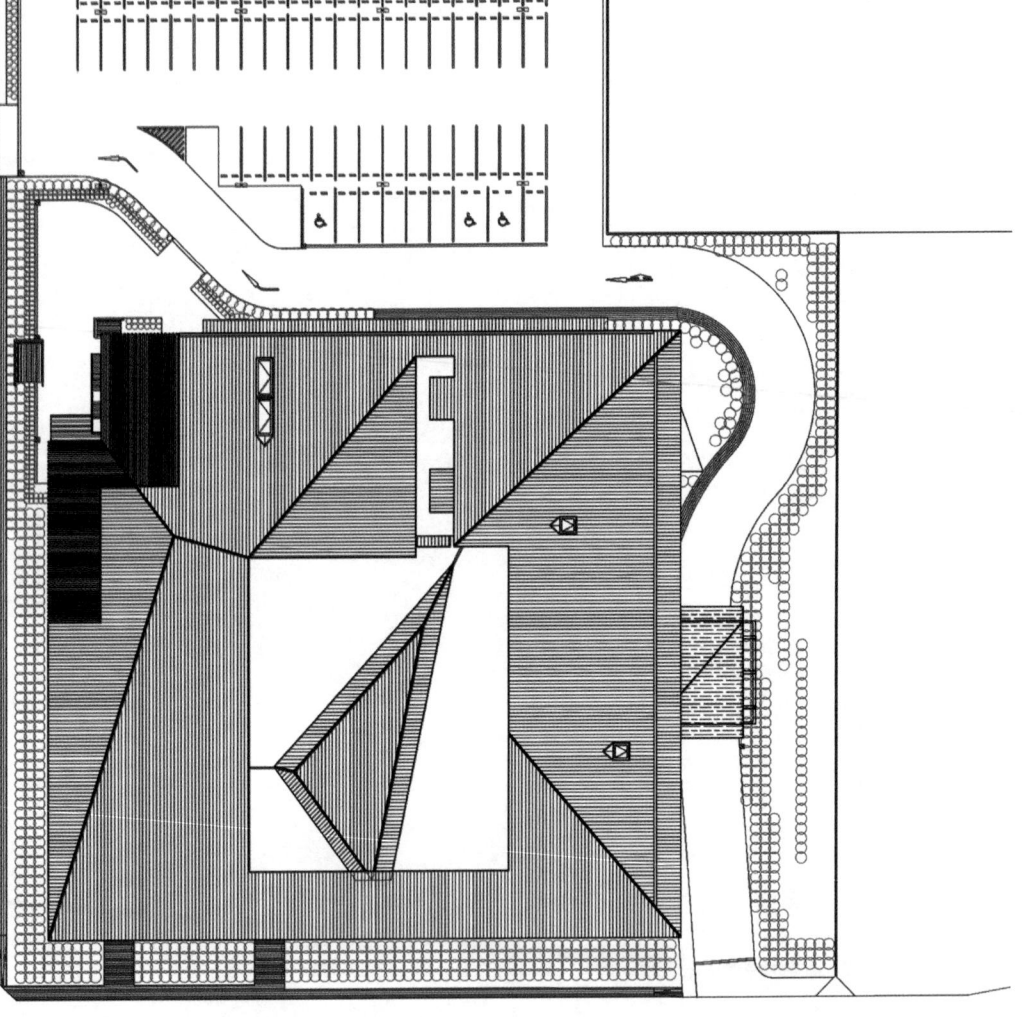

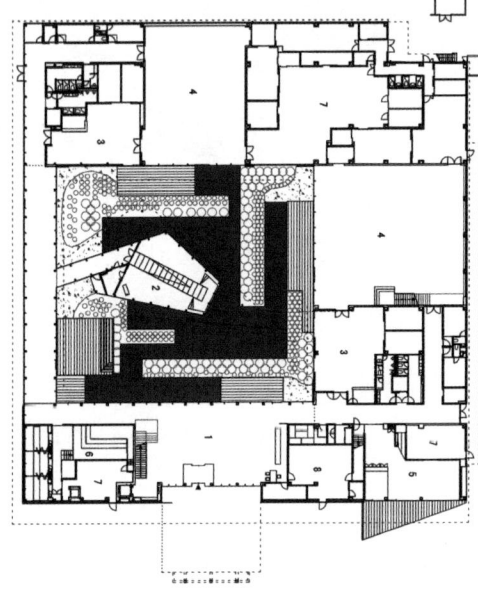

1階平面図

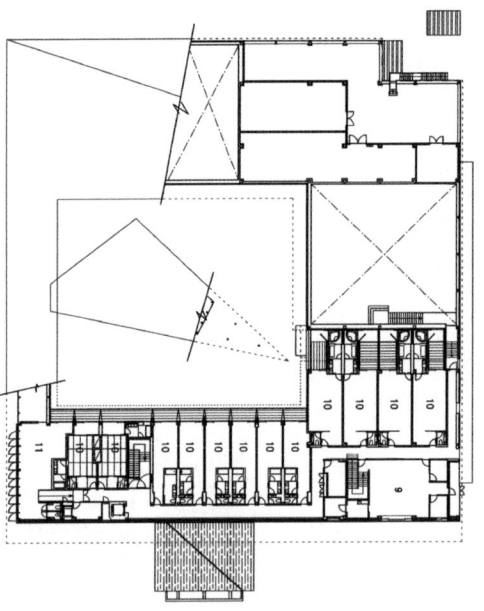

2階平面図

客室細竹ルーバー断面図　　客室細竹ルーバー立面図

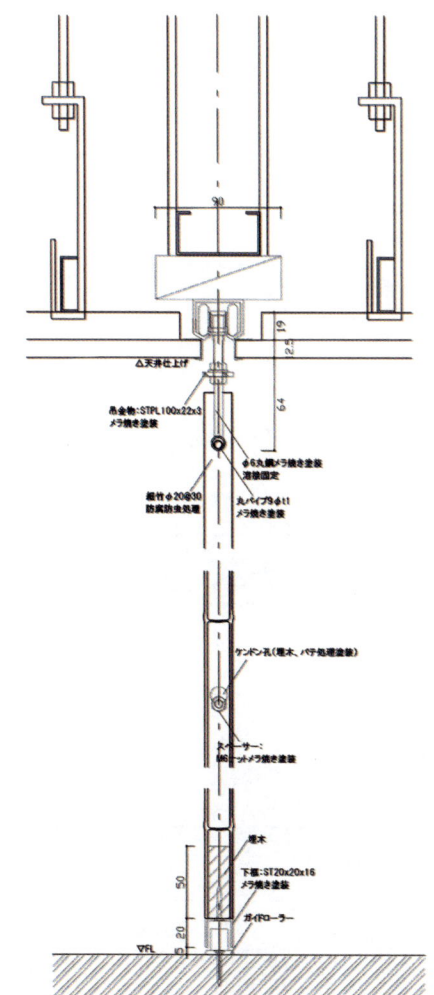
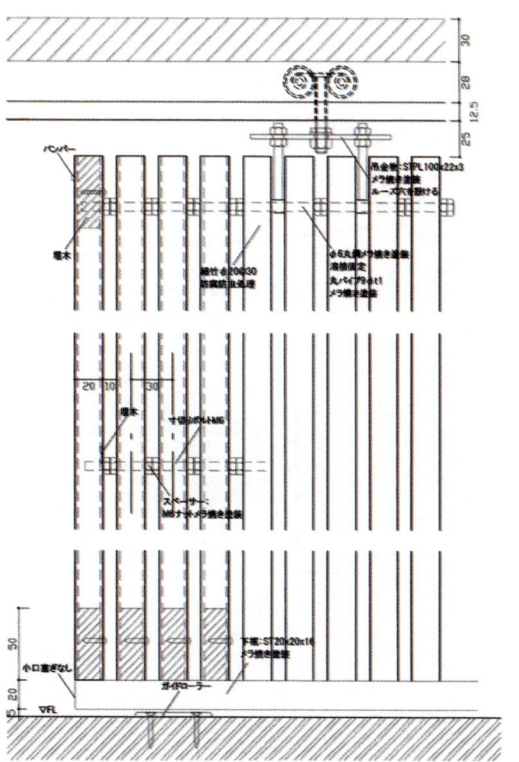
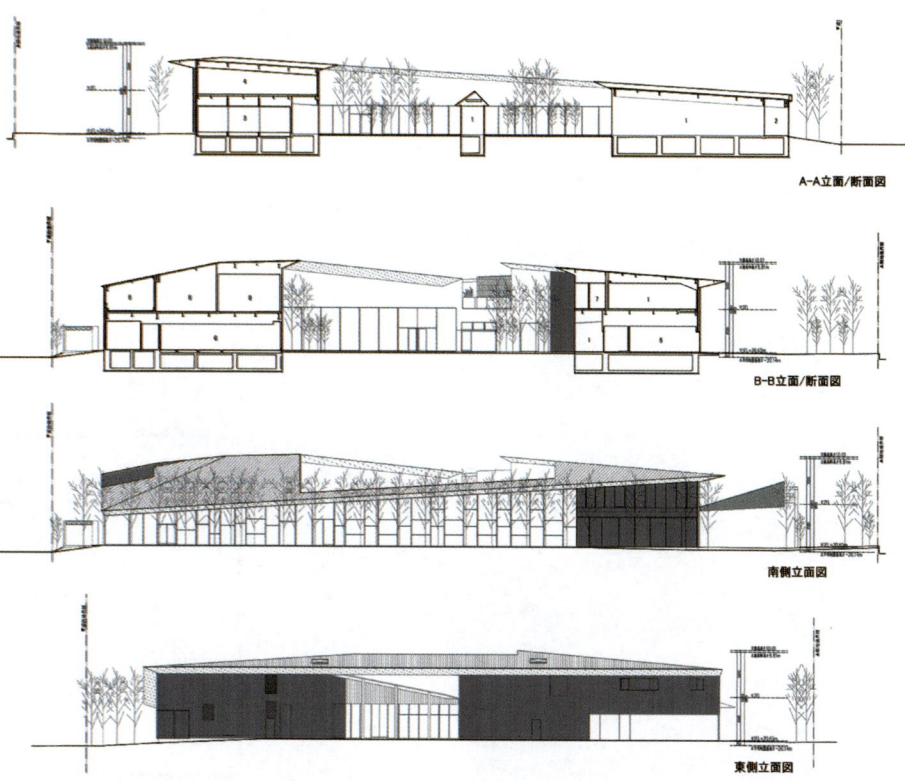

A-A立面/断面図

B-B立面/断面図

南側立面図

東側立面図

ROOF
39 GLASS/WOOD HOUSE
CASA GLASS/WOOD
New Canaan, Connecticut, USA (2012)

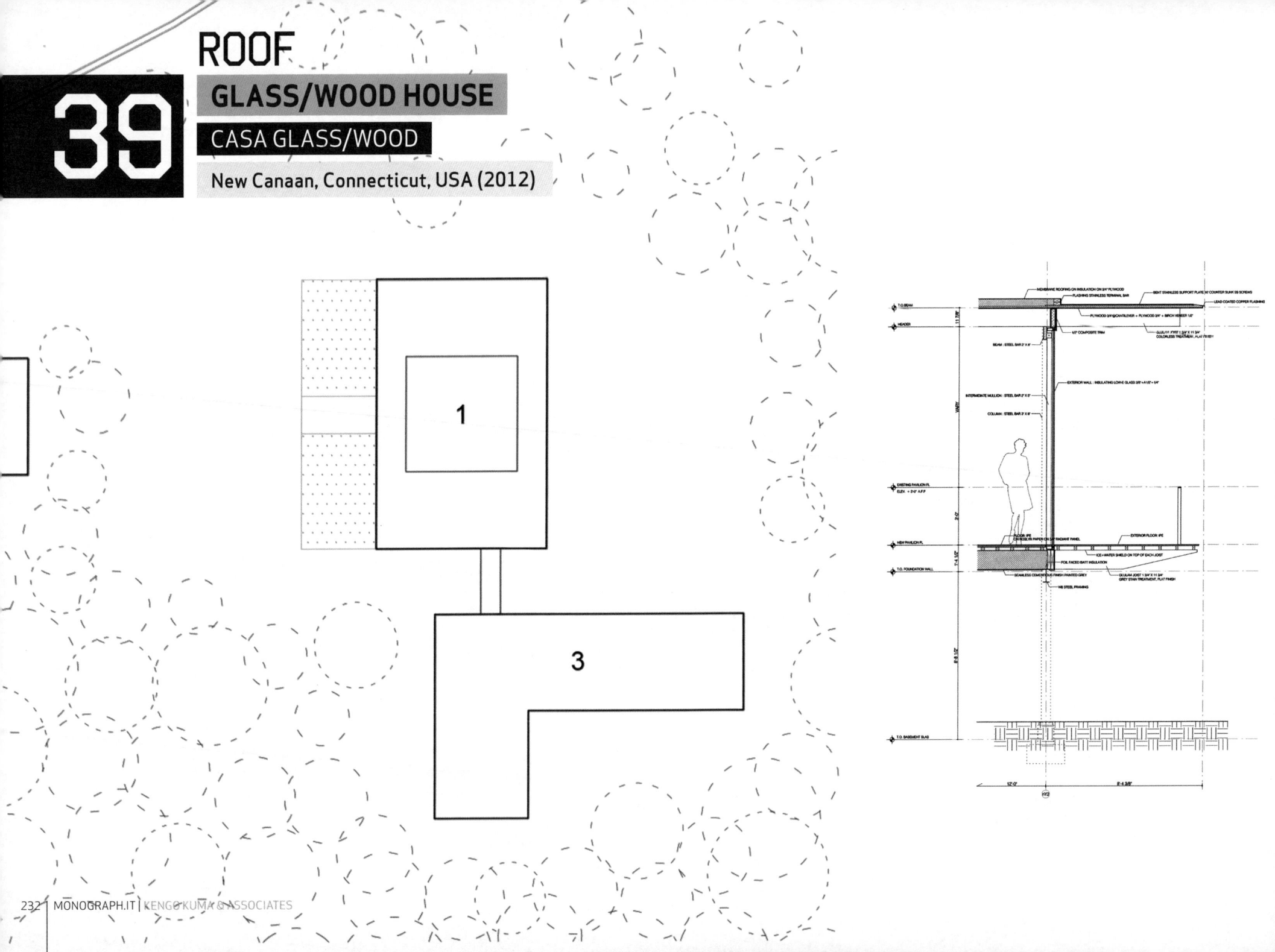

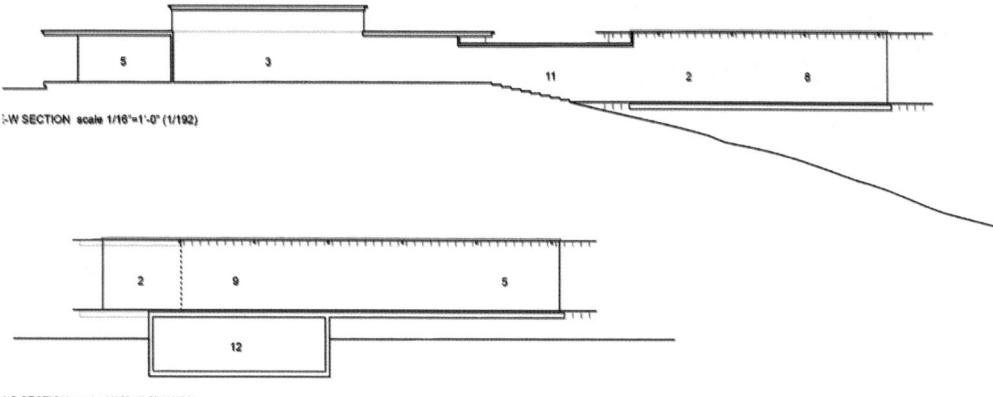

E-W SECTION scale 1/16"=1'-0" (1/192)

N-S SECTION scale 1/16"=1'-0" (1/192)

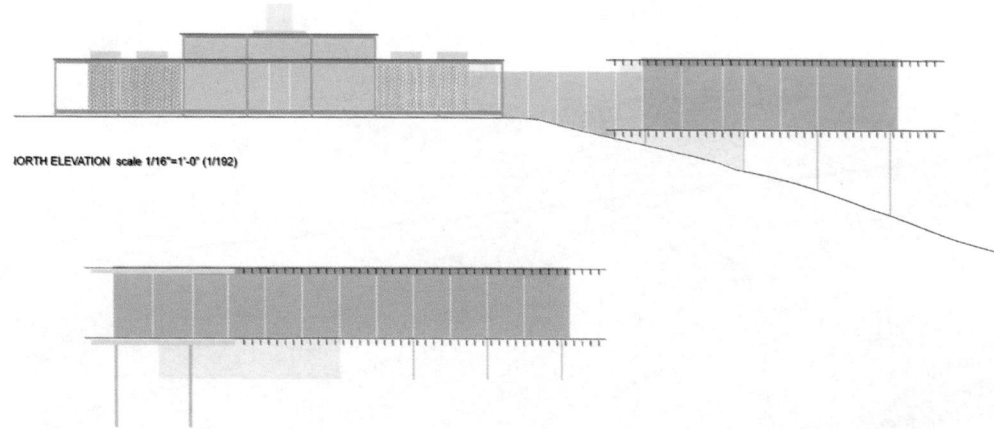

NORTH ELEVATION scale 1/16"=1'-0" (1/192)

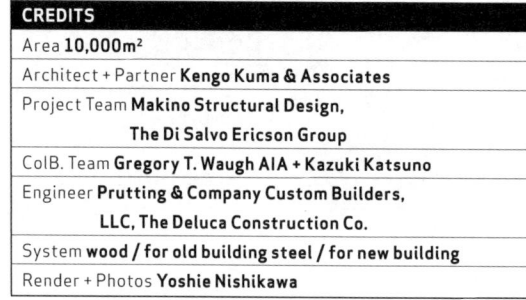

CREDITS	
Area	**10,000m²**
Architect + Partner	**Kengo Kuma & Associates**
Project Team	**Makino Structural Design, The Di Salvo Ericson Group**
ColB. Team	**Gregory T. Waugh AIA + Kazuki Katsuno**
Engineer	**Prutting & Company Custom Builders, LLC, The Deluca Construction Co.**
System	**wood / for old building steel / for new building**
Render + Photos	**Yoshie Nishikawa**

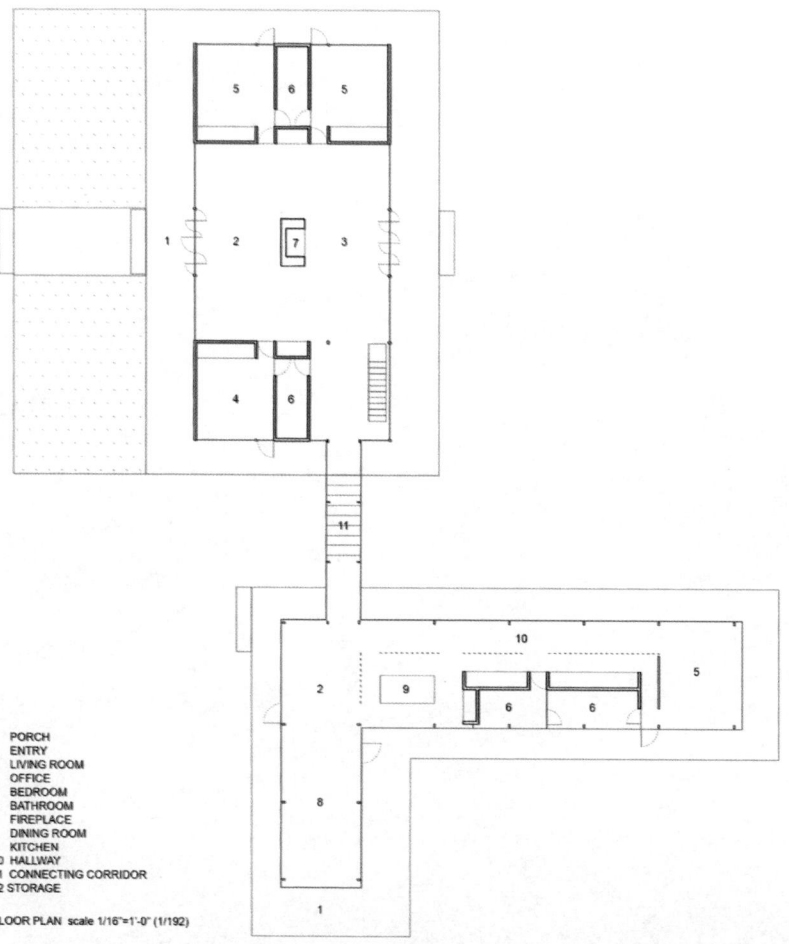

1 PORCH
2 ENTRY
3 LIVING ROOM
4 OFFICE
5 BEDROOM
6 BATHROOM
7 FIREPLACE
8 DINING ROOM
9 KITCHEN
10 HALLWAY
11 CONNECTING CORRIDOR
12 STORAGE

FLOOR PLAN scale 1/16"=1'-0" (1/192)

ROOF
MACDONALD PUBLIC FACILITY COMPLEX
COMPLESSO PUBBLICO MACDONALD
Paris 19th district, France (2014)

40

CREDITS	
Contest	**Macdonald public facility complex – general education and sports competition. 1st Prize**
Area	**11 000 sqm**
Budget	**39 500 000 €**
Client	**Paris City Council**
Architect + Partner	**Kengo Kuma & Associates**
Project Team	**Kengo Kuma, Nicolas Moreau, Jun Shibata, Charlotte Brussieux, Louise Lemoine, Shinku Noda, José Mateluna Pérez, Charlotte Duvernoy**
ColB. Team	**Kengo Kuma, Yuki Ikeguchi, Sebastien Yeou, Matthieu Wotling, Charlotte Brussieux, Louise Lemoine**
Engineer	**AIA**
System	**Concrete (existing) + steel**

STACKING ELEMENTS
CON-FIBER
CON-FIBER
Milano, Italy (2009)

41

|HAD some hunch that the Japanese synthetic fiber would remove the barrier that creational activities face in interior and products. It is essential that interior and product share common information. The 'transparent' concrete we used this time has a big potential as a structural material, not only as a decorative material for interior.

The fiber inserted in the concrete bricks, in combination with the bricks geometry, creates a "pattern of light" in addition to give transparency to the concrete wall

Con / Fiber

Exhibition title: Tokyo Fiber Senseware
Venue 1: La Triennale Di Milano / Viale Emilio Alemagna, 6, 20121 Milano, Italy
Exhibition Period 1: 2011.7.23 – 2011.8.21 in Milan
Venue 2: 21_21 Design Sight / Tokyo Midtown Garden, 9-7-6 Akasaka, Minato-ku, Tokyo, Japan
Exhibition Period 2: 2009.9.28 – 2009.9.27 in Tokyo
Installation

42 STACKING ELEMENTS
STONE MUSEUM
MUSEO STONE
Nasu-cho, Nasu-gun, Tochigi Prefecture, Japan (2000)

The project called for restoration and additions to a complex of old Nineteen-Thirties buildings in the zone of Ashino between Tokyo and Yamagata, originally used as rice warehouses. These were damaged during the war and are an interesting historical witness to a traditional stone Construction system – a system rarely used in Japan because of earthquake problems.
The basic idea for the project, commissioned by an important company that produces Ashino Stone and other stone materials, is to create a museum for exhibiting artworks in stone organized along a single pathway that moves between existing structures and new structures designed by Kuma; The overall project called for an entry hall, two galleries, three small exhibition halls, one tea room, a small library, offices, and miscellaneous services. The program layout on the lot and the distribution of buildings is quite complex because of the many heterogeneous components (pathways, architecture, materials) enlisted by the project. The entire system of buildings, three existing and and three newly designed, distributed on three sides of the rectangular lot, is connected together by a dense network of bride-pathways that cross the large central reflecting pool. This pool covers almost all the outside area as well as part of the covered area. The bizarre nature of this coming and going between buildings is only apparent: the open areas also have precise functions, creating reflecting pools and the central "plaza" for outdoor exhibition spaces. In this way the entire surface of the lot has been used for museum purposes without generating unused spaces.
The two main existing buildings function one as entry hall with cafeteria and sales area and the other as a space for temporary exhibits and conventions. Restoration of both structures called for insertion of new wooden structures along the walls to support the roof and substitute the old stone building walls, no longer up to standards, in their load-bearing task. The third existing building, very small in size, was transformed into a tea room. Here, the stone was treated at very high temperatures (1220-1500 degrees Celsius) to experiment with changes in texture and color.
All the new buildings, partly placed between the existing buildings and partly built on the opposite side of the lot, are a result of Kuma's search for "lightness" and "transparency" of the masonry by an original use of stone: the "heavy" material above all others.
One solution aims at obtaining "porosity" in the walls by stratifying slabs of Ashino stone and juxtaposing them in order to create openings where natural light filters in from the walls through very thin slabs of white Carrara Marble.
This experiment was applied to the group of new buildings on the north side of the lot, including gallery 1, the two exhibition halls and the offices.
On the opposite side, along the building that joins the services and the library, the uninterrupted wall adjacent the reflecting pool is designated to create – using the same material – a "transparent" effect.
Here Ashino Stone was used in thin strips positioned to create a sunscreen wall: light and air filter through this wall to totally "dematerialize" the masonry mass.

The combination of the stone and the light passing through the openings of the walls becomes a key element of the architecture.

242 | MONOGRAPH.IT | KENGO KUMA & ASSOCIATES

43 STACKING ELEMENTS
ADOBE MUSEUM FOR WOODEN BUDDHA
MUESO ADOBE PER IL BUDDHA DI LEGNO
Toyoura-gun, Yamaguchi Prefecture, Japan (2002)

the most simple architecture encloses this important Buddha statue, a national treasure. The layout of the adobe bricks allow the control of natural ventilation, avoids the need of air conditioned, otherwise required to strictly control the environment and to preserve the statue.

recently encountered a mysterious method of construction.

It was in a beautiful small town called Toyoura, facing the sea of Japan, located around 25 kilometers North of Shimonoseki. The property has a typical wall that wraps around it, but the wall is made from a strange earthen material. It is a very thick and monolithic one, consisting only of ochre earth, and a view of a broken section shows that it contains no wooden frame or gravel. Upon closer examination, it can be seen that the wall is made by piling up bricks, and has grout at regular intervals.

I immediately reached for my cell phone and called Akira Kuasumi, a plasterer. I said to him, "I just found a strange earthen wall." He immediately replied, "It's made from adobe bricks." Adobe (bricks made from sun-dried earth) is the same structural material that is frequently seen in American Indian houses and on the African savanna. Soil is hardened by kneading it, and then dried in the sun to make bricks. Differing from bricks that are made in high-temperature kilns, it is ecologically friendly since there are no emissions of carbon dioxide, and the bricks have a soft, pleasing feel. I had just found that this construction method was also used in Japan.

I had no experience with a heavy, sticky material without any segmentation, which is the main reason why I dislike concrete. However, I felt strongly drawn to the material since it consisted of bricks. This difficult material presented a challenge which interested me in much the same way as I had taken on the challenge of using heavy stones for the "Stone Art Museum", sprinkling them over the structure to transform the appearance.

The ability to make bricks from the soil on the site was very alluring. It represented the ultimate in melting into the surroundings. The material did not have to be transported any distance at all since it was already at the site. I had Akira Kuasumi come to the site right away to check the soil. What he told me surprised me even further. "Not only the wall is made from earth. Even the storehouses in this town are made from adobe bricks. I've never seen this before."

Both of us became very excited. But this presented serious implications. The structure we were building was going to hold an important cultural asset from the Heian era. The Agency for Cultural Affairs was at a loss for words when we suggested building the structure from earth. We stressed the humidity controlling and heat insulating properties of earth, and ended up compromising on the use of a concrete structure coated with adobe bricks.

The project called for a storehouse, but we made the proposal of using glass for one end in order to open up the structure and put the Buddha statue on display to the town. We thought that it would be great to have people visiting the town see this important cultural asset from the outside, and that it would become a new attraction.

One of the residents of the town said that it looked like the Buddhist monument at Bamiyan in Afghanistan when he saw the completed structure. The fact that the Buddha statue is exposed to the exterior is similar, but I think the fact that the material on the site is used for the structure is the most similar feature of all.

The project is located near the Hoshakuji station two stops after Utsunomiya. At the west exit is a round-about, and the east exit is closed, and had an abandoned rice storage house made of Ooya stone. Instead of making a modern station that is decorated with glass, aluminum, new materials, and illuminations that vainly try to appear bright and flowery, I wondered how I can design the vicinity of the station, that sits on the ground firmly, and which represent the image of this town.

Even when I was riding the train back, the image of the Ooya stone storage did not leave my mind. Ooya stone has two distinctive characteristics: "soil" and "porosity".

Soil is soft, and stone is hard. There exists a contrast, for sharp stone emerges from beneath like it rips the earth; however, Ooya stone is an unique one, which has the quality like that of soil, for it is soft, and is in harmony with the earth. Of all, the softest and the brown part of the stone called "miso", is the result of soil that got captured inside the stone. Then, it came to my mind that if I use this stone, maybe it is possible to create architecture that merges from the earth, or sublime from the soil.

The other characteristic of this stone is porosity. The whole Ooya stone have holes like that of a sponge, and miso is the largest hole out of all the others. Because of these openings hole the façade is more broken up rather than closed. In that way an inviting gesture is created.

"Soil" and "Porosity" seem like two opposing things, but within its self, they never contradict. For the construction of the Imperial Hotel in Tokyo (1922), Frank Lloyd Wright collected stones from all over Japan, and from the large selection, chose the Ooya stone, "a stone like the soil", which made everyone puzzled. Wright must have been moved by the fact that two qualities of stone that was believed to exist in contradiction was in fact in harmony within the Ooya stone.

I have been thinking to further purify these qualities of the stone, "soil" and "porosity", and create architecture that is soft, warm, and would not reject people. It is like an architecture that freezes the process which gradually sublimes from the earth to the sky. My idea was to also freeze the process of evolvement from the preserved, existing state of the stone storage house without any porosity, to the new state with much porosity, and make it architectural.

In order to solve this project theme technologically, Mr. Shintani, the engineer, Mr. Kenmoku, the stone dealer, and my colleagues and I brought together our knowledge and came up with the idea of this diagonal construction system. It is a construction system in which we use stacked Ooya stone in pairs, but at the same time weaved like a steel basket made of diagonally stacked steel plate. The stone is not only an applied material, but also an important structural element. It is stone-built, steel structured, which makes it a structural, as well as the finish material. Being in between these ambiguous double characteristics, this fabric was carefully weaved. While this irreplaceable characteristic of the double-sided quality is preserved, the soft substance slowly and gradually freezes. This fabric, even after it has been woven, will change into various different states. Such can be frozen and modulated. Over time, the stone and steel fabric will continue to modulate.

45 STACKING ELEMENTS
V&A MUSEUM OF DESIGN
MUSEO DEL DESIGN V&A
Dundee, Scotland, UK

V&A at Dundee will be an international centre of design for Scotland. It will celebrate Scotland's historic importance in design and host major exhibitions of outstanding international design that will appeal to the widest public and help develop understanding of our own and others' cultural heritage. V&A at Dundee will become indispensable to makers, teachers and industry nationwide as a place for the cultivation and exchange of knowledge, opportunity and design innovation. It will develop opportunities for diverse communities to engage with, learn from and enjoy design creativity of the past, present and future. V&A at Dundee will play a vital role in Dundee's ambitious plans for regeneration, symbolising the city's high cultural and economic aspirations.

V&A at Dundee will be the first design museum ever to be built in the UK outside London, and will be architect Kengo Kuma's first British building. The building envelope is created by methods of twisting, connecting and layering the City grid axis and the adjacent RRS Discovery ship axis, using a ring structure made of reconstituted stone and concrete to compliment the traditional construction materials used in Dundee and reflect the natural cliff structure of the coastline.

Additionally, due to the relationship with the water, the ideal building volume is defined to be extending upwards in order to minimise the building's footprint and maximize the interior spaces designed specifically for the required museum functions. The building's form creates dramatic spaces with an impressive main hall forming a public indoor plaza, and areas that overhang the external public plaza The external envelope draws people to the waterfront and generates a new migration route along the riverside promenade. The interior space of the main hall is filled with a gentle light emanating from apertures cut through the layered stone to create an open yet intimate public space. The ground floor comprises the building entrance, lobby, reception and cloakroom, museum shop, administration office, loading bay, back-of-house facilities, storage, and some plant. A generous area of public space located in direct proximity to the building entrance increases the potential for the building to cope with large numbers of people entering the building at once. Direct access is provided to the museum shop and the cafe bar from the entrance lobby and reception. The entrance core and dedicated lift have been configured so that the restaurant and learning studios, located on the upper floor, are able to open independently of the rest of the building outwith museum opening hours.

The main hall will be a welcoming social space - a 'living room for the city' designed to encourage the broadest public to interact with the building. It will be a fully programmed space hosting a variety of design-led events, a vibrant place for everyone to socialise and enjoy. This space will not only host pop up exhibitions, but also opportunities to engage throughout the day with design in all its forms – from catwalk shows to hands-on activities, dragons den style product testing to dance and live music.

This 'living room' will capture the imagination of visitors and will feel like an extension of the sequence of public spaces and plazas outside. It will create a strong integration between outside and inside, providing an offer that will appeal both to the citizens of Dundee and visitors from all over the world. Flexibility and ease of access is critical to the function of this room. This is achieved through the careful organisation and positioning of elements such as the reception desk, cloakroom, museum shop and main feature staircase. Consideration of visitor movement within the area is reflected in the layout of this space.

First Floor
The lunch room, offices and associated amenities are located on the first floor. The remainder of the space is predominantly dedicated to plant space and storage.

Second Floor
The second floor is dedicated to a suite of four galleries (two dedicated to Scotttish Design Heritage, and two dedicated to world-class touring exhibitions of design from the V&A. Next to these are the Learning Studios, auditorium, resource library and restaurant.

The exterior of the building made by blocks of reconstituted stone, is reminiscent of a cliff going down into the sea

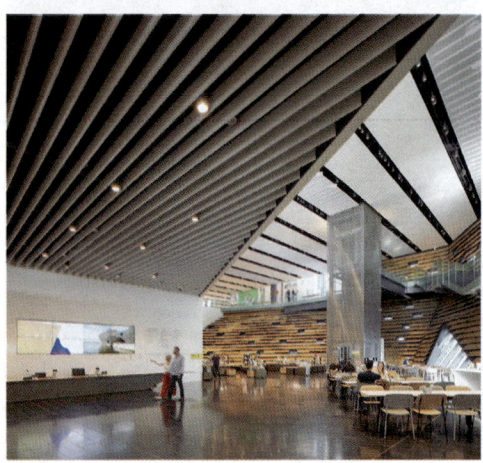

The interior of the "cliff" reveals a oak cladding to create a warm feeling for the main hall

STACKING ELEMENTS
41 | CON-FIBER
CON-FIBER
Milano, Italy (2009)

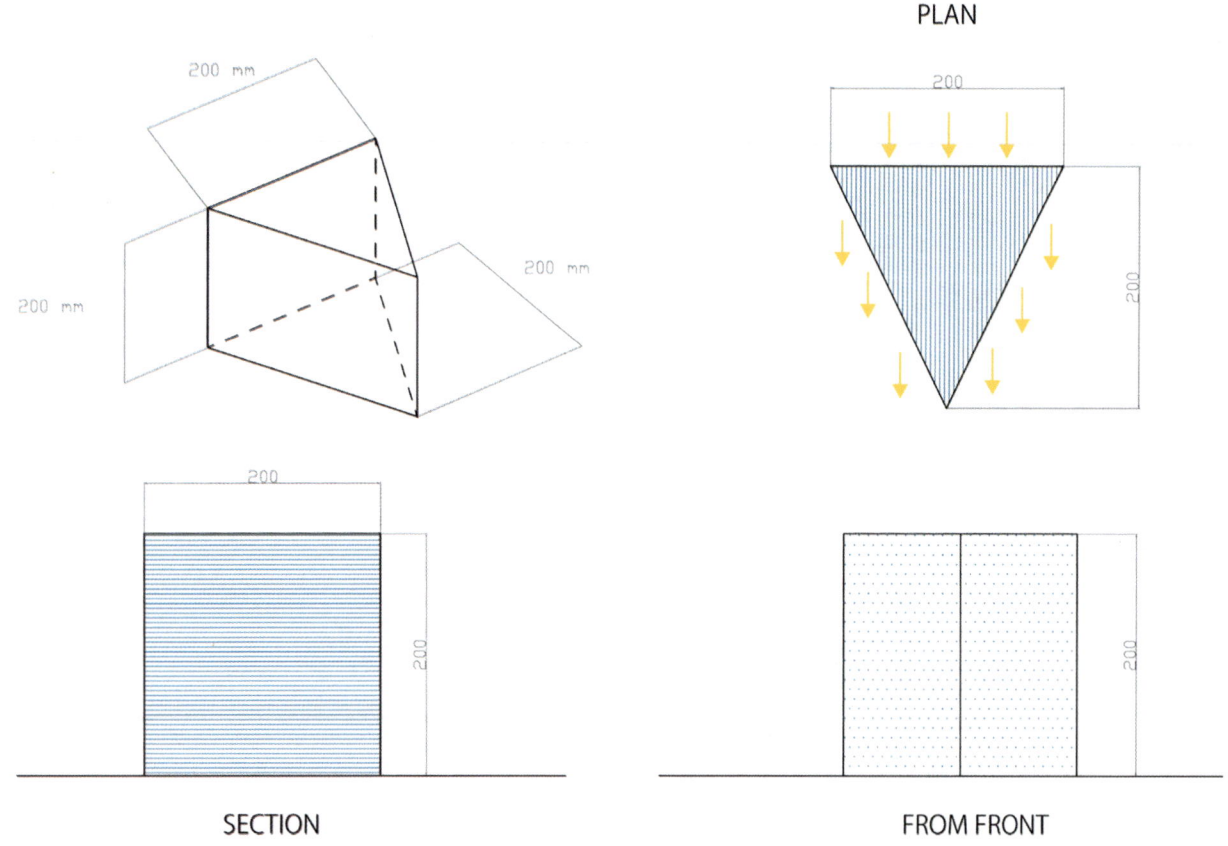

STACKING ELEMENTS

42 STONE MUSEUM

MUSEO STONE

Nasu-cho, Nasu-gun, Tochigi Prefecture, Japan (2000)

CREDITS	
Area	**532.91m²**
Architect + Partner	**Kengo Kuma & Associates**
Project Team	**Ishihara Construction**
Engineer	**K.Nakata & Associates, M.I. Consultant**
System	**masonry structure and steel frame**
Render + Photos	**Mitsumasa Fujitsuka**

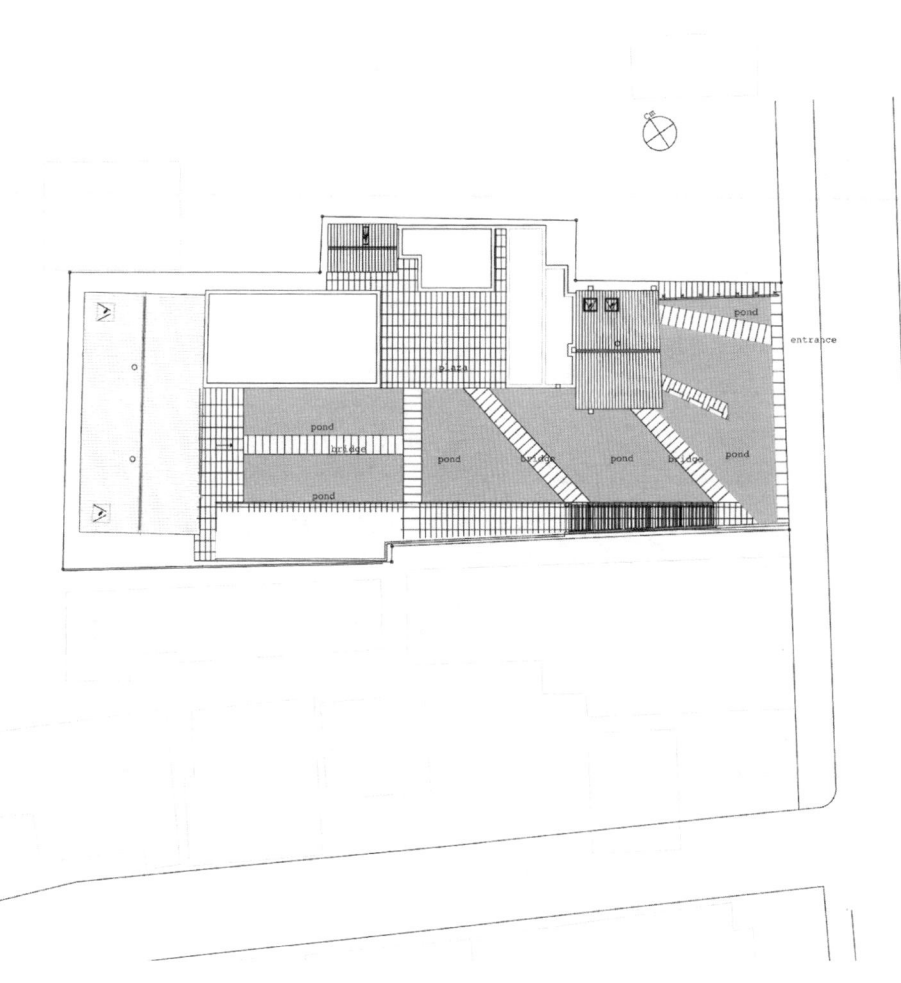

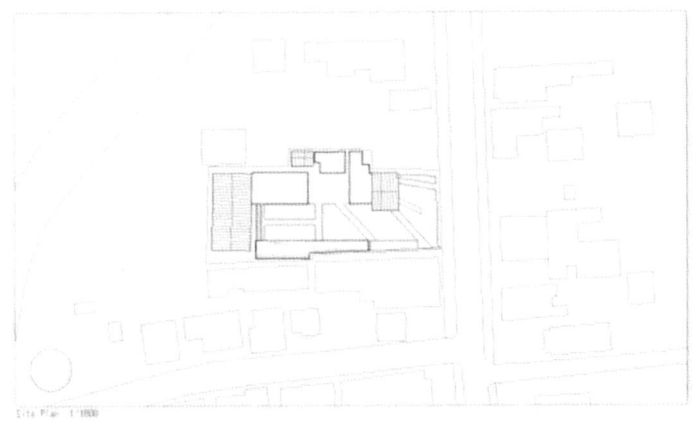

Site Plan 1:1800

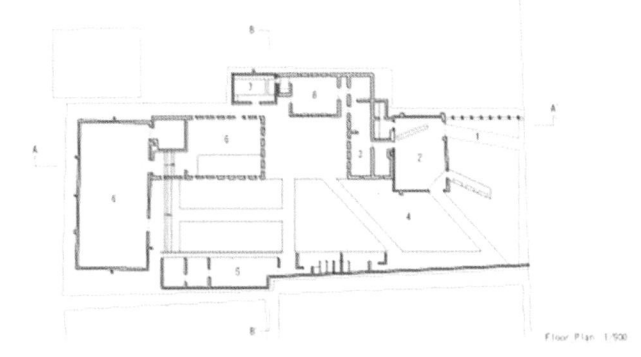

Floor Plan 1:500

1 Approach
2 Entrance Hall
3 Office
4 Reflecting Pool
5 Library
6 Gallery
7 Tea Room
8 Exhibition Space

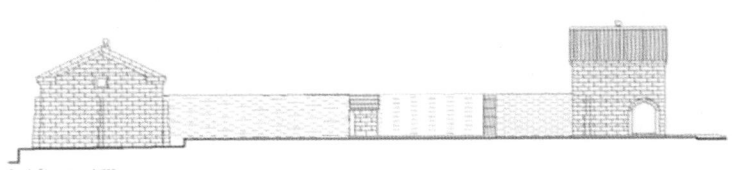

South Elevation 1:300

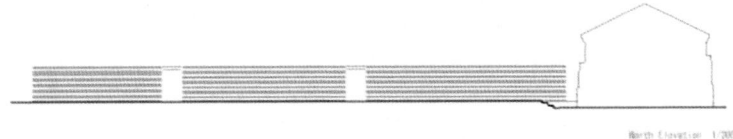

North Elevation 1:300

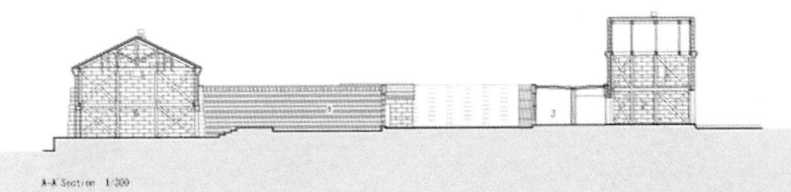

A-A' Section 1:200

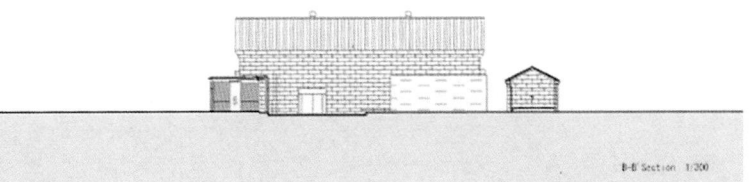

B-B' Section 1:200

43 STACKING ELEMENTS
ADOBE MUSEUM FOR WOODEN BUDDHA
MUESO ADOBE PER IL BUDDHA DI LEGNO
Toyoura-gun, Yamaguchi Prefecture, Japan (2002)

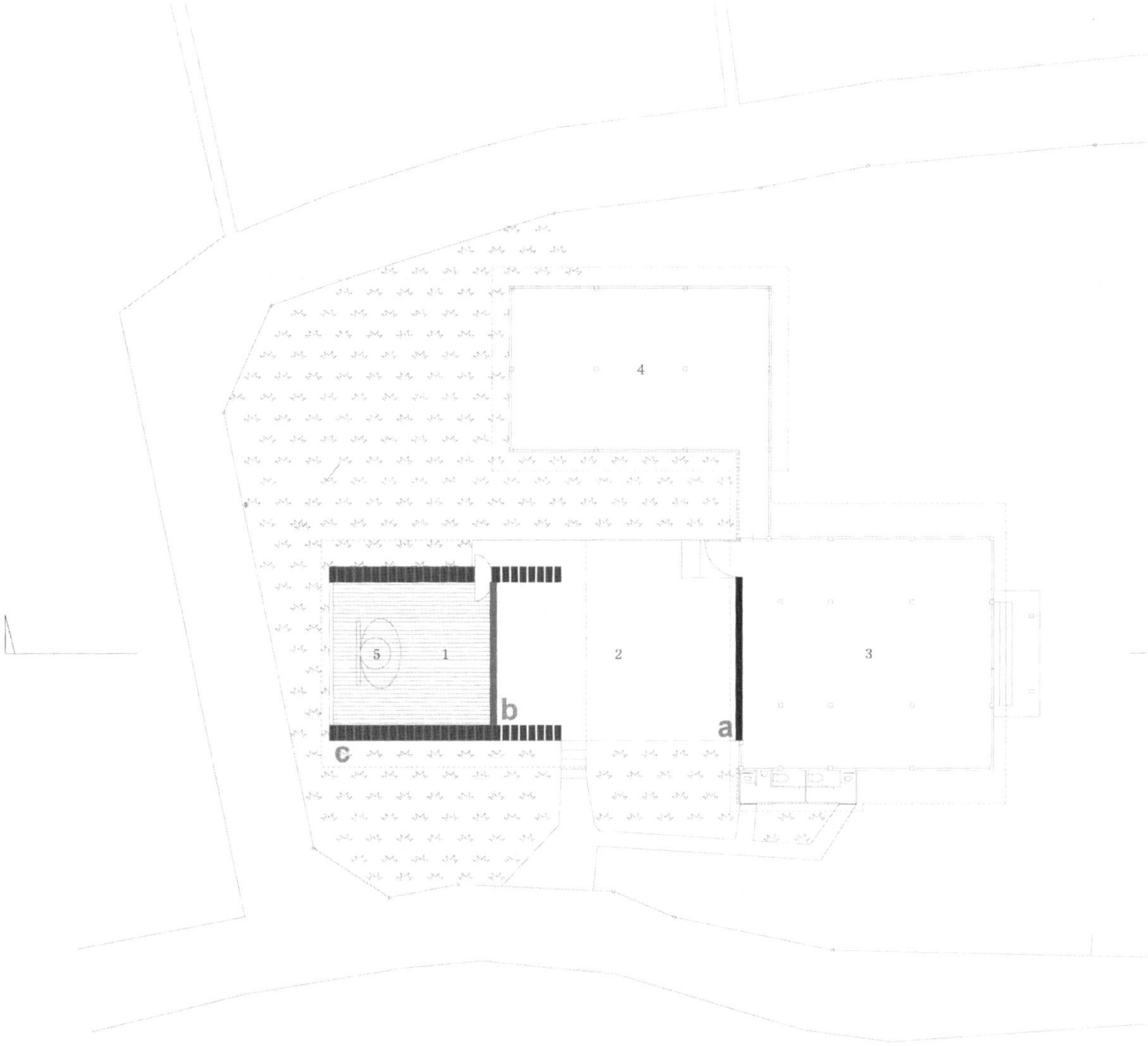

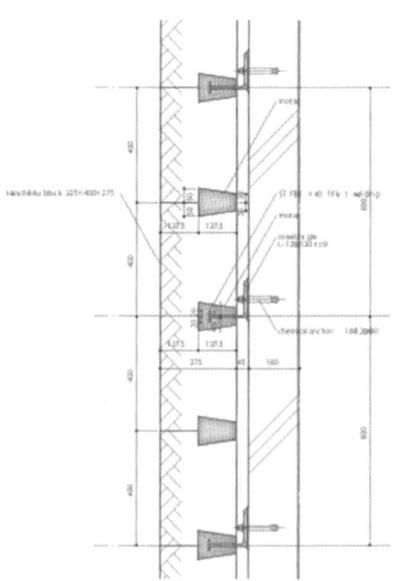

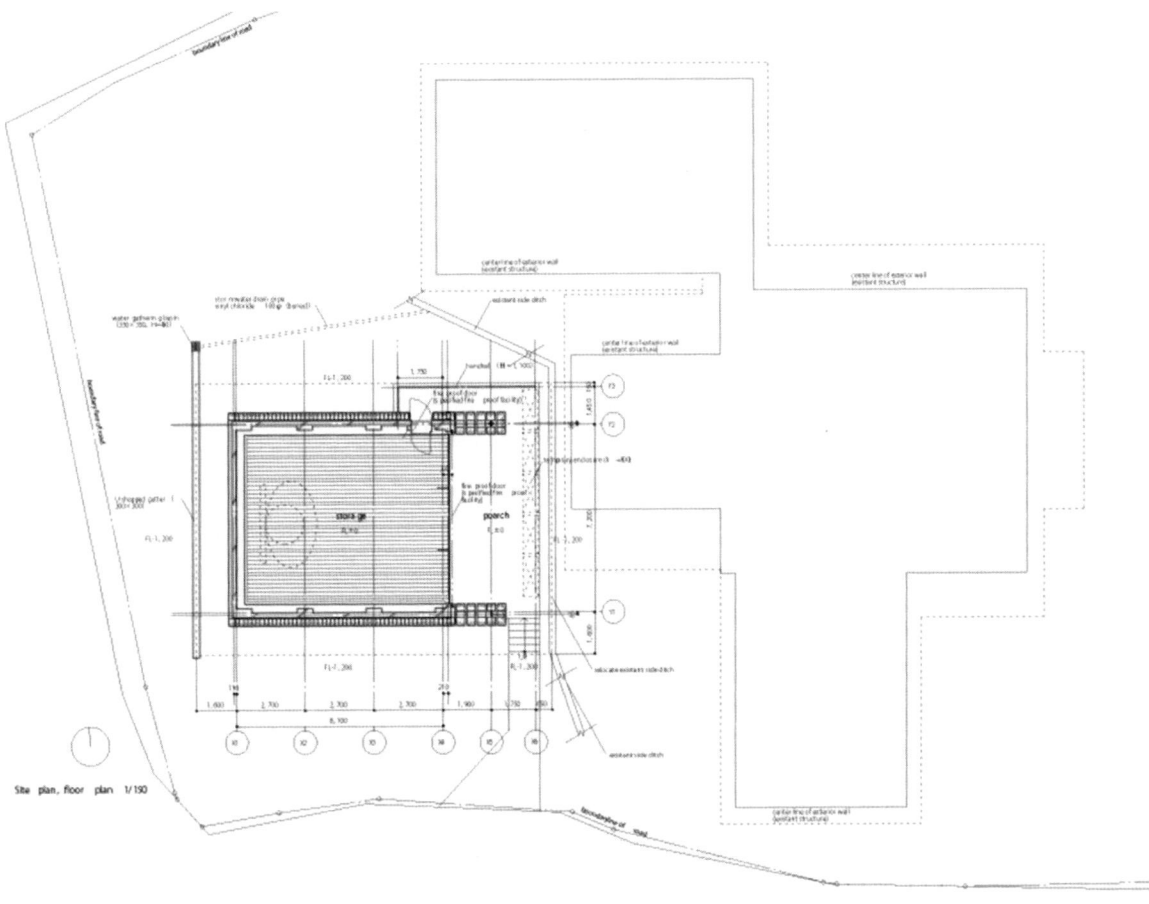

Site plan, floor plan 1/150

CREDITS	
Area	**1,975.3 m²**
Architect + Partner	**Kengo Kuma & Associates**
Engineer	**K.Nakata and Associates**
Render + Photos	**Daici Ano**

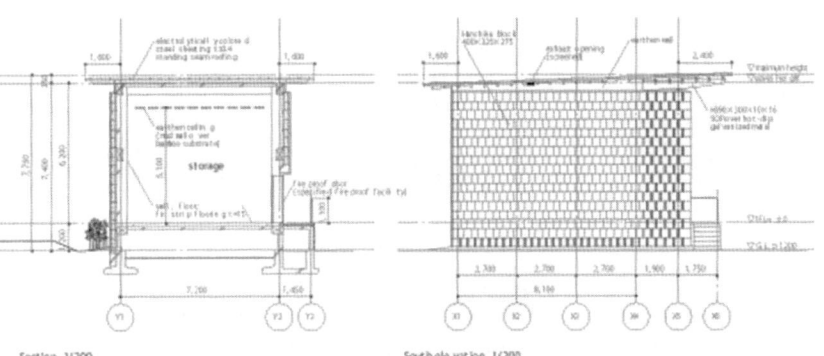

Section 1/200 South elevation 1/200

44 STACKING ELEMENTS
CHOKKURA PLAZA
CHOKKURA PLAZA
Takanezawa, Shioya-gun, Tochigi, Japan (2005)

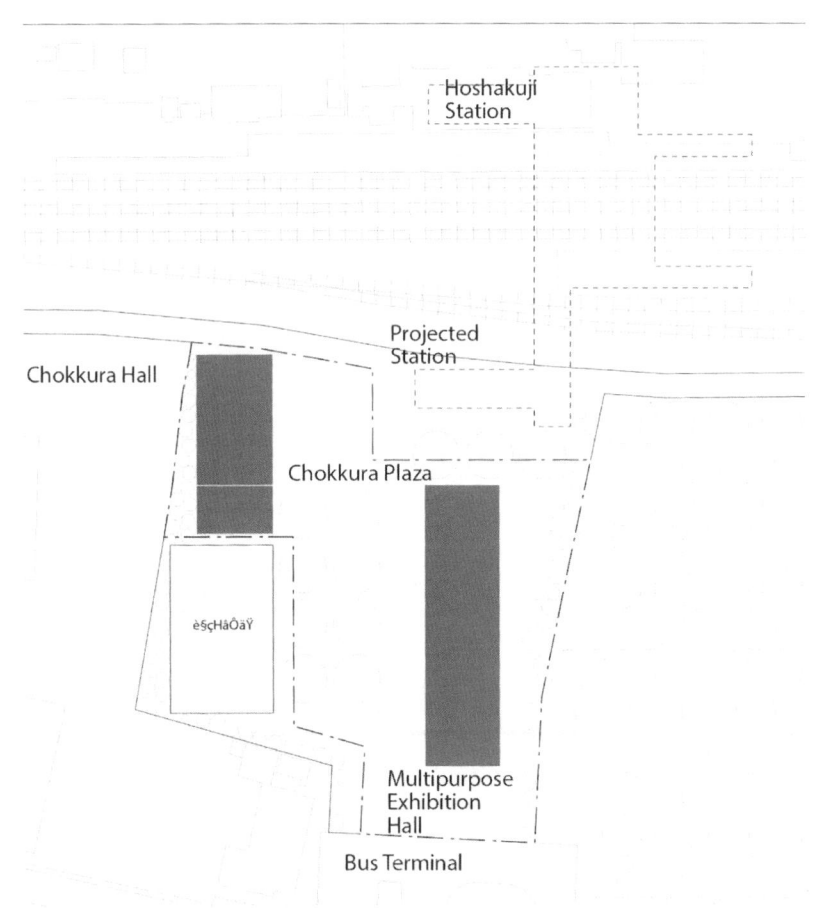
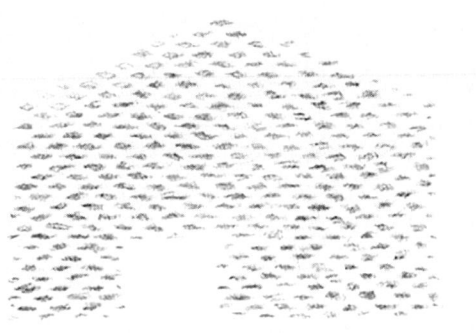
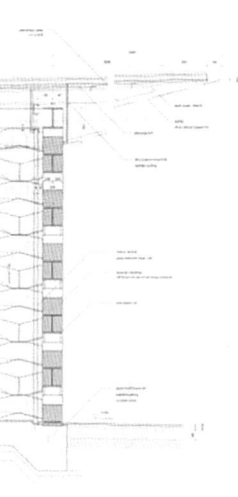

CREDITS	
Area	**87.30m²**
Architect + Partner	**Kengo Kuma & Associates**
ColB. Team	**Ohta Co., Ltd. + Fukuda doboku zouen Co., Ltd.**
Engineer	**Oak Structural Design Office**
Render + Photos	**Daici Ano**

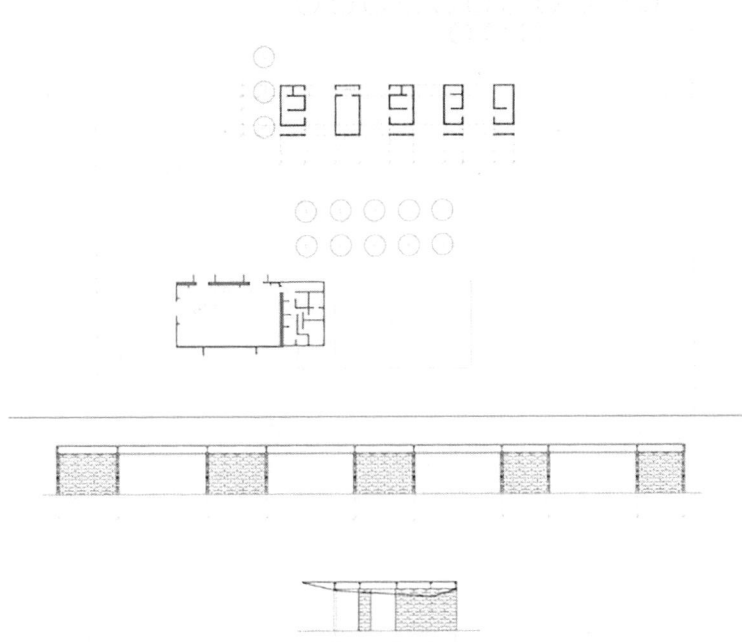
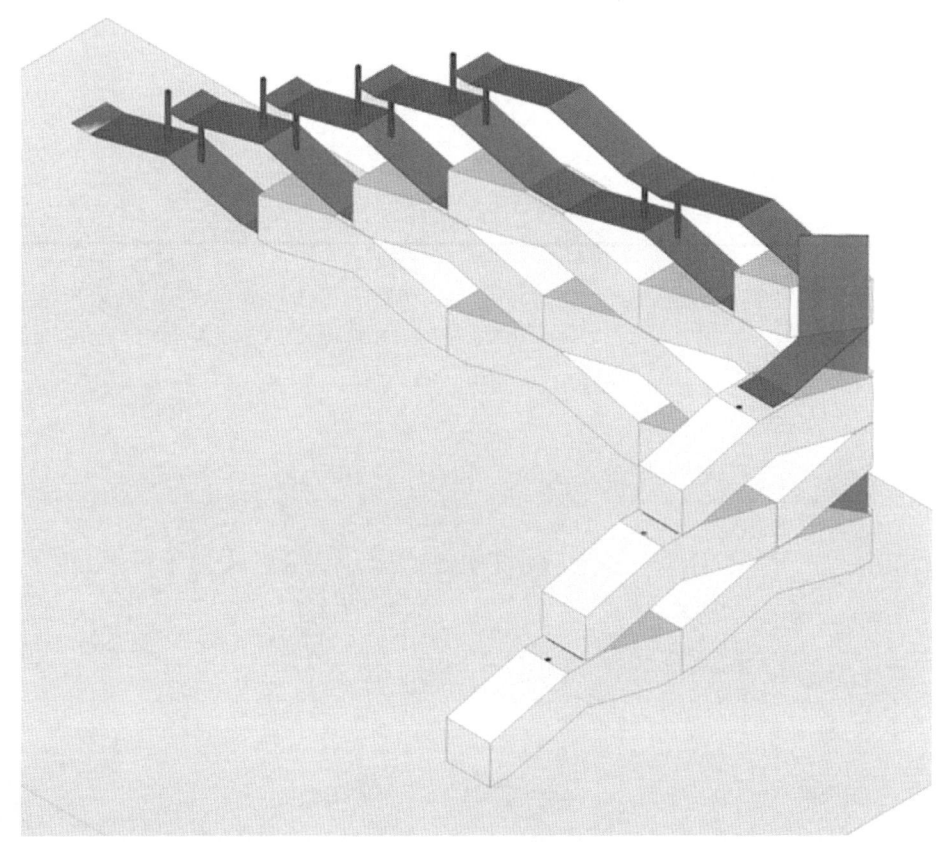

45

STACKING ELEMENTS
V&A MUSEUM OF DESIGN
MUSEO DEL DESIGN V&A
Dundee, Scotland, UK

CREDITS
Contest	
Area	**11,600 m²**
Client	**Dundee City Council, Design Dundee Limited**
Architect + Partner	**Kengo Kuma & Associates**
Project Team	**Kengo Kuma, Teppei Fujiwara, Maurizio Mucciola, Masafumi Harigai, Rika Hiratsuji, Hajime Kita, Kazuya Katagiri, Masaru Shuku. Hiroki Saito and Kimio Suzuki (visuals)**

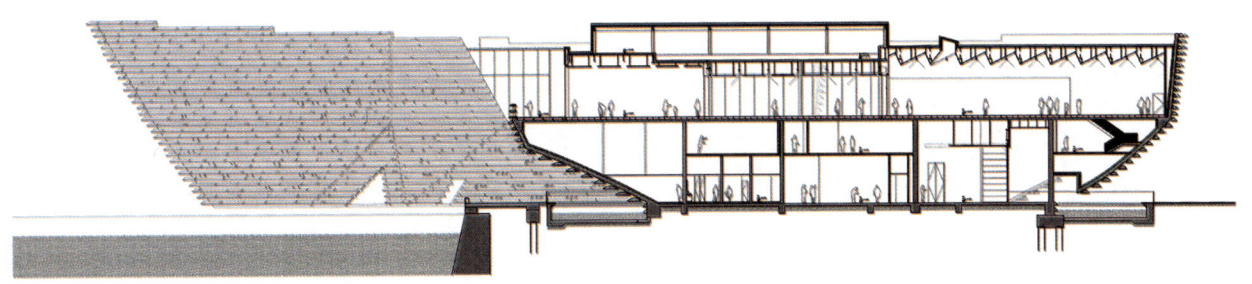

Section AA

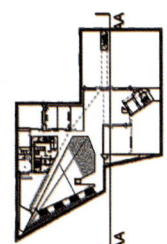

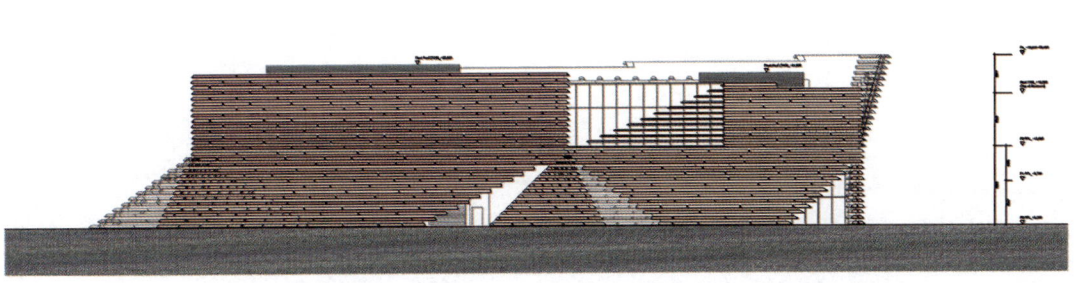

North Elevation

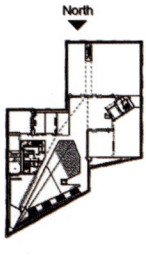

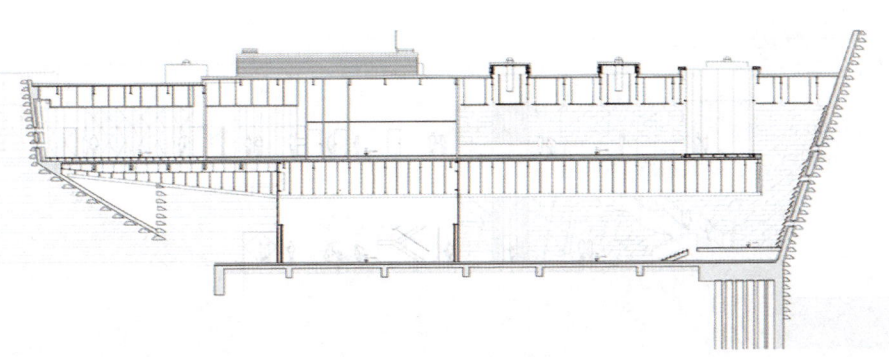

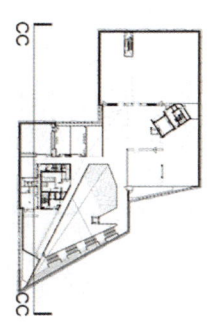

Published by
Pubblicato da
LISt Lab
info@listlab.eu
listlab.eu

Author/Autore
Pino Scaglione

Edited by/A Cura di
Maurizio Mucciola

Editorial Director
Direttore editoriale
Alessandro MArtinelli

Art Direction & Production
Direzione Artistica e Produzione
Blacklist Creative Partners, Barcelona
blacklist-creative.com

ISBN 9788898774050

Printed and bound in the European Union
Stampato e rilegato in Unione Europea
December/Dicembre 2015
October/Ottobre 2018 (re-print)

Series MONOGRAPH.IT

Prohibited total or partial reproduction of this book by any means, without permission of the author and Publisher

All rights reserved
© of LISt Lab edition;
© of the author's texts;
© of the author's images: (*)

Vietata qualsiasi forma di riproduzione totale o parziale di questo libro con qualsiasi mezzo, senza il permesso dell'autore e l'editore.

Tutti i diritti riservati
© dell'edizione LISt Lab
© dei testi gli autori
© delle immagini gli autori: (*)

(**) Takumi Ota, pp. 16, 18 - 19, 38, 40 - 41; Mitsumasa Fujitsuka, pp. 20, 22 -23, 162 - 163, 188 - 195, 240 - 243; Daichi Ano, pp. 34 - 37, 94 - 100, 244 - 246; Masao Nishikawa, pp. 42 - 45; Erieta Attali, pp. 47, 118, 132 - 135, 164 - 167; Edward Caruso, p. 48; Masaru Yutani/ Designing GYM, pp. 52 - 55; Antje Quiram, pp. 56 - 57; Nacása & Partners Inc., pp. 58 - 59, 239; p. 100 Marco Introini, pp. 102 - 109; Nicolas Waltefaugle pp. 119 - 121; Roberto Bartolomei, p. 124; Peppe Maisto, pp. 125 - 127; Yuji Takeuchi, pp. 158 - 161; Takeshi Yamagishi, pp. 196 - 199; Fujinari Miyazaki, pp. 210 - 213; Yoshie Nishikawa, pp. 101, 214 - 217; Hufton & Crow, cover, pp. 248 - 257; all remaining images "courtesy of Kengo Kuma & Associates"

Promotion and distribution
Promozione e distribuzione
distribution@listlab.eu

LISt Lab is an editorial workshop, based in Europe, that works on contemporary issues. LISt Lab not only publishes, but also researches, proposes, promotes, produces, creates networks.

LISt Lab è un Laboratorio editoriale, con sedi in Europa, che lavora intorno ai temi della contemporaneità. LISt Lab ricerca, propone, elabora, promuove, produce, LISt Lab mette in rete e non solo pubblica.

LISt Lab is a green company committed to respect the environment. Paper, ink, glues and all processings come from short supply chains and aim at limiting pollution. The print run of books and magazines is based on consumption patterns, thus preventing waste of paper and surpluses. LISt Lab aims at the responsibility of the authors and markets, towards the knowledge of a new publishing culture based on resource management.

LISt Lab editoriale è una società sensibile ai temi del rispetto ambientale-ecologico. Le carte, gli inchiostri, le colle, le lavorazioni in genere, sono il più possibile derivanti da filiere corte e attente al contenimento dell'inquinamento. Le tirature dei libri e riviste sono costruite sul giusto consumo di mercato, senza sprechi ed esuberi da macero. LISt Lab tende in tal senso alla responsabilizzazione di autori e mercato e ad una nuova cultura editoriale costruita sulla gestione intelligente delle risorse.